WHY

NOT JOY?

CHANGE YOUR MIND AND EVERYTHING
ELSE ALONG WITH IT

PATRICK KENNEY

Book cover design and interior layout by Ellie Bockert Augsburger of www.CreativeDigitalStudios.com.

Cover Design Features:
Happy businessman in front of a mirror where it looks reflected sad. isolated, white background. By Jr Casas/ Adobe Stock

Paperback ISBN: 978-1-7330055-1-7
eBook ISBN: 978-1-7330055-0-0

TO RACHEL,

BECAUSE YOU ARE

DESTINED FOR YOUR OWN

"COME UP HERE!" MOMENT. AND

WITH THANKS AND GRATITUDE FOR YOUR

SUPPORT AND ENCOURAGEMENT. IT WILL

ALL MAKE SENSE ONE DAY! WITH LOVE,

PAT K 5/28/19

TABLE OF CONTENTS

HISTORY

Do not conform to the pattern of this world, but be transformed by the renewing of your mind. Then you will be able to test and approve what God's will is—his good, pleasing and perfect will. (Romans 12:2)

"Change is hard!" How many times have you heard that? I'm not sure I've ever met anyone who says it's not. Changing is the topic of every self-help book ever written. It is the topic of this book as well, but I cannot honestly say that this is a self-help book. There are serious limits to how much help we can bring to ourselves; if you haven't been let down by your own ability to sustain the changes you've wanted to make, you are in the extreme minority. And, if you have never had any trouble making difficult changes I'm not sure you need to be reading any further! In substance abuse treatment settings we say, "If you could have made that change just by wanting it bad enough, it would have happened already!"

In my own life, I've hit just about every dead end a person could hit in the attempt to change. I've acquired bad (even destructive) habits without realizing what they would eventually cost me, let anxiety and depression dictate the terms I would live my life under, and made commitments to relationships that had no chance of bettering me or the other person. I've been strongly addicted to food, marijuana, cocaine, codependent relationships, and supremely negative thinking patterns. I wallowed in depression for most of my adult life and fought such profound despair that getting a phone bill for $250 when I was broke could immediately produce thoughts of wanting to die to escape the stress.

1

And I've lost just about every kind of thing a person can lose as a result of making those mistakes. I've been estranged from family, divorced, bankrupted, and watched a business fail - all despite my best efforts. At one point, I was contemplating having one of my feet amputated because I was in such chronic pain from carrying around 200 pounds of extra weight. I ate so much Tylenol, Motrin, and Celebrex during that time that my stomach started to digest itself from all the anti-inflammatories I was taking.

Okay, you get the picture! It was bad at times - *really* bad at other times. But, along the way, something else was happening without me knowing. Despite feeling like I was spinning my wheels, my prayers to find some sort of life that I could finally enjoy were being answered slowly but surely. But in some very unorthodox ways. Looking back, I can say with a smile that I was being set up. Set up for tremendous blessing! Of course, it felt like just the opposite for most of that time. I used to think that the only reason God would let things go well for me was so that when He pulled the rug out, I would fall far enough to pay for the mistakes I'd made.

It turns out I couldn't have been more wrong in my assumptions! In hindsight, every hurdle, setback, and stumble was part of a much larger picture that I was blind to while it was all happening. There was a day approaching where He would grant me the ability to see what I had been missing all that time, even though I felt utterly forsaken. It's only because of this relatively newfound clarity that I feel confident that telling my story can have value to those who hear it. I know I'm not the only one who has struggled with depression, addiction, and bad relationships, but I also know how to apply what has worked for me so that other people can get free.

I consider myself fortunate to have finally learned the lessons necessary to recover from addictions to drugs and food. I know the futility of addiction as well as anyone, and I'm grateful to have regained the freedom that has allowed me to avoid relapsing on chemicals for the past 26 years and also to have lost almost 200lbs. since then and kept it off for the past five years. But both of these victories pale in comparison to regaining the freedom to choose what kind of thoughts are allowed to dominate my thinking. The ability to discard the self- attacking and defeated mindset I used to ascribe to is my most treasured transformation! But, it is equally rewarding to have seen other people benefit from my experience. So much of the pain I went through was by choice and, now that I can see that, I get great pleasure in teaching others how to avoid the same mistakes in thinking. I'm so grateful for the opportunity to have counseled hundreds of people through some of the toughest times in their lives, and there are two criteria that I've used when deciding what to include in this book; it has to have helped me personally, *and* I've had to see it work for others.

I'm going to tell you a lot of stories throughout this book; I've chosen the ones that will best illustrate the principles that you can use to turn your life around as well. I'll tell you my story – even the embarrassing blunders, shortsighted detours, and painful truths. I'm also going to share several stories of the people I've worked with as a substance abuse counselor to clarify some of the points I'll be making. And I'm going to retell some stories from the Bible that will help you to see that these struggles are nothing new and that there are real answers there for people who are trying to make difficult changes.

This emphasis on stories is not accidental; we will look extensively at the power of our personal stories to influence the ways we approach change and what we believe we are capable of. We will also examine how the stories we choose to tell affect our ability to think positively about ourselves and others, set and achieve goals, and either assist us in growing spiritually or keep us locked in cycles of defeat.

This book is a distilled account of the ways I've seen these narratives (stories) affect people as well as how they have played a role in many of the setbacks (and breakthroughs) in my own life. Much of what I've written is what I have found myself regularly saying to clients, friends, and family who are having difficulty getting past certain hurdles. These are some of the insights you'll learn about before we're done:

- How you think about your past is much more important than what actually happened. Some people have terrible pasts, yet somehow "shake it off" and remain hopeful, while others have considerably easier lives but focus almost entirely on what went wrong. You'll learn how to avoid sabotaging yourself with a slanted view of the past and how to find the story that will maximize your forward momentum and, more importantly, allow you to enjoy where you are in the present.

- Focusing on a positive mindset is not nearly as important as having a flexible mindset. Being able to adapt quickly to changing circumstances is key to preserve our peace of mind. Can you adopt whatever mindset is appropriate to avoid discontent and quitting before you achieve your goals?

- How to create the kind of environment where you can grow as a person (spiritually). Without certain spiritual "nutrients" your attempts to change will be greatly limited. And this is true whether you consider yourself spiritual or not. Do you understand the relationship between spirituality and change?

A lot of what I've written sounds like it is specific to addiction, but the principles of how to change are the same regardless of what it is we are trying to accomplish. It's only the degree of difficulty that changes; I don't think there is anything more difficult for humans

4

than getting free of addiction. My aim is to provide information and inspiration that will assist any open-minded person who desires to experience difficult life change. If you are harshly critical of yourself, find clever ways to sabotage your own success, or compulsively use food, substances, or some other behavior to soothe yourself, the material we cover will give you some new tools to combat those things.

Some of the stories I share may be difficult to believe, but I promise they are all true (the names have been changed). But the point is not to convey the idea that I am in any way exceptional or deserving of praise. In fact, I spent many years unnecessarily committed to ways of thinking that held me back profoundly. The only advantage I can claim now is that I've lived enough years so that, when I was finally shown the big picture, I could make some sense of it. This book is the attempt to communicate some of that experience.

And, I don't want you to think that just getting out of an addiction is nearly enough. A miserable sober life is not much preferable to a miserable addicted one - trust me, I have lived both! But, having the self-control necessary to manage our various appetites is for sure the prerequisite to finding a satisfying life; there is no happy addicted life whether it is to food, drugs, bad relationships, or thinking negatively. Yikes, I just realized I'm writing to my previous self there!

I would be lying if I told you that maintaining sobriety, managing my weight, and finding relief from depression came easy. "Just say no!" is pitifully inadequate once compulsion and bad brain chemistry become involved. I wish I could say that I didn't have some spectacular failures as I learned how to get free, but the truth is that most of what I learned was done the hard way! There was more help available to me while I struggled than I realized, and my supremely negative mindset meant my progress was inconsistent and slow. It's my hope that some will be able to benefit from the mistakes that I have made as well as by hearing how God has faithfully played a key role in rescuing me from each of them. I am also confident that, if you can bring yourself to act on some of what is discussed here, you will spend less time in your own detours and not have to learn these same lessons in your own hard way. I'm going to teach you some shortcuts about how to set yourself up for transformation to happen – ways that will seem simple once you learn them.

I will be honest about the kinds of things that were said and done in my family of origin. It might sound gratuitous or disrespectful to detail some of these things. I am grateful that I was able to experience a great deal of restoration and healing before they died. I live with no bitterness or remorse about how things took place. On the contrary, it has only heightened my faith in God's ability to redeem even the most broken relationships. And it will not minimize the role that God has played. As God has faithfully performed the renewal and transformation mentioned above, certain areas of study and research have become more applicable and meaningful to me; I think it's important to mention those along the way.

There is a ton of new research about the power of mindset, and there are hundreds of books written about how to get a "growth mindset," a "warrior mindset," or a "miracle mindset." There are books about how to think like a millionaire, an Olympic athlete, or a Tibetan Buddhist monk. The one word that stands out among the titles of these books is "success." Each new book about mindset offers to help people succeed in some way they are currently held back. And for certain, there is a growing body of research outlining the connection between how people think and the success they experience in any given domain of life. Above all, I will work from the assumption that finding God's "good, pleasing, and perfect will" is the ultimate success a human can aspire to.

But this book will be a little different from most. This is not really a "how-to" book; it is much more of a "how-did" story. How did these transformations take place in my life and others' lives and what can you do to set yourself up for the same sort of experience? At heart, this is a story about the kind of transformation that is possible by "renewing your mind." But, I will not downplay just how difficult and frustrating that can be. Many people have been working (and praying) for that transforming power to reach them somehow, sometimes for many years – I know I did. Some spend many thousands of dollars trying to see themselves in a radically different way.

We will look at all three domains in life that require transformational change: mental, physical, and spiritual. And you will have some concrete action steps to address each of these when we're done. You will learn how to examine your own story for the plot points that keep things like addiction and depression coming back. I'll give you some ideas about how to take advantage of your brain's tendency to crave rather than be a slave to it. And how to create an environment where time can heal your wounds rather than prolong your pain and suffering.

The title of this book addresses the main idea we will look at from a variety of perspectives. That our current emotional state is mainly the result of choices that we make about what to emphasize or downplay in the narrative we tell about ourselves. And that, in most cases, we feel exactly how we have chosen to feel. If that's the case, why not tell the story that ends with us feeling joy? And I know from experience that choosing that story is not always as easy as it sounds.

We will also look at what it takes to "change your mind" about the kind of story you are telling as well as who the main characters will be. Originally, I was going to title the book "How to Change Your Mind" until Michael Pollan took that title to write a book about how psychedelic drugs offer some sort of enlightenment to those looking for meaning in life. That is about the exact opposite of what you will find here!

The concepts I will focus on are some of the most necessary for human beings to grapple with. And, when resolved, can be the most liberating. Whether it is changing my mind about what (and how much) I will eat, the drugs I will take, the people I will commit to, or the lens I will use to look at the world through, success in any one of these categories is priceless. Just ask anyone who has gotten there.

I will also mention my belief that God has "spoken" to me at various times in my life. Some of you will have no problem accepting that, while others might feel differently. I do not mean that I heard an audible voice coming down from heaven (although I believe that is possible). For me, the speaking I refer to is a sort of sudden, inner knowing that sharply intersects with how I would normally think. A distinctly different sort of intelligence that turns what I'm prone to think on my own upside-down. And always with life-changing potential in it. That is the best I can describe it, and to those who doubt the supernatural, I can offer no better explanation.

It amuses me when I think of the strange symmetry of events God has arranged for me. I spent the first half of my life progressively surrendering my freedom to choose and the second half fighting to get it back. I grew up in Malibu in the midst of the celebrities of that time and learned just about everything I could about becoming addicted during my friendships with Charlie Sheen and other recognizable people. For a time in my early twenties, because of Charlie's skyrocketing fame, I had access to the highest circles of Hollywood A-listers and supplied them with marijuana I grew within sight of Surfrider beach in Malibu.

When I had something to offer others in recovery, I changed careers and began by working with homeless clients where I found that their needs were not so different from the rest of us. Eventually, I ended up working for several years in Malibu at one of the most prestigious recovery centers in the world, where among my clients were, you guessed it, many of the Hollywood elite as well as sports stars and highly successful business owners. You will hear many of the same things that they happily paid a lot of money for.

So are these mind-changing events distinct, sudden "epiphanies" or the result of "nose against the grindstone" effort that finally pays off in breakthrough after months or years? At the end of the movie Forrest Gump, as Forrest stands at Jenny's gravesite and speaks to his lost love, he considers whether there is some ordained plan to life or whether things are just "floating around accidental-like." I'll borrow his words to answer the question above: "Maybe it's both."

IDENTITY

The condition or character as to who a person or what a thing is; the qualities, beliefs, etc., that distinguish or identify a person or thing; the sense of self, providing sameness and continuity over time.

I was a loser. I wasn't the worst possible loser, mind you, but if one guy was going to get the job, or if one guy was going to get the girl, it wasn't going to be me. How the word loser came to define me is still somewhat murky; I'm not aware of any single, dramatic event that convinced me to adopt that label. Instead, it was a slow, but meticulous, process of training myself from a very young age that the most important or defining aspects of me had to do with my losses, setbacks, or shortcomings. I also believed that it was preferable not to get my hopes up about things yet to come in order to protect myself from disappointment.

Without me even consciously choosing it, losing had become my story, providing a sense of "sameness or continuity" that I could rely on when thinking about my role in life as well as what to expect from relationships and the future in general. It made my life predictable and, because it was predictable, a little less anxious. I might enjoy isolated instances of success or seasons of blessing, but I could comfortably expect to lose at some point. I had an identity. This description of me was so tangible that my wife at one time said, "You always seem to find a way to lose!" I can remember playing tennis with a friend who mentioned how, after playing at a relatively high level for the first set or two, my game would invariably crumble when the possibility of winning got close. I found a way to lose despite feeling like I had a better all-around game than my opponent. I will tell you more about my own story later, but let's pull back to a bigger picture to set the stage better.

Human beings are obsessed with identity. We are always scrambling to protect or enhance it if possible. The diseases that attack identity (Alzheimer's, dementia, etc.) are some of the most feared and tragic. Try to imagine how you would feel if you suddenly forgot who you were and the events leading up to the present – for many, that is a terrifying prospect! Many cultures draw their identity primarily from their family or ancestry; if their actions reflect poorly on the family, they are struck with intense shame. And if the family is found to have a shameful secret, they are likewise tainted by it. They will make strong defenses of the family's "honor" even to very extreme ends.

Other people define themselves by political party or nationality, and we tend to make very broad attributions about what we think someone's character or values must be by who they voted for or their country of origin. Whenever you see a car with a bumper sticker that says "Proud parent of a _____," or with a license plate frame from their alma mater, you are seeing someone define their identity.

Many people choose tattoos that are meant to represent some part of their identity or immortalize their most important relationships. In the Maori culture, copies of facial tattoos were used in the same way we would use our signatures to identify ourselves. I was speaking to an older gentleman at the gym recently who was wearing a University of Southern California t-shirt. I said, "So you're a Trojan fan, huh?" He emphatically replied "No! I AM a Trojan." Even late in life, he continued to draw significant "sense of self" from his college experience. It signified something very much more important than just the location where he went to school.

Advertisers are constantly trying to form associations between their brand and a certain kind of identity of the person who buys their product; we are exposed to myriad messages daily about what the products for sale around us say about who we are, and what we buy can say everything from "(I'm) the most interesting man in the world" to "I'm a socially conscious protector of the planet." And if we lack solid, meaningful sources of identity, we will gladly accept faulty or even dangerous ones. This is what lies behind every young person's decision to join a gang. Or a compulsive shopper's desire for high-quality goods that they believe will signal to others that they are a high-quality person.

When the *Jersey Shore* reality TV show was popular, the stars were sent all sorts of expensive merchandise that manufacturers hoped would be seen on screen. The irony is that many times the stars of the show were sent these products not by the actual manufacturer, but by their competitor. The goal was to get their rival's brand tied to the identity of the show's stars, who were mocked for their perceived shallowness and vanity.

When asked "Who are you?" people will generally provide a set of facts about themselves that they think are most descriptive and appropriate. "I'm the mother of two children," or "I work in the financial sector," or "I'm from New York." When we answer that question, we talk about the relationships that we consider defining to who we are. And I use the term relationship broadly; our identity can revolve around our relationships with the goods we possess, or the kind of work that we do, as well as the family we belong to or our place of origin.

As we define who we are, the facts we use can be strung together as a loose story that provides an outline of our history and self-perception. In literature, this story is called a personal narrative. A personal narrative connects and explains a set of life events, whether true or not, and supports a particular view or conclusion about ourselves, others, and society at large. Narratives that humans create also invariably have moral and ethical aspects to them; we are usually

12

trying to convince others that we are "good people" or, if we are not, to provide a set of facts that will exonerate us and explain the bad we have done.

One area where the concept of narrative has become commonplace is in news coverage of our political system. Both sides of the political spectrum openly talk about trying to "control the narrative." This used to confuse me until I realized that each side was trying to string together various facts to create and tell a story that would prompt a desired response in the hearer. Each side emphasizes or ignores certain facts in their narrative in an attempt to generate anger, disgust, sympathy, or good-will towards a cause or political figure. The spin doctors on both sides go to great lengths to write over each other's narrative for one reason -because they know that whoever controls the narrative controls the emotional response the narrative generates.

As I write this, there are two competing narratives battling for control of public opinion about President Trump. What is truly remarkable is how starkly different these two narratives are; I cannot remember a time when the overlap between the Democrat and Republican narratives was so small. Listening to certain news outlets will expose you to the narrative of the President as an incompetent, corrupt, and possibly treasonous buffoon while other outlets put forth a narrative describing him as a master of negotiation who is "crazy like a fox," and being subject to the greatest miscarriage of justice since the crucifixion. And both sides rely on a particular set of facts that support the narrative they wish to establish.

Regardless of what you think of the President, it should fascinate you how intensely each side fights for the upper hand in controlling the narrative. Because, inside each of us, there is an equally important battle going on for control of the narrative about what we should think about ourselves and what kind of emotional response is appropriate.

These competing narratives, and the emotions associated with them, have consequences that strongly influence the choices we make.

Identity and narrative are inseparable because they both have everything to do with the history a person has experienced. The story (historical narrative) we tell, whether positive or negative, is what provides the "sameness and continuity over time" that constitutes identity and that humans are driven to create. We are the ultimate storytelling species, and it is not an accident that stories end up being so important to every culture on earth. We tell stories about how the universe was created, the origin of our species, the history of our family or culture, and to put our young ones at ease when it is time to sleep.

But not all stories are created equal. Just as there are happy fairy tales and epic sagas, there are also eerie ghost stories and tragic tales of loss. This also applies to the personal narratives we tell about ourselves – some are positive and inspiring while others are negative and depressing. Positive narratives tend to focus on our admirable character qualities as well as uplifting or redemptive relationships with people and things of the past. Negative narratives take shape when one determines that his losses, weaknesses, lacks, or incapacities are the most defining aspects of his identity. A negative narrative emphasizes relationships (with people, places, or things) that have been detrimental, abusive, or otherwise limiting.

There is a growing awareness in our culture of the importance of being able to control one's narrative; I recently saw a commercial for a new T.V. show where the main character says, "Now that I've learned to control my own narrative, nothing can stop me!" In my work with both the homeless and substance abusers, I have the perfect laboratory to get close-up experience with some very troubling narratives and, early on, I began to see some remarkable similarities in the kinds of stories that people tell about themselves. It became clear there were certain "families" of stories that shared important aspects regardless of whether they were being told by a homeless person who hadn't had a job in years or a pampered housewife who hadn't a care in the world. And, more importantly, I began to see that the progress people made in attempting to make difficult change was directly related to the success they had in changing their narrative.

I also began to see that relapse and backsliding had much to do with a person's narrative and identity as well. It was astonishing to see people make steady progress in their recovery up to a certain point and then, right on the verge of achieving a noteworthy goal, sabotage themselves by relapsing or running away. This made no sense to me until I looked at it in light of the stories these people were telling about themselves.

When someone whose narrative didn't include the possibility of earning above $40,000 a year found themselves on the threshold of landing a job much better than that, they suddenly decided that getting loaded the night before their final interview was a good idea. Or, when the wife whose narrative assumed that she was less powerful than her husband finally decided it was time to set him straight about his extramarital affairs inexplicably agreed to go on a vacation with him instead of attending the counseling session that she had arranged in order to confront him.

One of my earlier clients, Peter, was a homeless alcoholic who, after two months of sobriety, had begun to talk about finding a job again. All he needed to get employed was an I.D. card, and he wanted to finally get some long-neglected work done on his teeth as well. He had been a short order cook in the past, and we spent several sessions focused on taking action to merely look for a job. Forget applying for now - we just wanted to see what was out there. He came back excited to tell me he had found several jobs that were available to him in the area.

At the time, he was living in a "camp" cut out of the brush surrounding a golf course, and any of the jobs available would have allowed him to have a small apartment and continue to build on his success. We spent time talking about the kind of life he wanted to live when he had an income again, and he beamed as he thought of the options he would have. I got the DMV form out of my filing cabinet and, after he filled it out, signed it so he could go and get an I.D. card. I also made an appointment for him to see a local dentist who donated his skills to treat the homeless in the area.

When I saw him the next week, I asked how things went, and he told me he had lost the DMV form and that an emergency had arisen that prevented him from keeping the dental appointment. He and I sat down, filled the form out again and rescheduled with the dentist. He thanked me and swore that he would go straight away to get the I.D. and that he would be early to the dentist. It took repeating this process four times before I realized that something deeper was happening than just trouble with keeping track of a sheet of paper or getting to the dentist's office on time. As we talked about it, we found our way to the topic of identity, and he was able to describe what he thought his identity was. He was, in his words, "a lost soul," and it became clear that, in his story, lost souls live in cardboard and plastic houses behind the golf course, have rotting teeth, and, most certainly, don't have jobs.

After he had that realization, I didn't see him for several months and ended up bumping into him on the street one day. He told me he had been drinking heavily since the day he discovered that the words "lost soul" described him perfectly. He also told me he wanted to arrange another meeting with me to pick up where we left off, but I never saw him again. Evidently, lost souls also drink themselves into oblivion. All that devastation as a result of a little I.D. card. But it was such a threat to his identity that it had the power to literally destroy him!

At the heart of these examples is the truth that, when our identity and narrative about who we are is conflicting with our actual circumstances, the result is profound anxiety. The trouble is that it is much easier to change circumstances than it is to change identity. That is why Peter got stuck. While he made relatively quick progress toward his goals of sobriety, work, and self-sufficiency, his identity hadn't budged an inch the entire time. So the higher he climbed the ladder of success the more anxious he got when he looked down. Finally, he couldn't stand it anymore and renounced all responsibility until his circumstances and his identity matched. Instead of being a lost soul pretending to be something greater, he slid back down the ladder and became a lost soul living exactly how lost souls are meant to live. When we are attempting to change, we will run into this reality again and again as we climb toward our own success. And, if we do not have sufficient support to live with that tension while our identity evolves to accommodate our success, we will sabotage ourselves just like Peter did. It may not look as hideous as his example, but it will be just as limiting in its own way.

In my work with substance abusers, it is uncommon that I run into someone with a positive narrative and it's not hard to determine pretty quickly the kind of story people are telling about themselves. I've heard "I'm a bad seed," "I'm a worthless dope fiend," and "It sucks to be me!" among many others. There are as many narratives as there are people, but there are basically three broad umbrellas of negative narratives that all others fall under - *loser, victim,* and *villain*. Most people who adopt a negative narrative will gravitate primarily to one particular expression (or blend) of the three, but it is not uncommon for people to move between narratives depending on the circumstances or who they are relating with. A man could be a victim at work and a loser at home, a woman might be a victim in her marriage and a villain with her children. I have also seen people shift narratives from day to day as well as within a single conversation.

People in the loser narrative focus primarily on internal faults, flaws, and shortcomings and tends to see the bad things in life as being *inside* of them. They attribute the setbacks and losses they've experienced mostly to internal flaws or lacks. They might believe that society is unfair or that they've been shortchanged somehow, but they will still believe it is what they don't have inside is why they fail. These people generally have an exceedingly hard time accepting compliments and lean toward perfectionistic thinking and behavior. Losers almost all identify with this statement: "I have to be twice as good to be thought of half as well."

Because losers tend to accept all blame like sponges, they are usually burdened by intense guilt and shame. And, because they are accepting blame for things that are not authentic to them, they cannot receive the benefits that forgiveness brings. To feel better about themselves, losers will sometimes take a perverse satisfaction that they fail to effectively navigate the demands of work or relationship. They may try to make the case that because the world is "dog eat dog," it says something good about them that they don't fit in.

The victim, conversely, has successfully created a narrative that places the "badness" and blame *outside* of themselves. They see themselves as basically innocent and at the mercy of a world that can be counted on to hurt them again before too long. These people have difficulty admitting blame and will go to great lengths to avoid taking responsibility for their circumstances. Victims tend to be hyper-sensitive and can easily find reasons to take offense at other's treatment of them. We'll touch on the villain role shortly.

Both the loser and the victim roles have something called *splitting* in common. Splitting is something that happens in all of us when we are developing as children, and occurs because of the difficulty children have reconciling the simultaneous presence of positive and negative qualities in themselves and others.

There is a branch of psychology called *object relations theory* that posits the idea that infants and children "split" these qualities in order to "protect the good." In other words, splitting acts as a defense mechanism that allows the child to maintain positive feelings about his caregiver, even when the caregiver frustrates the child or is unresponsive at times. Because it is critical for the child to feel cared for, and because it is so terrifying to feel abandoned, the child separates the loving feelings he experiences when he is gratified from the furious feeling he has when his desires are thwarted.

As the child grows and learns to resolve this split, he will ideally be able to look positively at his relationships with others and see them as whole people. In other words, as people who are a mixed bag and who have both the desire to meet some of his needs (good), but also the inability to meet all of his needs (bad). Just as importantly, he will have the ability to recognize that good and bad exist simultaneously inside of him - *and that it is OK!*

Jean Piaget, the famed developmental psychologist, called the stage of development between ages 2 and 7 the *pre-operational* stage and noted that it was characterized by egocentrism. In this context, egocentrism means the inability of a child to imagine any difference between his own viewpoint and the viewpoints of others. He assumes that everyone feels the same as he does. In this stage, it is difficult, if not impossible, for the child to understand why he should be denied what he wants, and containing his anger when his desires are not met will be very challenging. When you see a young child rage at his mother because she tells him he cannot have some treat in the checkout line at the supermarket, you are watching someone split. It is not uncommon to hear a child say he "hates" the one who is thwarting him at that moment. The child has great difficulty holding on to the fact that his mother loves and satisfies him frequently enough at other times and he is only able to experience her refusal as "bad" in that moment.

When we fail to resolve issues of reconciling the presence of good and bad in others and ourselves (and we all leave childhood needing to work on this), we have only a limited range of responses. First, we have the tendency to harshly judge the bad in ourselves and others. Then, we deny and externalize the existence of good or bad either in ourselves or others. Because of difficulty reconciling the presence of both simultaneously, we make desperate attempts to get one of them outside of us. If the split remains unresolved, its influence can be seen in many of the mental illnesses that plague us as adults. Narcissism is thought to be closely related to the inability to maintain positive and negative views of the self simultaneously; the narcissist's view of himself cannot contain anything negative, and those who remind him of his shortcomings are quickly made the targets of wrath or marginalization.

It's easy to see why someone would want to deny the existence of bad in themselves – they get to feel the relief of being blameless victims. The only downside is that, because the victim projects his own badness on everyone around him to some degree or other, the world becomes a pretty threatening place with all those ill-willed enemies out there. But why would someone go the other direction and choose to deny the good in themselves? For some people, it is preferable to assign the "good" label to the people who are caring for them and to take the "bad" one for themselves (losers). This allows at least some relief from the child's anxiety; if they can project the good onto their caregiver, they feel somewhat safer because someone "good" is looking out for them.

In my own case, it made the solution to problems more possible, if only in theory. If the badness or "wrong" was in me, it could give me the control necessary to fix it. If it was outside me, it remained in others' hands. And the hands I had to trust in were not very capable at solving relationship problems. I also grew up with a mother who played the victim role and needed to place her badness outside of herself. I was trained from early in life that the path of least conflict was to just instinctively take the blame; it became natural for me.

In abusive, perfectionistic, or high conflict environments, children have greater difficulty resolving this dilemma that we all must pass through. The longer this split takes to resolve, the more experience a child gathers to construct a negative narrative and the more the identity (narrative) is defined by turmoil, loss, and blame. Someone who forms a victim narrative might have suffered some sort of very real abuse and was unable to reconcile a loved one hurting them so severely. The loser might have grown up exposed to subtle, or not-so-subtle, statements about their lack of intelligence, athletic ability, etc. In both cases, the split remains unhealed and gives fuel to the unfolding narrative. It's important to note that people who adopt negative narratives almost always have real-life evidence to draw on to support their stories.

The negative narratives essentially codify the good/bad split into the story we tell about ourselves and our relationship to the outside world. The loser is focused primarily on his internal badness and flaws, and while he may see fault in others as well, his own downside is so magnified that the faults of others pale in comparison. While the loser generally believes he deserves the blame, he can go to great lengths to provide explanations about why he should not be blamed for any one particular issue. He is also prone to reflexive statements that border on the ridiculous. Because he usually lacks the ability to take responsibility for just the amount of error in a single incident without being overwhelmed by his flaws, he may go "all-bad" and say something like: "You're right, I'm the worst. I can't do anything right!" Instead of being able to acknowledge he left the milk out again, he collapses inside, swears he will never drink milk again, and fails to resolve the conflict effectively. Anger and resentment toward those who point out his flaws is common, and the loser is a pro at avoiding conflict.

The victim is the polar opposite of the loser. She can fleetingly acknowledge that some fault may lie in herself in principle, but it is always necessary to minimize or deny the role her own issues may have played in any given conflict. When forced to examine closely her role in a conflict or failure, she may react with intense anger, blame, and a widening of the conflict. Victims tend to bring up unrelated previous conflicts or topics in order to muddy the water and bolster the evidence they need to support placing the blame elsewhere. The victim has a very fragile self-esteem that cannot tolerate accepting her part of a conflict, and win-win resolutions are very difficult to come by with a victim. They must always win, and the blame must end up on the other person or group they are in conflict with. Victims tend to feel morally superior to others and can be vicious when they feel they have a legitimate reason to be angry at another person.

Another important thing happens when the good/bad split is unresolved. The villain role becomes empowered to mete out judgment and punishment on whoever it deems inferior. When someone feels it necessary to deny the good that is in them and adopts a loser narrative, they become something less than human: they become sub-human. The villain's attacks are turned inward toward the inferior self, and the loser will punish himself mercilessly. The loser is also likely to be passive aggressive with others because he is conflicted about expressing his anger directly.

Someone playing the victim role becomes something other than human toward the opposite end of the scale: they become super-human. Victims are excellent score-keepers of wrongs done to them and use the outrage that is generated by the victim story to jump into the more powerful villain role and punish others without remorse.

And the more uncomfortable we are with both good and bad in us at the same time, the greater force the villain expresses itself with. If there is little to no good present in us, we assassinate ourselves with criticism, and if there is no badness or fault in us, we feel perfect liberty to judge others harshly. Conversely, when the split is resolved, and we can accept ourselves as lovable people who are also deeply flawed in ways, we become fully human, and the villain role is robbed of the power it needs to punish us or others with.

Louis is a good example of someone who shifts wildly between negative narratives. He had been a successful businessman for most of his life before he had a heart attack in his mid-fifties. It is not uncommon for men who have thoracic (chest cavity) surgery to experience depression afterward and Louis was surprised to find himself feeling depressed after his surgery. It was then that someone introduced him to crack cocaine and changed his life forever. He quickly became addicted to the feeling of power crack brought to him, and he progressively tossed everything he valued on the bonfire of his addiction to it. He lost millions of dollars, expensive cars, a custom home, retirement accounts, his marriage, and his beloved dogs. This savvy businessman spent tens of thousands of dollars on Nigerian bride scams not just once, but multiple times. When he had burned through his own money, he stole from his mother and other family members to keep feeding his addiction. While this process was unfolding, he ignored warnings he got from his closest friends and convinced himself he was immune from the consequences of his folly.

When I met Louis, he literally could not believe what had happened to him and frequently said with disgust, "What kind of person does what I did? I'm the lowest of the low!" He sobbed with regret about sacrificing everything he thought he loved for just a little more crack. When his thoughts were directed towards the lunacy he had perpetrated, he completely lost track of anything good inside of him, which empowered the villainous judge to pronounce all sorts of curses on himself. He ruminated obsessively and called himself an "idiot," "stupid," and "pathetic." He resisted any counsel to learn how to "let go" of what was lost and instead chose to constantly insult himself about what he had done. His internal judge would also demand that he compare himself to his companions in treatment and he lamented that he had found himself surrounded by types of people he previously considered to be weak-willed and inferior. As long as he was in the loser identity and focused on his role in the catastrophe, the villain was there to make sure he punished himself relentlessly.

But an interesting thing would happen every few days. For no apparent reason, Louis would turn that withering gaze outward to his housemates and the staff who worked at his treatment center. Rather than flogging himself for the devastation he had caused, he began to blame his wife for not stopping him, the false friends he surrounded himself with for taking advantage of him, or the stock market for turning on him. And when he did this, when he was able to project his badness onto others, the villain was freed to punish everyone around him. He made scathing judgments toward women about their weight or attractiveness and purposely made the lives of the staff who were trying to care for him miserable. Even though his housemates were generally happier than he was, he ridiculed them for taking the recommendations of their doctors and counselors.

Louis has extreme difficulty remaining human; he alternates between the sub-human loser and super-human victim on a fairly predictable timetable. It is easy to determine which one of these narratives he is operating from – all you have to do is listen to who he is spitting his venom at.

Just as there are three broad negative narratives, there are also three broad positive narratives that correspond: *victor, overcomer,* and *hero*. These narratives don't just represent believing the opposite of the negative ones. They represent the resolution of the split and the acceptance of reality rather than the denial characterized by the negative narratives. And where the theme in the negative narratives is judgment designed to punish the "inferior," the positive narratives suspend judgment and embrace struggle from a fully human position that accepts the reality of our faults. Just as the villain role expresses itself differently depending on whether its energy is directed inwardly or outwardly, the hero role takes different forms based on whether its focus is internal or external.

The victor is not fixated on only his shortcomings but sees the potential inside himself as well. He believes that the expression of his God-given gifts, talents, and abilities will eventually produce success and that acting in faith and taking appropriate risks will produce positive results, even if he fails in the short term. He recognizes that there are flaws inside of him, but knows that many people have succeeded in realizing their dreams despite great shortcomings. Nor does the victor feel compelled to win every time; he can admit his part in a breakdown and ask for forgiveness when necessary. He takes action and remains accountable to prevent his immaturity from infecting his thinking and stifling his progress. He moves from seeing his internal resources as his doom and instead begins to see his internal world as a source of strength, despite his flaws.

The victor embraces the challenge of struggling against his character flaws, distorted thinking, and destructive habits. And, unlike the loser, he does it without the crushing burden of self-judgment. The victor fights from a place of confidence, knowing that he can trust God to provide the insight and assistance he needs at the right time. Accessing this narrative also makes it possible to enjoy the process of difficult change. Change almost always goes faster (and is a lot more fun!) if one can approach it with this mindset.

The overcomer narrative is engaged when struggle against external resistance is undertaken. In contrast to the victim, the overcomer does not demand fairness or concessions from others or the world, and instead applies effort to achieve goals and form relationships. Because judgment of others' flaws (humanity) is minimized, the overcomer moves away from the statement "The world is against me," and instead reaches out and risks hurt to form meaningful, trusting relationships. The overcomer does not let the mistreatment of others remind her of her powerlessness, but instead, when she encounters mistreatment, uses it as a reminder of how powerful and resilient she really is. Because she is not threatened by admitting that her own flaws can sometimes hurt others, she is open to express forgiveness to those who have hurt her.

The overcomer begins to see the external world as possessing many needed resources and, despite the presence of flawed people, acts on the belief that the risk necessary to access these resources is worth taking. The overcomer resists the temptation to demonize others and affirms their humanity even when they are opposed to her.

This non-judgmental stance is what gave Gandhi or Martin Luther King Jr. their moral authority. Both of them lived at a time when circumstances could easily support a victim mentality and the outrage that comes from it. Even in the face of great prejudice, they did not revile the people who stood between them and justice, but understood that a non-violent approach preserved the obvious moral superiority of their position and saw great breakthrough as a result.

The overcomer does not waste time focused on blame, because when one person or group puts the blame on another, they are also identifying where the power to change lies. The victim's obsession with blame is essentially an admission that someone else has the power. And when blame is the only response one has when facing opposition, you can be sure the victim narrative is in charge. Coincidently, the anthem of Dr. King Jr.'s civil rights movement was the old spiritual "We Shall Overcome," which is a powerful affirmation that, with gentle but persistent faith, there is no evil that cannot be dethroned.

The hero understands that the challenges of life are not meant to break him with discouragement or teach him that it's futile to hope. He instead relishes the challenges ahead, whether they are internal or external, because only then can the hero in him be most fully expressed. No hero ever became recognized as such without some profound battle against injustice or evil. The hero normalizes the resistance present inside of him as well as outside and continues to persevere in whatever task he believes God has set before him. In contrast to the villain, who is frustrated by the resistance reality presents and who generally subscribes to a "screw them before they screw you" worldview, the hero remains resolute in his belief that behaving with integrity and honor in the face of evil is of ultimate, even eternal, importance. He is not focused on finding evil to punish, and he is not demoralized by the abundant amount of it in the world.

Why does any of this matter? Because people *always* live out the narrative they have created. When I was playing tennis with the friend I mentioned earlier in this chapter, I could feel the tension build inside of me as the points became progressively more important. And the only way I knew to control the anxiety I was feeling was to anticipate that I would lose. I preferred to prepare myself for the likelihood of that outcome rather than the uncertainty of winning. I didn't consciously make errors but, instead of playing to the strengths that had gotten me that far, my mindset caused me to alter my style of play just enough to allow my opponent to take advantage of my weaknesses.

That's how a loser narrative plays tennis, but what about a victim or villain? How would the same circumstances play out from those stories? I would suggest that you go back and look at some John McEnroe footage to see the answer. McEnroe was a stellar tennis player who dominated the game in the late '70s and '80s. Despite having the skill to outplay almost anyone on the planet, McEnroe was renowned for his pettiness and temper tantrums on the court. He would frequently take issue with minor mistakes in officiating and punish the offender with contempt and ridicule. I challenge you to watch one of his tantrums (some of which last for several minutes) without wincing as he screams, "Are you kidding me? You're a disgrace!" or "You're the absolute pits of the world!" to well-mannered tennis umpires.

As talented as he was, his narrative leaned strongly toward the victim, and he used the protest from being mistreated to quickly access the villain's power. He never seemed to make peace with the human error that could not be eliminated no matter how angry he got. And the victim in him could never accept the idea that his opponent was subject to the same officiating errors that he was and that, over time, he would benefit from them as much as he would suffer.

Just like I consistently found a way to lose at tennis despite having enough skill to win at least some of the time, the story one tells about who they are in the present is the most certain predictor of what their future will contain. Losers will frustrate others with their negativity and over-emphasize their failures, leading to more losses. Victims will gravitate towards people who hurt them in similar ways they are familiar with and, because their response is limited to blame that must forever remain where they put it, they will never effectively resolve conflict. And villains will always find an abundance of inferiority, either in oneself or others, to vent their rage on and further alienate themselves.

There is a test, called the Thematic Apperception Test (TAT), which assesses personality based on the narration that people create in response to a series of provocative, but ambiguous, drawings. The TAT is similar to the Rorschach Test, which uses ink blot shapes that provide clues to what the viewer is thinking. Except the TAT drawings depict various sorts of interpersonal interactions designed to elicit information about the narrative used by the viewer. The story that people use to describe these drawings can provide insight into the narrator's opinions about themselves and others; takers of the test commonly import their own conflicts onto the characters depicted in the drawings. In short, whatever narrative we use to make sense of our history is the same sort of narration we will project on to every aspect of our interactions with others.

Most everyone would prefer to be living out the three positive narratives if they had a choice, but the problem I've seen others come up against, and experienced personally, is the frustration at how persistent the negative ones can be. It is exceedingly hard to convince someone they have a heroic story inside of them if they have considered themselves damaged goods for many years. For most people with a negative story, the most painful part is how they speak to themselves. The self-attacking and self-defeating thoughts that are common in these narratives can be very toxic. And anyone who has struggled with thoughts like these can attest to how frustrating it is to challenge them. You feel like a pretender who is lying to yourself about having a shred of worth, or whether there is an iota of hope worth hanging on to.

You might have noticed I use the terms narrative, identity, and role almost interchangeably. Another way to conceptualize these ideas is as a sort of life script that we read from as we relate to others. We use the script to prompt us about what we think other people's motives are and what the proper response should be. We consult these scripts when we make important decisions, attempt to resolve conflict, or determine how we should behave in relationships. Many of us carry around negative scripts, which have usually been handed to us by others who have also consistently reminded us which lines are ours: "Here, you read the lines that say loser." Some of us are fortunate enough to have recognized that a more positive script is available to read from.

These narrative roles can also be helpful to distinguish patterns in how our behavior is working for or against our goals. Jessica was a client who had a generally decent family life until, at 14, caught her father in an affair. This crushed her and, to make matters worse, her father manipulated her shamelessly to keep his secret. She began using a variety of drugs and, while still a teenager, married a member of a white supremacist gang, which put her in close contact with some very dangerous people and, in the middle of a drug deal, she ended up being gang-raped in a hotel room. This victimization led to some devastating choices afterward. Jessica actually arranged situations where the identical events could be replayed. But, in her fantasy, she would turn the tables on her attackers and, instead of the powerless victim role, she would play the villain and exact her revenge. More than once, she carefully recreated the event, even down to the particular hotel room where it took place, but, despite her efforts, never did have success at getting revenge on those who took advantage of her. In fact, she ended up re-victimized several times.

We talked about this pattern, and she was able to trace the origins of it all the way back to her father's betrayal and manipulation years earlier. From the outside, it was easy to see how the victim/villain roles still dominated her behaviors, but, because of how natural they felt to her, she was struggling to identify how her behavior was affected by her faulty narrative *as it was happening* - until one day when circumstances conspired to open her eyes to it.

Because she had suffered a seizure and loss of consciousness in a previous treatment center, her driver's license had been suspended, and she needed a doctors certification to have it reinstated. As we filled out the paperwork together, I noticed there were areas where she was not fully honest about the event and its severity. She lied because she was afraid that, if she told the truth, the DMV would not let her drive for a very long time. I warned her that the doctor was unlikely to certify the claims she was making, but she insisted that she needed him to sign the paperwork as written. She asked me to sit in with the doctor and answer any questions that he might have about her current treatment. I had no idea what I was about to witness!

As I expected, the doctor balked when he saw what Jessica wanted him to attest to, and gently explained that he was required to tell the truth on the form and would not sign it. I could see Jessica slump and begin to beg the doctor to reconsider. She told him, "You realize I can't get a job without a driver's license, right?" One after another, she reminded him of all of the reasons she needed her license back in an effort to manipulate his sympathies, but he would not budge. After a short while, when her appeals had been exhausted, I saw a remarkable change. Suddenly, her back straightened and her tone shifted from powerless victim to enraged villain. She ridiculed him for being so "petty," and holding to his integrity. She screamed, "You're no doctor! Doctors are supposed to help people!" among other more foul things. If the devil himself had shown up, I doubt he could have come up with more ingenious insults than Jessica did. That poor guy had no idea!

But, as this was happening, I saw we had a great opportunity to make progress. As she was spewing out insults, I asked her, "Jessica, what role are you playing *right now*?" She paused, let out a deep breath, and said, "I'm all villain right now!" Then, she quickly realized that she had assumed the victim role when the doctor thwarted her attempt to mislead him. And, when she found that she could not get him to yield by manipulating him, she felt justified in venting all the victim's rage she could on him; she then turned to the villain to execute judgment and punishment on her behalf. The light had come on for her, and she was able to see the outworking of her narratives and how quickly they could destroy her relationships. After a few minutes, she was able to apologize and thanked the doctor for his help. When we debriefed after the incident, she marveled at how automatically she had operated from her default roles as well as how seamlessly she moved between the victim and villain roles. She had been able to see the connection between certain feelings and the corresponding narrative for the first time. It would be a great deal later that she would be able to choose different responses when those feelings arose, but I did see her make some progress before she left the treatment center.

We've covered the very basics about the positive and negative narratives and I'm pretty sure that, if you've identified yourself in one of the negative ones, you'd really like to shut its mouth when it tries to convince you of those profound lies that it pushes as the truth. Can you remember a time when you found yourself operating from one of the negative narratives? Or maybe you can identify a friend or loved one's narrative. If you're not clear yet, just try to focus on being aware that you have a narrative that is influencing your thinking, actions, and decision making. Because, just like Jessica realized, these stories we tell ourselves are so second nature that they can feel automatic and beyond question in the heat of the moment.

But we will question them as we proceed. I'll tell you about some people who've succeeded at changing their narrative and how they did it. And you'll learn how to diagnose where your own story is letting you down. More importantly, you'll have some techniques that will allow you to root these lies out and replace them with truths about your identity that will make the positive narratives second nature to you.

We'll also look at how shifting our narratives and perspective radically transforms things like self-esteem, goal-setting, and hope. A portion of what's ahead focuses on ways to manage the difficult emotions that change creates when it pushes us out of our "comfort zones." And we'll revisit some familiar stories from Scripture to see what they can tell us about the "renewing your mind" process.

Remember, controlling the narrative means that we also control the emotional outcome that the story generates. So, the most important question to answer at this point is, "Do you have a choice about the script you will read from?"

EXPECTANCY

To have faith is to be sure of the things we hope for, to be certain of the things we cannot see. (Hebrews 11:1)

"Where does hope come from?" It's a question I frequently ask clients in a group setting. I do it because I know where the discussion will inevitably lead and I can't wait for the fireworks to start. Most people will look at you like you're a little dense and tell you that hope obviously comes from the future. But then we start to examine the question a little bit more in depth and the group begins to see that hope isn't about what will actually happen in the future - it is about what they *expect* will happen in the future. When people consider hope a bit further, they find that it comes as the result of a forecast about the future that is based on very much more than just the basic facts about current circumstances. How we come to form these expectations of the future, and determining if we can change them, is of vital importance.

We are the ultimate forecasting species. We forecast the weather, the stock market, the price of consumer goods, and just about everything else under the sun. When I ask the group how we come up with these elaborate forecasts, they pause for a moment before someone will finally answer, "We look at the past!" And it's true - we scrutinize every scrap of data about weather patterns we can find to come up with more and more reliable predictions. There is a huge controversy right now about privacy concerns related to the collection of "big data." Humans have developed the ability to store incredible amounts of information about the past, and it is done for only one reason: to better predict the future. To predict what you will buy and when, to predict where you will go on vacation, even to predict who is likely to commit terrorist acts and on what timetable. If we want to know what to expect from the future, we always refer to the past. Maybe you've noticed how the banner ads on the websites you visit change based on your browsing history. They are trying to predict your behavior!

When I said I loved the fireworks that come out of this discussion, it is because talking about forecasting the future always separates the group into two factions, each of which shakes their heads at the other in wonder and disgust. No, I'm not talking about Trump and Clinton voters! I'm talking about optimists and pessimists. These two groups are each sure they have the proper way to filter through the data to come up with the most reliable forecast about what the future will hold. Ironically, one side is so certain about the reliability of their forecasts they have even renamed themselves. Pessimists only reluctantly allow themselves to be called pessimists; whenever I ask people if they are pessimists they frequently reply, "No, I'm just a realist!" Now, as a formerly committed pessimist, I totally understand this statement. My friends used to call me Eeyore. There was no silver lining I couldn't find the dark cloud in. And I called myself a realist as well. When pessimists listen to optimists share positive thoughts about the future, they snicker to themselves and say something like, "Oh brother, if you only knew what I do about the future, you'd be just as sour as I am!" And optimists are equally mystified by pessimists seeming inability to see even the possibility of positive outcomes. They can't understand why someone would want to look at the world through such a dark lens.

But here's the secret many pessimists don't want optimists to know: they're jealous of you. They oftentimes wish they could throw off the restraints of "realism" and just relax about the future the way many optimists seem to be able to do. When I was a pessimist, I felt the same way. I was curious about what it would feel like to just suspend the worry and contingency planning for all the ways something could go wrong, but to do so felt like a complete repudiation of why I even had a brain in the first place. Wasn't the point of memory to be able to remember everything that had gone wrong in the past so I could safely avoid those things in the future? It seemed so obvious to me.

In his book called *The Time Paradox*, psychologist Philip Zimbardo has identified a phenomenon he calls *"time perspective bias."* I sometimes open a group by telling them this will be our topic and ask who would like to go first. I enjoy the quizzical looks I get and quickly let them know I'm only joking. But I know that before too long they will realize they are experts in time perspective bias. Because we all have one. Let me explain by summarizing some of Dr. Zimbardo's research and adding a few of my own observations.

We all orient ourselves to time in relation to three spectrums, one each for the past, present, and future. We will look at the present and future biases later on, but for now let's focus on the past. How we view the past runs on a spectrum that is positive on one end and negative on the other. Past-positive people tend to look with fondness and warmth at the past. These people are likely to spend time and energy creating scrapbooks or other types of memorabilia, and they usually value family traditions and rituals highly. They speak with loving recollection about the past and its continuing influence on them.

Past-negative people, however, have a different view of the past. They highlight the losses, betrayals, and letdowns above the good times or high points. They tend to be skeptical or dismissive of nostalgia. When I ask a group if anyone is willing to identify themselves as past-negative, there are usually only a few who will readily confess that they are. Others feel enough shame about being negative that they are slow to admit it. Many will say some version of this, "I can't stand how I think! I always have to find what's wrong with things." Some of them will express annoyance or even distrust of positive people.

It's also interesting to see the reaction of people who are not past-negative to the ones who are. They are not shy about expressing anger toward the past-negative people they are close to. Whenever I give them the opportunity to talk about what it's like to interact with a past-negative person, people will usually say, "It's so draining! They just suck all the life out of you," or "I get so frustrated trying to get my boyfriend to just be happy. No matter how much I try to get him to look on the bright side, it just bounces right off of him." Most past-negative people will express the desire to be more positive, but will also express frustration (even despair) at how difficult it is to sustain thinking positively for any appreciable amount of time.

Now, it's important to realize that thinking negatively about the past has a good purpose: it teaches us what not to repeat. A proper amount of focus on what went wrong, what it felt like to suffer a loss, or, in the case of my addicted clients, how unpleasant it is to be strung out on heroin, can keep us making efforts to avoid recreating those unpleasant circumstances. It's also interesting to note that too much past-positivity can also have a downside. These are the people who are always rhapsodizing about "the good old days" and how things "just aren't what they used to be." They can idealize the past to such a degree that they get stuck there and the thought of change or newness becomes unappealing. In my addicted clients, this shows up as a romanticization of the addiction and an inability to properly assess the costs of their behavior. I have seen people relay devastating details of what their addiction or abusive relationship has cost them and watched a small but noticeable smile gradually creep on to their face as they recount the horror they have been through. That is past-positivity gone haywire.

Now hopefully, you can see the relationship between one's time perspective and where one falls on the optimism/pessimism scale. The more negative one is about the past invariably correlates to how negative one is about the future. Past-negative people don't just suddenly turn their gaze toward the future and find it to be a rosy place. This is where our story-telling nature becomes important, because we select our narratives to provide that sense of continuity that is necessary to form a solid identity. We avoid telling discontinuous stories or we classify them as fairy tales.

This is why people who have a past-negative bias struggle so hard to be positive in the present. It is not possible to clip the present moment off from the ones that have preceded it or the ones we are anticipating in the future. As desirable as it is to "live in the moment," the moment we are in cannot be cleanly divorced from the stream of past and future moments it is a part of. Our lives resemble a movie with thousands of individual frames which, when run at the proper speed, appear to be a seamless image. To examine a particular frame in isolation from the rest of the movie is not meaningful in the context of the movie. Only when it is added to the film and run at the proper speed does it find its true context. The individual moments that make up our lives are like those frames, and our narrative is like the voiceover to the entire film.

One's orientation to the past (positive or negative) determines the tenor of the narrative going forward. If one is telling a generally negative story about the past moments and forecasting a continuation of that story in the moments to come, it becomes a herculean task to be positive in this one present moment. In the negative story, one has to work against the momentum of the narrative to be positive. But when one chooses to use the set of positive facts about his past to change his narrative, his expectation about the future will instantly change to accommodate the new positive story. In the positive story, the present moment is just one positive "frame" in a generally positive "movie" and being positive is literally effortless.

Some people like to interject at this point that there is nothing good about their past that could enable them to change their forecast. This is never true. Even lives that have incredible abuse or trauma demonstrate the resilience and fortitude of the one who has survived it! That is a good thing, even a heroic thing. When examined from the proper perspective, everyone has an abundant positive body of evidence available in their past to forecast from.

So where does hope come from? It comes from our past. It is forward-looking, but backward rooted. Our ability to look positively into the future is dependent on the viewpoint we use to look at our past. When I explain this concept to clients who voice how hopeless they are, I ask them how they are going to get a new past. They usually shrug with a defeated expression until I tell them there are two ways to get one. I also tell them that one way is mandatory and has slow but steady results over time, but the other way is optional and can have miraculous results instantaneously. The mandatory way is to begin taking new action in the present so that when one looks back in three months, six months, or a year, they will be forecasting from a different body of facts. It is this new body of evidence that will enable them to find a good reason to hope.

This is one reason why programs like Alcoholics Anonymous help people to recover; they provide support while people create new pasts "one day at a time" until they can sustain hope that they could not before. As they clear the hurdles involved in staying sober, they establish a track record of success they can refer to when contemplating the future. When they are confronted with a lack of information or skills necessary to make progress, they learn that there are people available who can teach them what they need to learn. Over time, the practice of reaching out, and finding, assistance and comfort allows one to look much more confidently toward an uncertain future. Hope arrives slowly but surely.

The second, optional, way to become hopeful is more what this book is about. It has to do with giving ourselves permission to look at whatever evidence we want to in order to change from a narrative that keeps us in pain to one that celebrates the healing that comes with renewing our minds. For the Christian, this means identifying where our narrative conflicts with what God says about His children and choosing to embrace the truths found in Scripture about His intimate involvement in every circumstance of our past, as well as what we can count on Him to provide going forward. I said this optional way to get a new past has miraculous power, so let me explain how I came to understand this.

SIN CITY

Taste and see that the Lord is good; blessed is the one who takes refuge in him. (Psalm 34:8)

One of the Scriptures I learned soon after I became a believer mentions that God is able to do "exceedingly abundantly beyond all we can ask or even imagine" (Ephesians 3:20). I always loved how big that made God sound, but honestly, I really thought I could imagine some pretty big things and kind of doubted that He would go lengths half that great for someone as ordinary as me. But now, I can say with the strongest certainty that God is well able to exceed my wildest imaginations about what He is capable of! This chapter is the account of how I came to believe that.

Before these events took place, I was as past-negative as someone could be and had a well-entrenched loser narrative that leaked out of me constantly. I was so committed to looking at life through a dark lens that if someone had said God could somehow intervene to set me free, I could not have begun to think how He would even find a way to approach the problem, much less do anything about it. It was absolutely unthinkable to me that any other lens was available to view the world through. I will touch on more of that later, but for now, please do your best to suspend any preconceptions you have about where and how God will act, except that He is unbelievably kind, merciful, and wise.

I grew up in Malibu, California in the mid-sixties before it became as glamorous as it is today. I happened to make friends in kindergarten with a kid named Carlos Estevez, who would later change his name to Charlie Sheen. He and I became close friends and spent quite a bit of time together over the first 26 years of our lives. We had very compatible senses of humor and spent a lot of time cracking each other up as kids. As teenagers, we both discovered a love of marijuana and Led Zeppelin that became central to the time we spent together. Because there was no high school in Malibu at that time, we had to drive to Santa Monica every day (about 25 miles). Charlie drove his BMW 320i, and I rode with him along with another friend. The traffic from Malibu to Santa Monica on weekday mornings was always bumper to bumper, and we would open the sunroof to blow out huge clouds of smoke on the way to school. What a sight that must have been. Yikes! Most days we would arrive late, look at each other with skepticism, get back in the car and head to Westwood to play video games and see a movie.

For a time in my early twenties, when his fame was exploding after he did the movie *Platoon*, I was employed by him as a sort of professional tax write-off. Being on a film location is nowhere near as exciting as it sounds, with long days (and sometimes nights) and a lot of time spent waiting for shots to get set up. Having familiar faces around is a welcome comfort, and by employing me as a "trainer," Charlie could write off my salary on his taxes and have a friend accompany him on location who could take care of some of the little things that make life easier on set. I drove us from the hotel to the set, ran errands on occasion, shopped for food, and otherwise did what I could to help him out. I should also mention that this is during the time when my addictions to marijuana and cocaine began to become more ingrained, and one of the things I ended up good at was supplying drugs to the cast and crew of the movies we were filming. My ability to speak Spanish was particularly useful when we were on location in Spain filming *Navy Seals*. I made regular trips into the plaza to bring back cocaine and hashish for anyone who placed an order with me.

This was also the first time I was able to watch the addiction process unfold in someone else. One day after work, Charlie came out of the bathroom and, with a measure of concern, said, "Dude, I'm addicted to everything!" He ran down a list of all the things that had become troubling to him and ended by saying, "I'm even addicted to Visine!" I don't remember what I said, but I do remember feeling ill-equipped to offer any good advice.

One of the places we spent time in Spain was called La Manga, a beautiful city on Spain's southern coast a short distance northeast of Cartagena. La Manga is built on a spit of land that shelters a large bay called the Mar Menor (Little Sea) and is a very popular tourist destination in the summer months. It is reminiscent of the Florida Keys due to its geography, but is developed much more densely. It is full of vacation homes, high rise hotels and condominiums that are all packed in the summer months. The only problem was that we were there in the absolute dead of the offseason. Aside from the hotel we were staying in, the city resembled a ghost town with just the locals and the minimum staff necessary to run the resorts sticking around for the winter. One of the few things there was to do was visit the casino, which we did nearly every night while we were there. It was here that Charlie introduced me to the table game that would one day be where God would meet me with the answer to many years of prayer and supplication.

Charlie loved roulette. He loved it so much he wanted to play at more than one table at a time. So one of my duties became placing bets for him on one roulette table while he played on another. This went on for a time until his losses mounted and he scaled back to just one table. While, due to factors I mentioned earlier, I have limited memories of our time there, I do have a memory of him directing me to consistently place bets on several numbers one night, one of which I forgot to place on one spin. Of course, that was the number that hit, and when he saw it from the other table, he rushed over excitedly to claim his winnings. When I sheepishly told him I had forgotten to place the bet on his favorite number (17), he shook his head slightly and looked at me as if to say, "You had one job...!" Oh well!

Bear with me while I explain some basic facts to those who are not familiar with the game. Roulette is played by placing bets on where a small white ball will land on numbered slots in the roulette wheel. The European wheel contains the numbers 1-36 (half red and half black) as well as a single green zero space and is laid out in random fashion. There are many ways to place bets but, for our discussion, it is enough to know that a $1 bet placed on any single number will be paid $35 in return if the ball falls into that slot on the wheel (35-1). Proper payouts on the European table should be 36-1, but the casino pays out as if the zero space does not exist; it constitutes the house edge and gives them a 2.63% advantage, which, over time, makes all those casinos profitable. This knowledge about odds will come into play later in the story.

As I became familiar with the game, I began to play my own money and gravitated to certain numbers on the table. To my surprise, I began to win with some regularity, and I pocketed quite a few pesetas over the span of a few weeks. I got curious about the numbers I was playing and examined the card that casinos distribute to players that shows the layout of the wheel and where past rolls can be recorded. I noticed that the numbers I had settled on playing were grouped in what looked like quadrants of the wheel. It seemed more than coincidence that the numbers I was playing created several small clusters of space on the wheel and I got the self-satisfied idea that I must have discovered a "system" that accounted for my consistent wins over time. I was thrilled and when we left La Manga, and I looked forward to visiting Las Vegas at some point and continuing my winning streak.

Not long after we finished filming, I accompanied Charlie to Las Vegas for some sort of celebration I can't recall clearly and had the opportunity to test out my system. I was eager to play and felt utmost confidence about my chances when I sat down at the table. It took only a few minutes to lose the first $100. I considered this an anomaly and quickly got $200 more in chips, which I lost in about the same amount of time it took to lose the first $100. I was a little stung and stepped away from the table to assess what had happened. To my dismay, I noticed that there was a completely different layout of numbers on the wheel and not just one green space but two! There was now a double zero in addition to the single zero I was used to. Not only is the American wheel laid out in a different order from the European one, the presence of the double zero means that the house edge is doubled on the American wheel (to 5.26%).

So I grudgingly let go of my dream of employing some sort of system to make money playing roulette on the American wheel, but, in the back of my mind, I always entertained the idea of finding a European wheel to try it out again. After some years, I visited Las Vegas again and noticed a single zero wheel at one of the casinos. I was thrilled, but as I approached to play I noticed that the minimum bets allowed were much higher than I wanted to risk. In exchange for the privilege of playing the wheel with more favorable odds, I would have to play at least $100 per spin of the wheel. I had no intention of gambling at this level of risk and walked away disheartened.

Now, it's important to remember that I told you I considered myself a loser. And part of why I was disheartened was because of that nagging desire every pessimist has to let go of thinking about what is likely to go wrong and believe that winning just might be possible. I wanted to believe that I could have the confidence necessary to step up and face the level of risk required to play at those higher stakes. But, when one is convinced that losing is the likely outcome, the most sensible thing to do is to make every effort to minimize risk. If losing is probable, then losing in small nibbles is far better than large bites. Keeping risk small seems the wisest course; this is called "playing it safe." So, for years, I secretly harbored the desire to one day step up to the table and set aside my fear of losing just long enough to have a bit of fun and test my old system.

It was around Christmas time in 2014 and my year was not going well. I had separated from my wife a few months before, and my family was not eager to talk with me. I was unemployed and living in a house I had inherited when my mother passed away the year before. I had attempted to sell the property, but the escrow fell through at the last minute because of some arcane fire department regulations having to do with water flow through the fire hydrants in the neighborhood. So no permitting would be allowed without spending hundreds of thousands of dollars to upgrade the system. I had even offered to reduce the price of the property by the amount required to upgrade the neighborhood water main, but no one wanted the profound headache that managing the project would have been.

And on top of it all, the city was threatening to turn off the power and water because of the current status of permits. I had to beg them to keep the utilities on so the landscape wouldn't die. So I had an ostensibly very valuable piece of land with a manufactured home on it that I could legally neither develop nor inhabit due to permitting issues. I was essentially squatting in a neighborhood filled with million dollar homes hoping that the authorities would not find out I was there and evict me. Talk about a loser narrative!

As Christmas approached, I began to wonder what I would do for the holiday. I was estranged from my family, and they were going to visit my ex-wife's family in northern California anyway. I had a few friends who would gladly have opened their homes to me had they known I was alone, but, not being very sentimental about holidays (past-negative) I decided I would go to Las Vegas instead. Just to treat myself to a couple of shows and a few good meals and to take my mind off of everything that had gone wrong during the year. So I made reservations to stay at the Bellagio hotel for two nights (Dec. 23rd & 24th).

As I drove into town, I had no reason to think that this Christmas would be any different from the previous ones, although I was somewhat relieved that I would not have to spend time with in-laws or extended family. The first night I was there I had dinner in the Bellagio buffet which is an extensive feast full of all you can eat delicacies. There are numerous salads, pizzas, roasted meats, seafood, and desserts available. I ate like a king and left the restaurant on my way to watch the Bellagio fountains for a few minutes and see a Cirque du Soleil show at another casino. But I was about to walk into one of the greatest blessings God has ever given to me. And how He did this will forever boggle my sensibilities about where He is likely to show up.

It was then that I saw it! On my way through the casino floor, I saw a European roulette wheel. All the other tables were crowded, but because of the higher minimum dollar amount to play, there was only one other gentleman playing this table. Twenty-five years of history was suddenly recalled as I weighed the decision about whether to play or not. I remembered fondly the times in Spain, but more than that, I remembered that I wanted to be someone who did not reflexively back away from risk every time it appeared in front of him. The time had come! As I got closer, I noticed the table minimum of $100 per spin and made the uncharacteristic decision to play. I had the intention of staying for only one spin since losing $100 was all I cared to let go of in the minute that it would take to spin the wheel.

From the moment I decided to play there was a very subtle, almost imperceptible, voice that began whispering in my mind like a sort of background tape. As I reached for my wallet, this tape reminded me "But you're going to lose." I got to the table and asked for four $25 chips to place on my four favorite numbers, and the little voice said: "But you're going to lose." As I placed the chips on the

46

numbers 0, 17, 23, and 35, the voice dutifully told me "But you're going to lose." And, as the wheel spun and the ball bounced around inside of it, I let myself enjoy the excitement of the anticipation because I was utterly convinced it would be the only excitement I would get. I was totally, unequivocally certain that the ball would drop into some other slot and I would walk away proud (and somewhat comforted) that I had been able to predict the outcome: I was a loser.

But then the unthinkable happened. After bouncing around the wheel haphazardly, the little white ball settled into the zero hole! I slapped one hand against the other and exchanged a satisfied look with the other player at the table. Then, instead of walking away $100 lighter the dealer pushed $875 in front of me. I tipped him $25, put the rest in my pocket, and walked down a broad aisle between the rest of the table games. No doubt I was already elated and in a state of mild shock, but I was even more surprised by what happened next. As I was walking outside to see the fountains, I felt as if God was providing His own very subtle, almost imperceptible background voice to the event. There was a message being conveyed at that moment that was unspoken but clearly communicated. It was as if I heard Him say, "You know, Pat, I could come through for you in some really impressive ways if you could just bring yourself to PUT IT IN PLAY!" It stopped me in my tracks. If I had to put a tone of voice on what I heard I would say it was 98% tender love and 2% mild frustration mixed with urgency.

To be clear, this was *not* a call to loosen up and play roulette with more confidence. This was an alarm that God was ringing in my ears to stop letting fear of the future freeze me in my tracks. Up to this time, my relationship with risk was based entirely on avoidance of it, and it had reached the point where it was hindering me from fulfilling my potential in every way. My faith was deep due to 22 years of pursuing Him diligently and learning from good teachers, but almost totally mental. It had very little power to influence my actions at all. I talked myself out of applying for jobs, pursuing relationships, and putting myself in any situation that I couldn't predict the outcome of. I was engaging life from a passive and powerless position because I was scared to assume responsibility for the outcome of my choices; I avoided leadership, even of my own life, like the plague!

This was God's wake-up call to me that it was not acceptable anymore to shrink back from the risk necessary to live a fulfilling life. It was also a potent reminder that, if I was going to have success, it would have a lot to do with *acting* on the belief that He actually was backing me up. Most importantly, it finally sunk into me that it was His great desire to "come through" for me in ways that I literally could not imagine - if I would just PUT IT IN PLAY!

Up to that time, I was acting on the assumption that God would bless and uphold anyone who came to Him humbly in need – except me. I had tons of hope that if you needed something from God, and you did your part of the work (even if that was just asking), you had every reason to believe that He would intervene on your behalf somehow. But I was, because of my loser mindset, excluded from that hope. It was as if the sun was shining on a thick, black cloud that hovered over me and blocked out almost all the light. I knew the sun was shining, but the feeling of warmth on my spiritual skin could rarely penetrate my negative mindset. I would experience happiness or joy briefly, and then, despite reveling in them, I would watch them quickly recede and leave me again with an anguished loser narrative. Because of the manner in which I came to know God, I remained steadfastly certain that my afterlife was secure but, because I could not imagine His goodness reaching me on this planet, I longed for this life to end and relieve me from the burden of having to wake up for another day.

I spent another day and night in Las Vegas diverting myself with a visit to the spa, another show, and some good food. I lost the money I made at the roulette table (and more), but I felt a bit lighter by what had happened. Hearing God say something very personal, even if it is convicting, can do that. On the drive home I had no idea the extent of the change that was taking place in my thinking, and I certainly had no idea that lifelong depression was about to be utterly shattered. He had begun the process of showing me that my predictions and forecasts about the future were unreliable and hope, which was an almost totally alien concept to me beforehand, was about to come alive in an amazing way!

CERTAINTY

And without faith it is impossible to please Him, for he who comes to God must believe that He is, and that He is a rewarder of those who seek Him. (Hebrews 11:6)

Psychologist Leon Festinger first described the principle of cognitive dissonance in the late 1950s. Cognitive dissonance is what occurs when two contradictory thoughts are present in one's mind at the same time. Like two musical notes that are jarring to the ear, thoughts that cause dissonance are unpleasant to experience and prompt us to adjust our thinking in ways that produce consonance, or harmony. Someone who considers themselves an honest person will feel dissonance when they cheat someone else. They may attempt to justify their actions by minimizing the loss the other person incurred or by convincing themselves their victim somehow deserved to be taken from. Or they might feel compelled to make amends to relieve themselves of unpleasant feelings of guilt.

Elliot Aronson, another prominent psychologist who studied cognitive dissonance, describes it this way: "Dissonance theory does not rest upon the assumption that man is a rational animal; rather, it suggests that man is a rationalizing animal – that he attempts to appear rational, both to others and to himself." In hindsight, there was nothing more irrational than stubbornly holding on the idea that the most sensible prediction I could make about the future was that I would sooner or later become a loser. I went to great lengths to rationalize my refusal to allow for the possibility that things could turn out other than dreadful. This is especially dissonant when one considers all of the incredible promises and reasons to rejoice available to anyone who puts their faith in God. Scripture is full of astonishing statements about our value to Him and all the good things we can expect when we come into His family. I would have staked my life on the fact that all those promises were true – just for other people.

After I left Las Vegas, the next few days were spent pondering the cognitive dissonance that had manifested in my thinking when I won at the roulette table. It wasn't the amount I had won (I had inherited quite a bit of cash from my mother as well, and it had not improved my attitude one inch in over a year), and it wasn't that the bet was such a longshot (I had a 10.8% chance of winning) - it was how absolutely certain I had been that I would lose. The story that I was telling myself at the table left not one iota of space to allow for the possibility of winning. When the dealer pushed that money in front of me, the loser narrative that had been playing in my mind like a low hum for many years was suddenly, glaringly wrong: the loser had won! How would I make sense of that?

When I returned from my trip, I began to dissect the experience to find out if there was a bigger application to it. I sensed it had value to think about further, but did not yet understand the deliverance God was quickly bringing. I had always taken great pride in using logic and reason to guide my thoughts and actions, and I put a high value on using them to make rational and consistent decisions. I honestly believed that my pessimism was the logical expression of what I had learned in life to that point; I thought I was only being "realistic" when I forecast that something negative was likely to happen soon. And I incorrectly reasoned that pondering all the ways that a setback could arrive would make me both more prepared and more able to withstand the shock of it.

One of the coping skills I had to learn to deal with depression was not to give myself the luxury of having two different schedules or routines based on how I felt that day. I put this as having an "above the line" day or a "below the line" day. When my depression was at its worst, I would come home from work and curl up in bed for two hours, but the point is I went to work even though I wanted to curl up in bed before I ever left. Whether my day was tolerable or miserable (because they were never great!), I would not allow myself to alter the schedule I knew I needed to keep to reach my goals. I got up at the same time each day, performed all the same grooming routines, and generally tried to keep my schedule predictable whether I felt like dying or not.

Part of that lifestyle includes the habit of regular, vigorous, aerobic exercise. I found that, after I had done it consistently for several months, it had the power to reliably change my mood for the better. There were many times I got on the stair-climber ready to cry, but got off feeling much better. I have a saying I use now with my clients, "It's hard to have a bad day after a good workout!" Over the past several years, I have used the time on the exercise bike at the gym to pray, meditate, and ask myself questions I don't yet know the answers to. That was what I planned to do when I went to the gym after I got back from Vegas, but I had no reason to think anything unusual was about to happen. I couldn't have been more wrong!

I can best express what happened to change my thinking that day as a conversation between God and me. And if I had to guess how He felt having it with me, I would have to say delight: delight about knowing what He was about to do for me. Looking back, the relief that He brought was so profound that I have a hard time believing He wasn't walking me through the argument in a very personal way. It took only a few minutes (seconds?) for this exchange to take place, and while it is more accurate to say it was more of an intuitive conversation, it is easiest to convey it as a dialog that God chose to have with me. It went like this:

God: So Pat, of these two possible futures, the one where what happens is positive and the one that is negative, which one of those futures actually exists right now?

Me (on the recumbent bicycle): Well, the future has not happened yet, so I would have to say that neither one exists right now.

God: So then, when choosing between two things that do not currently exist, how do you use logic and reason to determine which one will occur?

Me: That's a good question. I suppose I look at previous experience.

God: Is that what you were looking at when you were standing in front of that roulette table?

Me: It must have been.

God: Then how did you forecast it so poorly?

Me: I must have been using the wrong information about the past.

God: (with great force) EXACTLY! And when you forecast with certainty all the other negative things that you see in the future, all the other things that currently don't exist, is it at least possible that you could be mistaken about those as well?

Me: It would be logical and reasonable to admit that it is.

God: Then why do you think you consistently forecast that you will lose?

Me: It must be because I have a bias toward looking at the negative in my past.

God: And what if you were freed from that bias and the constraints of "logic and reason" when you looked to the future and could use whatever evidence from the past you wanted to in order to make your forecast? Is there any difference between expecting something negative to happen and expecting something positive?

Me: Well, I spend a lot of energy planning on various contingencies, and I waste a lot of time worrying about things that almost never happen. Because I think the future is basically painful, and the present is constantly sliding into the future, I have dread about what is likely to meet me when I get there. And, despite doing this to give myself peace about being prepared for what is coming, all it ever does is rob me of the ability to feel happy RIGHT NOW! I have to fight off so much heaviness to enjoy the moment I almost never can.

God: And what if you could bring yourself to forecast out of the positive parts of your past? Out of the things you have overcome and seen Me deliver you from or out of the victories and gifts that I've given to you so that you and others could be blessed. Would that be a different experience?

Me: (imagining how that might feel) Hell yes! I could believe that you were already there in the future tending to all the contingencies and I would not have to carry that burden anymore. The future would become an adventure that I collaborate with you on moment by moment in the present. Life would become a gift and joy would be a main character in the story I tell.

God: (unspoken) You're welcome!

Me: (stunned silence)

So I got up from that 30 minutes of cardio an entirely different person! God had done for me in a very personal way what Isaiah wrote when he spoke the word of the Lord to Israel, "Come now, and let us reason together..." Isaiah finishes the thought by saying, "Though your sins are like scarlet, they shall be as white as snow..." (Isa 1:18). God's "reasoning" had made my sin plain to see; in my negativity, I had utterly mischaracterized Him, and it led me to discount the gift of being given breath to live another day!

Until then I had concluded God was indifferent, distracted, or primarily interested in teaching me a hard lesson while He got on with the important things that had nothing to do with me. I saw life as a drudging and repetitive duty that one had to endure before finally entering God's kingdom after death. I believed that whatever plan He was working on was much grander than my small life and had very little to do with my day to day circumstances. Over and over, I had made the mistake of excluding myself from the benefits promised in Scripture and completely missed how kind, generous, and wise God really is. My narrative about my worth and potential was constantly clashing with what the Bible teaches and I lived with those dissonant thoughts 24/7.

Now, I am in no way comparing my suffering to that of Job, but I am amused by the parallels between my story and his. In both cases, a limited human being experiences significant loss and struggles to reconcile what he knows about God to his circumstances. In both cases, there is a wish for God to finish the job and bring the relief of death: "Why is...life [given] to the bitter of soul, to those who long for death...who search for it more than for hidden treasure...if only God were willing to crush me, that He would loose His hand and cut me off!" (Job 3:20-21, 6:9). In both cases, when God decides to intervene, He asks a series of questions designed to give the limited human a different perspective of reality: "Where were you when I laid the foundations of the earth?" (Job 38:4).

And in both cases, when the grandness and purpose of God can finally be seen in the circumstances of the past, the response is similar: "...I have declared that which I did not understand, things too wonderful for me, which I did not know...I will ask You, and You instruct me. I have heard of You by the hearing of the ear; but now my eye sees You; therefore I retract, and I repent in dust and ashes" (Job 42:3-6). Like Job, I had been attempting to declare something too "wonderful" for man to understand - how the circumstances we see and experience on earth could ever be reconciled with the existence of an all-knowing, all-powerful God, who is only motivated by love. Job was angry with God and was experiencing some cognitive dissonance of his own, namely, "How can this God, who is so loving and supposedly concerned with fairness, let all this wrong happen to me?"

If the answer doesn't boggle you, you aren't thinking about it right! It's either true or false that God is incapable of evil: "For You are not a God who takes pleasure in wickedness; No evil dwells with You" (Ps. 5:4). If God is good, then every single event that has ever happened has come through that good gateway to reach mankind. Now, I am not saying that everything that has happened is, in and of itself, good. Some things are inherently evil and cannot be endorsed. But, no matter how wrong or out of order an action is, there is no way to erase the possibility of good arising from it. That's how powerful and wise God is!

The only limiting factor is our willingness to examine and alter our perspective to make room for the goodness of God to express itself. This is the remedy that God applies when He speaks to Job. He doesn't bother explaining the nuances of exactly why tragedy had happened to Job; He simply changes Job's perspective from a narrow field of view focused only on his pain and suffering to one that sees the entire range of God's activity in creation. God ignores Job's complaints about his loss and instead reminds Job who it is he is accusing. This acts like a splash of cold water on his face and reawakens Job's faith in God's wisdom. And a complete faith includes the assurance that, at some point in the future, possibly the distant future, the goodness and wisdom of God in allowing circumstances to take place as they have will certainly become evident.

It would be appropriate to use the word slave to describe my relationship to both cocaine and negativity. As hard as I tried to get away from each in my own strength, I was unable to move them at all. In retrospect, the experience at the roulette table had shaken loose the moorings of my negative mindset. The miracle had actually happened at that moment, but the full expression was still unfolding (and continues still as I write this).

56

A few years after this experience, I came across a body of research having to do with something called *memory reconsolidation*. Psychotherapists Bruce Ecker and Lauren Hulley have created a branch of therapy, called Coherence Therapy, which takes advantage of the brain's ability to reconsolidate, or alter, memories that have been previously stored in one's long-term (consolidated) memory. The theory arose after they observed certain occurrences in treatment that led to profound, immediate breakthroughs for their clients.

Coherence Therapy (CT) focuses on what Ecker and Hulley call implicit core emotional memories or learnings. These learnings begin very early in life, even before the child has words to describe them or make sense of the environment around him. As the child ages, these learnings are organized into what CT calls a construct or schema, both of which roughly correspond to the idea of narrative that we've already covered. Ecker calls these constructs the "projection of the past onto the present," which, when they replay trauma or dysfunction, sounds a lot like the past-negative time perspective bias that the negative narratives all operate from.

The coherence Ecker describes is defined as the "necessity" of the symptom in light of the schema or narrative that underlies it; they cohere or "stick together." In my own example, because the anxiety produced when I accepted responsibility for the choices and outcomes of my life was overwhelming, it was necessary to remain paralyzed by depression and futility. My schema assumed that I was going to lose, and for that emotional core learning to remain true, I had to exhibit the symptoms that would support that assumption. This was me living out my story.

The most interesting part of CT has to do with what Ecker and Hulley discovered to be the factors that led to those breakthroughs I mentioned. Rather than focusing on counteracting a client's negative symptoms or teaching them how to better cope with their presence, Ecker and Hulley noticed that, when a person could be provided with an experience that "mismatched" what they expected to happen, the memories that supported the core emotional learnings became malleable, or moldable, allowing the person to adopt a totally different schema that no longer needed the negative symptoms.

The key experience that CT attempts to create is one where a person's schema (narrative) is fully activated and brought to conscious awareness before providing the person an experience where "prediction error" can cause the consolidated, long-term memories that support the negative narrative to be reconsolidated without the previous connection to negative emotions and symptoms. In other words, the memories that used to automatically bring anxiety, sadness, or terror, are no longer connected to those emotions and a person is free to assign whatever meaning and emotion he wishes to the memory.

I was astonished when I realized that this was exactly the experience that God had arranged for me to have in front of that roulette table. As I repeatedly affirmed, "But you're going to lose" in front of that roulette wheel, my loser narrative was in full bloom until I had a profound "prediction error" moment when the ball dropped into the zero hole. The shock of that, coupled with His gentle encouragement to assume more risk in my life, was exactly what I needed to adopt a new narrative where despair and negativity were no longer part of my story. The loser narrative melted away effortlessly and allowed me to consciously choose a schema (narrative) that cohered to the "symptoms" of hope, joy, and gratitude.

Evidently, there is a mechanism built into the human brain that can allow for memories, or groups of memories, to be disentangled from the emotions that were appropriate when they were originally consolidated. This has amazing applications for all sorts of psychological problems; if my depression, which was unshakably present with me for 48 years, could be relieved, then it is not unthinkable that anyone laboring with a narrative that requires them to suffer can find similar relief.

The encounter I had with God in Las Vegas was the second time that He had intervened and tipped the scale back to balance. Just as He had, twenty-two years earlier, suspended the compulsion to use cocaine and allowed me a 50/50 choice on whether to use drugs or not (more on that later), He had used the roulette table to first demonstrate my folly of committing so strongly to the loser narrative and then to give me a 50/50 choice about whether to remain a pessimist or not.

Needless to say, I was overjoyed to receive the gift of freedom to choose my mindset and shed the old way of thinking that had dominated me for so many years. The experience was very similar to when God first intervened in my mid-twenties; I saw the world (and myself) in an entirely different way. But what would change as a result of this meeting with God? Everything it turns out!

IMMEDIACY

If it is disagreeable in your sight to serve the LORD, *choose for yourselves **today** whom you will serve... (Joshua 24:1, emphasis mine)*

I spent many years living with very deep depression. The seeds were sown early in life (elementary school) when I had difficulty understanding why *some*thing existed rather than *no*thing. I couldn't solve these existential questions and I was tormented by the meaning of life. As a child, I sensed that death was the only way to answer the questions I had about the purpose of life. I would either meet whatever God existed there or go out of existence myself and not care anymore.

As a teen, I tried hard to get pleasure from the kinds of things that seemed to please my peers at the time, but I never could find the same sort of satisfaction that they did. One of the few things that I did find satisfaction in was calorie-dense foods like fatty lunch meats, dairy products, and peanut butter. I found early in life that I could numb myself to the pain of feeling isolated if I had the company of food. By the time I was a teenager, I was 30-40 lbs. overweight and felt much heavier than that. I lost much of the weight when I played football in high school, but my body image was so distorted that I cut the size tags off my Levi's even though I had a normal waist size.

I had a few close friends, but because of shame about being overweight and the low self-esteem that came with it, I always assumed I was disposable to them. Because I had no strong sense of self beyond my loser story, I struggled to find a group of people where

I felt I belonged. During my senior year in high school, I dreaded lunch because this sense of being without community would become painfully obvious every day. I would arrive at the quad and survey the different cliques of people who always sat in the same spots or under the same trees. I was not bullied or ostracized, but I have a feeling I was a total enigma to my peers at the time; they didn't know what to make of me - probably because I didn't know what to make of myself. I would approach one circle of people and gently insinuate myself into their conversation until I realized within a few minutes that I had little to no interest in what they were talking about. Then I would repeat that process two or three more times until I realized that there were no groups where I felt I belonged. And after football season was over there was no practice to attend, so I would quietly slip away to the bus stop, head back to Malibu and smoke weed to forget the confusion I was feeling.

This alienation set the stage for some decisions that changed the trajectory of my life going forward. The decision-making process I used to consider what to do after high school was ruled by doubt about my ability to make the right choices, and because I felt that there was a lot at stake, my fear was heightened to a paralyzing degree. In hindsight, it's tough to say the choices I did (or couldn't) make were mistakes because I believe they were necessary to get me to where I am now. But I did have to go through a period of grief to let go of the loss of who I might have become had fear and avoidance not dictated the terms of how I would face the adult world.

I felt powerless to take action that would bring anything good into my life, and I was conflicted about approaching women. I had seen a very distant relationship between my mother and father, and operated from a basic assumption that women tolerated men, but did not really like them. There was one girl who I had formed a connection with throughout high school, but, even while we spent hours together each day, she sent me mixed signals that alternately drew me close and made me wish I could walk away. At one point, despite knowing that I wanted her to be my girlfriend, she confided to me that she had a crush on my best friend. But not even that could convince me to let her go. My self-esteem was so compromised by this time that I did not believe I would find anything better.

I was so codependent in that relationship that I stayed devoted even after she got married just after high school. During that time, I tried over and over to pull out the cables that had kept me connected to her, but it seemed that, just when I was about to finally cut the last one and be free, she would call me and reconnect them all in an hour. I attempted some other relationships through my twenties, but I always found myself available when she came back around. She struggled in her first marriage and used me as a confidant to tell her troubles to. Eventually, she divorced him and we married after a year or so. But, despite loving each other, we were in near constant conflict and spent significant time separated from each other over the next 21 years. We were both loaded with baggage from our early years, addicted in our own ways, and living out two narratives that brought out the worst in each other. After our first year of marriage her 5-year-old daughter, Ellen, was diagnosed with terminal brain cancer and given only six months to live; this type of stress splits most couples up, and we were no exception. She ended up living for seven years, and while she was a delight to all who knew her, her condition demanded almost all of the emotional energy we could summon as a family.

After high school, I started working as a landscape contractor because I was too scared of the kind of commitment college would require. I was certain I would pick the wrong school, the wrong major, and the wrong future – the loser narrative had infected every aspect of my thinking by that time. I had great difficulty turning the kind of profit that was possible as a landscape contractor and a lot of our marital conflict was about money. It didn't help that my wife was a compulsive spender who used money to soothe her own low sense of self-worth.

I became a very creative and capable landscaper and eventually found out I was bidding for the same jobs that some very high-profile companies were. I had a meeting one day with a landscape architect who complimented my work by saying, "You do better work than the guys who charge $900 a day!" And that was in the early '90s. I'm not sure that she knew I was making about a quarter of that amount, and my jaw dropped that anyone could have the courage to charge that much. And, even though I knew I was worth significantly more than I was earning, my loser identity prevented me from pricing my work appropriately.

At one point, I was managing a crew of six and wearing every hat possible for a business owner. I say now that I was an excellent landscaper, but I was a terrible businessman. I was hollowing out the business to cover our personal expenses because I was so averse to having the necessary conflict with my wife about finances. She was much more comfortable in conflict and, because she was always willing to escalate to a higher level than I was, she won before we even started. I resented her for her dominance and hated myself for my passivity. I used to take large checks into the bank - enough to pay the bills, payroll, and materials, and walk out in tears because I knew I had to do it again in just a few days and I didn't know where it would come from. These problems snowballed as my foreman became an alcoholic and my crew started feuding among themselves. Eventually, I realized that it was costing me more money to go to work than it was to stay home.

My wife and I were splitting up again during this time and, because we had bought a house during the housing bubble and run up a huge line of credit, my finances were unsustainable. I left the house, folded up the business, and went bankrupt for almost a million dollars. I was shocked when I added up all of the liabilities that I had taken on, and I took it as a backhanded compliment that I had that much debt. Nobody who was as much of a loser as I thought I was would have been able to get that much credit in the first place!

I had various sayings I let echo around my head all those years. When I was in the loser narrative I begged, "Somebody please destroy me!" and when I was playing the victim it was, "F...ing world, never gives me what I want!" I said each of those thousands of times to myself for years. I used to tell others that the reason I knew God did not answer prayer is because I was still alive – and, even though I said it jokingly, I secretly meant it.

At the time, I described the self-loathing I had by saying that, if the intensity of my negative thoughts about myself could be made physically manifest, I would become a pile of ash. I bargained with God by offering to take the place of some innocent drunk driving victim so that tragedy could be avoided. For many years, I wished that there was a switch on the wall that would have stopped my heart. If it were that easy to die, there is no way any ten people together could have prevented me from flipping it.

This passive suicidal ideation was present even in elementary school. In 6th grade, I took a large bottle of Tylenol with me to school with the intention of taking them all at lunch. I told one of my friends about the plan, and he wrestled the pills away from me and threw them over the playground fence; Andy Margolin, thank you if you're out there! My brother and I shared similar genetics, upbringing, and mindsets; in March of 2011, he rented a hotel room in Costa Mesa, CA and asphyxiated himself with helium gas while in an alcohol binge. He weighed over 500 lbs. when he died. It was a shock but not a surprise.

I considered myself such a certain loser that thoughts about letting my family down or hurting others did not have any effect on my suicidal ideations – they would be better off without me. The only thought that kept me from ending my life was that I would appear before God. I do not believe that suicide is unforgivable and I imagined when I arrived in His presence He would look at me with deep understanding of my pain and despair. But I feared hearing Him say something like, "If only you had waited one more day, I had your comeback all planned out!" I've spoken to many people who readily identify with the kind of statements I mentioned above. These are incredibly painful thoughts, and perhaps the worst torment of all is sensing how close relief really is. If I could just stop judging myself so harshly, let go of the persistently negative assumptions about the future, or stop insulting myself about how I must look in the eyes of others, the depression would float away and leave me happy.

This sounds so easy, but these dark thoughts become so ingrained that they begin to feel necessary and utterly true, and to deny their "truth" feels ridiculous and a pretense. And, after a long enough time, to suggest that there is any choice involved in whether to endorse them or not can be infuriating. Every depressed person has chafed while listening to well-meaning people say, "You have everything in the world going for you, why can't you just be happy?" Now, because this thinking is so painful, you would think people would do all in their power to root it out and replace it with more pleasant thoughts. But, everyone who suffers from depression nods in understanding when you mention the "sick comfort" of it. I remember feeling like I was in some sort of spiritual underground prison cell and that if someone could cut a hole in the wall and lead me out into the sunshine, part of me would be reluctant to step out.

There is something called *institutionalization* that I did not fully understand until I worked in residential treatment centers and sober living environments. Institutionalization happens when a person, after repeated negative experiences trying to handle adult responsibilities, becomes willing to trade the privileges of adulthood for the security of a supportive structure that will buffer him from the full force of the adult world. These structures exist throughout our society – rehab and prison are two of the most obvious, but even codependent families and government assistance programs can foster the same sorts of dependent behavior. It is somewhat amusing, but also telling, that the word *adulting* has recently come into being. Younger people use this term to refer to duties that adults typically carry out, but that people in their generation have difficulty doing consistently.

This trouble handling responsibility can happen because of deep-seated fears and insecurities, the presence of addiction, or some other mental illness. Because of difficulty solving adult problems, managing adult stress, obeying adult laws, and facing adult anxiety, some people accept an outside structure limiting their freedom for the relief of not having to perform at a fully adult level of capacity. There is a "sick comfort" to it. And despite stating a strong desire to regain their lives and function fully again, many of them subtly sabotage themselves literally on the eve of stepping back into society. But, until I was plucked out of depression in front of the roulette wheel, I didn't understand that institutionalization can happen in a purely internal way. We can learn to accept, and even welcome, limits on our God-given freedom without the presence of an external "prison." All we have to do is think like a prisoner!

As my mindset shifted from loser to something else (I hadn't yet considered what other identity might be available to me), I began to see that depressive thinking had institutionalized me in just that way. It had relieved me of the necessity to take action that could possibly have a positive impact on the future. I've come to describe depression primarily as the mental and physical malaise experienced when one believes that he is powerless to influence the future with any action that can be taken *right now*. When one adopts that idea, it necessarily drains out all motivation to take action or make decisions; there is no meaningful difference in the future between any of the actions or decisions that can be taken in the present. It is as if time is made of some very thick substance that will not carry ripples forward into the future to effect change.

Behind the willingness to accept the limits of being institutionalized is a profound fear of being proven inadequate. This fear of being exposed as insufficient can manifest in any life domain: educationally, relationally, vocationally, etc. And, because some of us have accepted the idea of being irreparably flawed in ways that make success unlikely, it is desirable to avoid putting ourselves in any situation where these flaws will become obvious.

Although I wasn't fully aware of it at the time, this was behind some of my weight gain. Because I was afraid of being rejected for who I was (an internal inadequacy), I gained weight so that I could explain rejection as something due to external factors (my weight). I also dreaded success because, when you believe success is more luck than anything else and are sure that your luck will certainly reverse one day soon, you seriously doubt your ability to maintain it. And there is only one thing worse than failing - failing after initially succeeding. It became preferable to fail due to insufficient effort or indecisiveness rather than to make a good-faith effort and fail. Failing by delay, or not trying, leaves open the slim possibility that one might actually have what it takes to make a risk pay off; failing after putting in effort only confirms the nagging suspicion that one really is unable to meet adult demands.

The depressed mindset serves a purpose; it allows someone to plausibly excuse himself for not taking action or for being indecisive. When I was thinking in the prison of depression, it could explain why I was not experiencing the sort of success in life that would otherwise be expected of me. Just like a prisoner cannot be held responsible for not achieving what might otherwise be possible because he's behind bars, I had a similar limitation I could lean on that would explain my circumstances. Except my cell was made up of an intricately designed web of negative thoughts and conclusions that was further reinforced with endless rumination. No wonder I wanted to be destroyed!

And, in exchange for this relief from the anxiety of handling the stress of adult demands, all I had to do was constantly punish myself mentally for failing to live up to my potential. It was a negative feedback loop that reinforced itself for years; my futile thinking led me to shrink back from necessary risks, quit early, remain paralyzed in front of important decisions, or otherwise sabotage myself, and then I could use the resulting failure to affirm my futile thinking. What a trap I had found myself in!

When God handed me back the freedom to choose whether or not I wanted to be pessimistic anymore, it was as if I had recognized I was in a cell that I believed had always been securely locked. When I began to question my commitment to negative thinking, one of the things I questioned was whether the door to my cell was really locked at all. Imagine my surprise (and horror) when I stood up and, after 48 years of confinement, decided to test the door to find that it had been open all along! I say horror because of how many years I spent there *voluntarily*. I had only assumed it was locked – I was thinking like a prisoner who had come to welcome the limitations provided by the cell. Even though it was small and spare, it buffered me from the fear, anxiety, and responsibility of the unpredictable outside world. It had a "sick comfort."

Happiness is not the opposite of depression. As I mentioned, depression is the exquisite frustration of feeling powerless to influence the future. It is the opposite of hope. Hope embraces the notion of human freedom and the individual's power to effect change in his circumstances. People who hope believe that they can take action that will send ripples forward in time that will influence what kind of future they will inherit. And people who live in a hopeful fashion understand that every goal they set is composed of a series of smaller steps that wind up finally accomplishing that intended goal. These preceding steps are like ripples being sent backward in time from the goal. And hope is the awareness of the truth that those ripples (steps) coming backward in time from our future goals don't stop next year, next week, or tomorrow – they stop *at the present moment!*

"I'll start tomorrow!" I can't tell you how many times I've heard people make that promise. I've made it myself hundreds of times. It sounds perfectly sensible, like someone has thought through the problem and determined to make some necessary change starting at a convenient time in the future. But that is exactly the problem. Change in the future is not a real thing; if I'm not changing *now,* I'm not changing at all. The only moment available to respond differently is this present moment. It is the only moment available to forgive someone who has wronged you, love someone dear to you, or refuse to take that drink you normally would. It is the only moment available to truly, authentically connect with God and other people. Change in the future is a nonsense concept because the only marker we ever have to measure change by is what we do differently *right now*! Because the future does not exist yet, change cannot happen there, and by telling ourselves (and others) these reasonable sounding fables we rob ourselves of the most powerful thing in our possession: this moment.

You see, the choice to hope (and it is a choice), comes with the acknowledgement that, unless one's actions *right now* line up with accomplishing the desired goal, there is no good reason to believe that it will ever come to pass. If you are intending to lose weight but never end up holding the fattening sauce, choosing leaner options, or skipping the second helping, you are "starting tomorrow." Those who set goals to change, but do not let that ripple coming back through time connect to this present moment are not acting in hope – they are merely wishing for a miracle. They are the ones "starting tomorrow."

In the movie *Tomorrowland*, George Clooney plays a scientist who has invented a machine that can show the future. When he finds out that the villain, Governor Nix, is using the machine to hasten the

Apocalypse, he tries to stop him, and they battle at the film's end for control of the machine. Hugh Laurie, as Governor Nix, gives the standard villain's monolog during their final conflict, and what he says captures this idea perfectly. After Clooney begs him to reconsider his plan, Nix refuses and justifies his decision to rid the earth of its inhabitants, saying, "In every moment, there is the possibility of a better future, but you people won't believe it! And because you won't believe it, you won't do what is necessary to make it a reality. So you dwell on this terrible future, and you resign yourselves to it for one reason - because *that* future doesn't ask anything of you *today*!"

There is certainly a burden that hope requires us to carry; choosing to hope places immense responsibility on us to act according to that hope and imbues every moment with the dignity that God granted it when He created the universe. We are either honoring the moments that have been granted to us or squandering them.

FLEXIBILITY

Set your mind on the things above, not on the things that are on earth. (Colossians 3:2)

I mentioned earlier that leading groups about our bias toward time inflames the tension between optimists and pessimists. Believe me, the battle lines are drawn deeply and quickly! The most heated part of the discussion always involves to what degree biological factors influence thinking. This happens because of disagreement about how much choice one has regarding their mindset. Optimists usually lean toward the belief that thinking negatively must be under the control of the individual. After all, they feel a measure of freedom to think negatively *if they chose to do so*. And they can't fathom why anyone would choose otherwise.

Depressed pessimists (and not all are), on the other hand, almost always react forcefully to that idea. They feel, by and large, at the mercy of something that no sensible person would choose if they had a choice. And, because they have such difficulty sustaining positive thoughts, they gravitate to more biological explanations to make sense of their perceived lack of choice. Accusations fly back and forth between these two camps: optimists tend to accuse pessimists of some sort of weakness that makes them lean toward the negative, while pessimists accuse optimists of callousness and insensitivity to their plight.

And a disclaimer up front right now about medications. There are many people who get significant relief from mental illness symptoms by taking various medications; I have absolutely no interest in entering the debate about the effectiveness or prevalence of these drugs. One thing that is certain though, is that our culture focuses heavily on the bad brain chemistry side of the equation and very little on the bad thinking side of the equation. These two factors interplay with each other and form a negative feedback loop, with bad chemistry producing bad thoughts and bad thoughts worsening bad chemistry. But it is impossible to know which comes first – the bad chemistry or the bad thinking. Over the years, I took several different pills for many months with no appreciable improvement. I attribute this now to having no success at confronting all the lies and distortions that I had let dominate my thinking. Even if a pill could have lifted my mood, it could not have done anything to rid my mind of the poor thinking habits I had practiced for so long.

I can remember hating to hear people recite easy aphorisms about mindset such as "Attitude determines altitude!" (an aviation reference referring to whether an airplane's nose was pointing up or down). Obviously, the nose-down plane would wind up crashing while the nose-up plane would soar above the clouds. My condescending response sounded something like, "Oh yeah, well what determines my attitude?" And I said this *as if it wasn't me!* Viktor Frankl, the noted psychiatrist who survived the Holocaust, once said, "Everything can be taken from a man but one thing: the last of human freedoms - to choose one's attitude in any given set of circumstances..." And here I was willingly renouncing the most elementary (and valuable) freedom a human is granted by God – the power to choose what to think.

We've nibbled around the edges of the topic of mindset in previous chapters, but now it's time to bite into the dead center of it! This is a topic that is highly studied and written about over the past few years, and how you define the term depends on what best-seller you've read lately. Steven Covey, in *The Seven Habits of Highly Effective People*, talks about the *scarcity* and *abundance* mindsets while Carol Dweck, in her book *Mindset: The New Psychology of*

Success discusses the research she has done that revolves around what she calls the *fixed* and *growth* mindsets. The imagery that most people who talk about mindset use to convey their ideas is that of a lens or pair of glasses that we look at the world through. A simple example is the "glass half-empty" lens that pessimists use when they look at the world around them. And the focus of much of the current research is why, when looking at the exact same circumstances, someone else will see the "glass half-full."

This "lens" we look at the world through is made up of assorted statements and assumptions about the self (self-worth and effectiveness), others (reliability, value, and trustworthiness), and society at large (beneficial or detrimental). We create these lenses to operate as a sort of filter to simplify the overwhelming amount of data that is constantly streaming into our brains. The working definition I use is this: "Mindset is the collective set of beliefs and assumptions that one acts on *as if* true, whether or not they actually are." As you can see, this definition of mindset leaves room for the possibility of distortion creeping in, and even assumes that there will be some distortion present in even the most well-adjusted of us. Both of the books I mentioned above have their own way of describing that distortion and use different language to describe many of the same things.

No matter what descriptive terms one uses to identify how distortion expresses itself in our mindsets, the most important factor to consider is this: are we free to change them? If we are able to, whenever necessary, change the lens we look at the external world through, we have something I call the *flexible* mindset. The flexible mindset incorporates the optimism/pessimism distinction we touched on earlier, but is not limited by the need to remain "positive" in every circumstance. Being pessimistic is not always the wrong perspective. But, it is a huge problem when that is the only "lens" available to look at the world through.

The main characteristic of the flexible mindset is its suppleness when responding to challenges, stress, or new situations. Its opposite is what I call the *static* mindset, which allows for only a very limited range of responses no matter what the situation calls for. The word static means "lacking in movement, action, or change, especially in a way viewed as undesirable or uninteresting," and that definition perfectly captures the concept here. A static mindset is unable to respond with creativity when confronted with unfamiliar or stressful situations and prevents us from seeing opportunity that is right in front of us.

A flexible mindset allows one to adopt whatever belief or assumption is optimal in any given circumstance. Flexibility protects one against resentment by making the most generous assumptions about whoever is acting in an inconsiderate way toward us. It protects us from ungratefulness by reminding us that God is the one in charge of supplying our needs when we are tempted to feel entitled or overlooked.

The flexible mindset looks at failure and setback through a non-judgmental lens and is able to interpret it accurately. If the failure is due to lack of skills or good faith oversight, the flexible mindset will allow one to assess these things without the need to ruminate in regret or blame. It will simply let go of the outcome and learn whatever can be gained from the experience. And if the failure is due to poor judgment or character immaturity, the flexible mindset accepts that one has done the best he could with the maturity that he had *at the time*. This allows mistakes to be examined without judgment and shows us clearly where we need more accountability and support.

Gary was a middle-aged man who had lost his business in the Great Recession in 2008. He spent significant time unemployed after that and his alcoholism accelerated rapidly during that time. He also struggled with self-doubt that he could make a comeback to his former success. He spent almost two months in residential treatment followed by several more in sober living. During this time we worked on finding a narrative that would support enough confidence to re-enter the work force. After some progress, he decided that it was time to begin looking for work. Because he could not find anything in his former field, he began looking for whatever he could find that was local, convenient, and low-stress. The goal was just to get used to getting up and going to work again.

After submitting his resume to numerous suitable employers, he was hired by a hotel to handle customer service and various other tasks that he considered "entry level." Despite the convenience and low-stress of the job, Gary found himself quickly resenting the owner of the hotel, who he considered to be of lower intelligence and class. Instead of being able to recast his circumstances as temporary and beneficial while he re-acclimated to going to work again, Gary seethed with bitterness about the owner's success. Gary would tell me all of the ways that the owner was "making a killing" by taking advantage of his employees. But in the next breath, he would express strong envy and scornfully say "Who does he think he is?"

It didn't take long for Gary to contrive a reason to storm out of work one day. As we were talking about that decision, I asked him if he had been able to feel appreciative or thankful for all of the aspects of the job that were ideal for him while he made his comeback. He snorted and said, "Are you kidding?! I was wasting my time there!" His mindset was static about the importance of gratitude and the value of a job that would let him practice some of his rusty work habits. He was immovable in his conviction that showing the humility necessary to enjoy the job was beneath him; he couldn't even see how the experience might be helpful with some low-grade social anxiety that he was struggling with as well. In truth, he was overqualified for many of the duties the job required, but his stubborn commitment to feeling entitled to something more led directly to his downfall. Not long after, Gary relapsed at the bar of the very hotel he had quit from just a few weeks earlier.

Because the flexible mindset adapts beneficially to whatever circumstances are present, it gives the greatest possible chance of success no matter what our goals are. There are no guarantees that things will work out in our favor in all cases, but there is always a way to think about a problem or conflict that gives the best possible chance at a good outcome. The flexible mindset finds, *and is then free to act*, on that idea. That sounds great to most people, but there are some hurdles to clear in order to become more flexible. When we try to adopt these new ways of thinking we are fighting against some of our most deep-seated natural tendencies. And, the frustrating part about some of these hurdles is that they can be helpful things in other situations.

In computer science there is a term, *heuristic,* that is defined as a "rule of thumb for solving problems without the exhaustive application of an algorithm." In the mindset context it means that, over time, we gradually gather information about other people (and ourselves) and find ways to classify and rank that information based on its perceived usefulness to us. And then, once we have determined the relative importance of past experiences, we can use it as a sort of shortcut in our decision making processes about the kind of people we are dealing with, what their motives might be, and what responses to choose in the present.

These "problem solving" shortcuts can be lifesaving at times, but they also cut the other way and hinder our flexibility. For instance, racism is an example of heuristics gone wrong. Racism is the application of a heuristic that elevates racial differences above shared values and personal integrity. Racists believe they know all they need to know about a person based on a person's skin color or ethnic origin.

Another way our flexibility is limited is through our vulnerability to something called *confirmation bias*. Confirmation bias is the human tendency to apply a heuristic (mental shortcut) that lets through information confirming our previously held beliefs but filters out evidence that would disconfirm those beliefs. While it gives us the benefit of saving the mental energy of having to shift positions based on constantly changing information, confirmation bias causes us to commit too strongly to our current positions and ingrains our distorted perceptions. Let's use the racism analogy mentioned earlier. A person who believes that all black people eat fried chicken and watermelon has his bias strengthened every time he sees a black person eating those foods. But confirmation bias minimizes the impact of seeing a black person eating other foods. If one holds the bias that all Asians are good at math, then seeing an Asian who is good at math confirms his bias, but seeing one who is average does nothing to prompt him to challenge his preconceptions.

The key to managing these hurdles to flexibility is to examine our own certainty periodically. We all have the ability to deceive ourselves when it serves our purpose, and any mental shortcut we make that has bias or error in it will infect every conclusion that follows after it. As Bertrand Russell said, "In all affairs, it's a healthy thing now and then to hang a question mark on the things you have long taken for granted."

Jill Bolte Taylor is a neuroanatomist who had the (mis)fortune of experiencing a major stroke. I say it that way because, as she says in her much-viewed TED Talk called "A Stroke of Insight," it provided her with valuable direct experience of something she could never have learned in the laboratory. Dr. Taylor's stroke occurred in such a way that she was able to experience the loss of one hemisphere of her brain. This enabled her to distinguish between the operations performed by the two hemispheres. She goes on to describe the workings of the two hemispheres of the brain as complimentary processing units. The right hemisphere is only concerned with receiving the data that is streaming into our nervous system at this moment. It is the way the energy present in the world around us interacts with us.

The left hemisphere, on the other hand, is constantly attempting to provide context to all that data; it is trying to turn it all into information. It does this through the process of recall: bits of data are plucked out of the incredible stream of energy that is pouring in and selectively categorized and prioritized according to their perceived usefulness. And their usefulness is determined by comparing these bits of data to other useful data that has been observed in the past. This process is called *attending*.

And maybe now it is clearer about how negative narratives and biases become ingrained. Past experience shapes what we attend to in the present. Our mindset "lens" acts as the aperture through which we attend to the facts at hand, with confirmation bias highlighting facts that we feel are relevant to the narrative and filtering out facts that are not. If we have an inclination to assign higher priority to remembering traumatic or painful circumstances so that we can avoid them in the future, we will attend more closely in the present to the facts that remind us of those events in the past. And what we attribute those past events to (our own incompetence, the indifference of others, the unfairness of society, etc.) will determine the nature of the narrative that takes shape.

Our attention and our attitude are closely linked. If we have trained ourselves to think like losers, victims, or villains, we will filter out evidence to the contrary; we will attend to the facts around us that verify our shortcomings and/or the shortcomings of others. We will focus on the unfairness present in how circumstances are unfolding in our lives and what we think we ought to have but currently lack. Obviously, if this is the content of our thinking, our attitude will suffer and hopelessness, anger, anxiety, and depression will be difficult to fend off. We will lose flexibility as our "lens" faithfully magnifies the facts confirming our previously determined story and filters out any disconfirming facts. And we all have met people who, when facts are not available to support their negative narrative, will simply make them up if necessary.

Is this starting to make more sense? This is why people who have PTSD (post-traumatic stress disorder) attend to, and assign importance to, very different bits of data than people who do not. A backfiring car can trigger extreme psychological (and physiological) distress in the combat veteran with PTSD while another person might not even notice it. We all apply a heuristic to the tidal wave of data streaming into our bodies at any given time; we filter out what we have learned over time is background noise and retain what we believe to be important. This is related to something called the cocktail party effect. It is how, in the middle of a crowd, you can detect your name out of the low hum of discussion going on around you. There are certain stimuli that, because of our mindset, we are primed to notice and, when they show up, they command our attention above the "background noise."

The flexibility of our mindset (and attitude) is directly related to the amount of attention that we believe is under our control; if we believe that we have no choice in what we notice about ourselves, others, and society, our ability to change our attitude will be sorely limited. If, however, we can bring ourselves to believe that we are able to attend to whatever facts we choose depending on how we want to feel, we have the power to adapt instantly to any challenging life circumstance, setback, or failure. Finding gratitude, forgiveness, and courage will be very much easier if we have the flexibility to focus on the evidence that is always present to support those attitudes.

Because God created us in this way, He is constantly providing instruction about what to pay attention to. Scripture is full of exhortations meant to help us stay flexible and experience life as the gift it is meant to be. Consider the following verses:

"Finally, brothers and sisters, whatever is true, whatever is noble, whatever is right, whatever is pure, whatever is lovely, whatever is admirable—if anything is excellent or praiseworthy—*think about such things*." (Phil. 4:8 *emphasis mine*)

"Since, then, you have been raised with Christ, set your hearts on things above, where Christ is, seated at the right hand of God. *Set your minds* on things above, not on earthly things. For you died, and your life is now hidden with Christ in God. When Christ, who is your life, appears, then you also will appear with him in glory." (Col. 3:1-4 *emphasis mine*)

So Joshua called together the twelve men he had appointed from the Israelites, one from each tribe, and said to them, "Go over before the ark of the LORD your God into the middle of the Jordan. Each of you is to take up a stone on his shoulder, according to the number of the tribes of the Israelites, to serve as a sign among you. In the future, when your children ask you, 'What do these stones mean?' tell them that the flow of the Jordan was cut off before the ark of the covenant of the LORD. When it crossed the Jordan, the waters of the Jordan were cut off. *These stones are to be a memorial to the people of Israel forever*." (Josh. 4:4-8 *emphasis mine*)

These Scriptures are just a few of the many that God has given us to act as a corrective on our thinking. And it is interesting to note that God wants to help us to change our time perspective biases in all three time domains: past, present, and future. All of these passages are meant to help us change our attitude *in the present*, but they all appeal to different domains of time in order to do so.

In the Philippians passage, Paul addresses our tendency to dwell on the negative by listing uplifting things that are available for us to focus on *right now*. The Colossians passage bolsters this by exhorting the believer to remember promised *future events* (the glorification of the saints) that are sending a ripple backward in time to us in the present. And the Joshua passage anticipates the need for people to be reminded about what God has done *in the past* so that they can effectively battle fear and anxiety in their present-day circumstances. He essentially commands them to not forget the redemptive acts He has taken on their behalf.

Taken together, these passages are the bones of a very different kind of narrative taking shape. The flexible mindset is characterized by the recognition that one has significant internal freedom to choose which information to emphasize or ignore. A flexible mindset is capable of shifting attention, whenever necessary, to the set of facts that God recommends is beneficial for humans to think about. This is God instructing us about how to "control the narrative."

SLAVERY

Do you not know that when you present yourselves to someone as slaves for obedience, you are slaves of the one whom you obey, either of sin resulting in death, or of obedience resulting in righteousness? (Romans 6:16)

I must have been around 11 or 12 when I went to see my doctor for a routine checkup. He had been seeing me since I was born and had my entire medical history in his charts. At the time, I was showing signs of obesity, and my mother was concerned about my weight. He examined his records and determined that I was around age 6 when my weight started to deviate from typical children. He asked me if there was anything noteworthy about that age and I told him I couldn't remember anything unusual happening. But, in hindsight, I can say that is when I first discovered the power of food to change my brain chemistry and mood. And I certainly had incentive to try to change my mood.

I grew up in a high conflict family that had great difficulty resolving the ongoing problems among its members. My brother, who was eight years older than me, acted as a black sheep and pretty consistently frustrated my parent's attempts to control his behavior. We had a regular mealtime tradition that started with uneasy silence around the table until my mother would be unable to contain herself any longer and would have to tell my father about my brother's misbehavior that day. There would be a short fact gathering discussion focusing on the bad behavior before the conflict moved to between the two adults at the table.

Because my parents were divided among themselves about the proper response to put forward, they turned on each other with blame and accusations, and the dinner table became a battlefield where they could have the same argument they had been having for years before I ever showed up. I had only my food at that time to act as a comfort, and I ate my meal in the presence of mystifying conflict and the anxiety it produced in me.

After years had gone by a subtle shift had taken place in me. Where it used to be "mealtime is conflict time," it gradually became "conflict time is meal time." And my boundaries were so compromised that I was "conflicted" about nearly everything, which meant I spent more and more time trying to soothe myself by thinking about (and eating) food. I didn't realize it at the time, but I had learned how to manipulate my brain chemistry to make myself feel better when I was stressed, and because food was a reliable and powerful means of relaxation, it became my first drug of choice. As much as I began to love food, I had some well-meaning help establishing a full-fledged eating disorder. It was not a coincidence that every being my mom fed became obese; my parents used to have significant conflict about how overweight our dogs were. My mother was the first person I realized had a victim identity and narrative. And for good reason, I'm sure. She never related much about her childhood to me, but as I look back as an adult, much of her behavior can only be explained by the trauma she experienced early in life.

Regardless, she looked through a lens of victimhood when making sense of the world and there was inevitable collateral damage in her kids' lives. Because she had so much difficulty facing the parts of her that were imperfect and hurtful to others, like all victims, she went to great lengths to excuse herself or blame others for her problems. She could not tolerate anger being expressed at her and when I would, on occasion, protest something she had said or done, she would withdraw completely, leaving me scrambling to figure out what I had done so wrong that I should "lose" my mother. So I went away feeling guilty and frustrated until, at some point she would return, not with an apology, but with my favorite food. And so, motivated by her guilt at abandoning me emotionally (and unable to apologize directly), she would bring me "love" in the form of a cheeseburger. As a result, I learned to confuse the feeling of acceptance and warmth that comes from a mother's love with the feeling of eating calorie dense foods.

As I slowly gained weight, it came along with the thoughts and feelings one would expect. I began to get teased for my weight and grew to hate my name: my classmates called me "Fat Pat." Since I had seen my brother rebel against the family and be marginalized, I went to the other extreme and tried to comply as best I could. I attempted to be "no trouble" even to the point of wishing I could be invisible. The wounds I experienced growing up were not the overt, easy to identify type such as result when physical or sexual boundaries are crossed. It was the more subtle type caused by the emotional incompetence and mishandling of stress and conflict by the adults in the family. And I sometimes think that it might have been easier if the abuse had been more overt and easier to identify. Because it was a more gentle warping, it went on longer before I could realize the type of damage that had been done.

As I mentioned, the breakdown in the family had begun before I arrived, and I watched it play out with unsettling, and unpredictable, regularity. I have one memory of my parents sleeping in the same bed before they moved to separate bedrooms, ostensibly due to one or the others snoring. And because there were essentially two separate households set up in the same house, I saw limited cooperation and sharing of positive emotion between husband and wife. My parents both vented to me about the faults of the other; I realized at one point in my teens that, if I listened to my parents, I was half "bitch" and half "asshole."

So, along with the weight, I gained shame about how I looked, self-doubt about my ability to succeed in relationships, and a very low self-esteem that was bordering on self-loathing even in my teen years. And, perhaps most importantly, I had lost the ability to "trust my gut" to guide me about how to repair relationships, take initiative, or protect myself from being hurt by others.

Part of my mother's victim identity included a pattern that I didn't identify until my late teens. I came to call this pattern "rewriting history." It would happen when conflict would arise between her and me, usually when she thought something I had done was insensitive or inconsiderate. In an attempt to bolster her argument, she would refer to something seemingly unrelated that had taken place within the past few weeks, but she would alter the facts to support her claim that I was in the wrong and needed to apologize. This new history always left me holding the blame and allowed her "villain" to discharge its venom on to me. When I was young, the certainty she had when imposing this new version of reality left me unable to discern whether my recollection of events was correct or if she knew something I didn't about what had taken place.

And this pattern repeated itself enough to instill a deep despair in me about my ability to make sense of the world. This is sometimes called "gaslighting" or "crazymaking" behavior because it forces the person on the receiving end either to adopt a false reality (go crazy) or, as in my case, to remain in unresolved conflict. I hated conflict so much that I chose to adopt the false reality. And because it is natural for a child to trust his parents to interpret the world to him while he learns to do it for himself, I was at a pretty serious disadvantage toward achieving that goal.

It wasn't until I was around 18 that an incident occurred that finally allowed me to see what had been happening. I used to enjoy growing vegetables in our family garden, and one year I grew a special sweet corn variety that is not commercially available because it takes too long to ripen. This means that the corn has more time to create sugars than typical corn. When it was ripe, I begged my mother to eat some with me right in the garden. It was so sweet that it does not need to be cooked; it tasted like warm vanilla ice cream right off the stalk. But my mother refused because she was on some fad diet that didn't include corn. I tried to change her mind several times over the next week because it ripens at once and then is gone, but she remained committed to her diet.

A few weeks later (always about three weeks), she took issue with something I had done that she thought was hurtful and said, "Just like you and your father sat out there and hogged all that corn and didn't give me any!" I was stunned. But it was the first time I could clearly see what must have been happening all along. It was an eye-opening experience for sure, and I remember feeling a certain relief that what my gut had been telling me for all those years wasn't wrong after all.

While I felt more able to trust my intuition after that event, I also was left with a lot of anger about what had been done to me. I would later describe what this felt like by saying, "In order for the relationship to be sane, I had to go crazy." I had a strong desire to get my mother to see this part of herself and admit the wrong of what she had been doing. But it was not to be. The victim identity was so ingrained that I could not make a dent in her conviction that it was her that was being wronged, not me. So I did the next best thing, I unwittingly looked for a romantic partner with the same trait who I could replay the same dynamic with. And I found her!

My father's main coping skill to manage the ongoing conflict was avoidance and mental escape. He spent time in his room reading adventure and spy novels and used to tell me "Books are friends." That might have meant something to me if I felt like he was close to me as well. But, I came away feeling like I knew him only vaguely. I have a vivid memory of the surprise I felt at his memorial as his business associates spoke of a man who had a willingness to listen and valuable insight to offer them both personally and professionally. At one point, I chuckled to myself as I momentarily wondered if I was at the right funeral service. They were describing someone I never met, but would have liked to; I cried for more than one reason that day.

My father had graduated college early and was an intelligent man in many ways. Dealing with women was not one of those ways. I took a risk as a 16-year-old and told him I was having problems with a girlfriend. I was shocked to hear him say, "Don't worry, one day you will give up on them." I remember thinking that I had exhausted the help that I could get from my dad at that point; that I was on my own with the problems that adulthood would bring.

This was further reinforced when the time to make a decision about college arrived. I had scored well on all the standardized tests and was a moderately regarded high school football player. I received hundreds of brochures and recruiting literature that I kept in two stuffed dresser drawers because I didn't know what to do with it all. I didn't notice it at the time, but several years later I recalled with some consternation that no one had attempted to help me make that decision. No one noticed that I was overwhelmed by what direction to take and had any assistance or wisdom to offer. I had a scholarship offer to a prestigious Ivy League school that I left on the table because the decision was beyond me. This was one of the first instances of the loser narrative affecting my life's direction; because I doubted my ability to make the right decision, I chose not to decide instead. My self-doubt and fear of failing kept me paralyzed at the crossroads of a major life choice. This would not be the last time either.

OK, so you get the picture. I was pretty much left on my own to manage the demands of approaching adulthood and was woefully unprepared to meet them. I had unresolved anger, growing depression, and morbid fear of being called on to make important life decisions. The allure of drugs as a means of tolerating stress and anxiety grew as I got closer to graduating high school. Ironically, I didn't even know I was feeling anxious. My senior year, I rode to school with my dad and would experience stomach pain that increased as our destination neared. It became so troubling that I went to a gastroenterologist for a barium x-ray scan. Of course, it showed nothing obviously wrong, but neither did anyone seek any further explanation. My solution involving ditching school to smoke marijuana and play video games with Charlie. I would often miss most of the day at school and show up for football practice in the afternoon.

The role food played at this time was becoming secondary to marijuana and cocaine. These newer ways to change my brain chemistry provided more effective relief from the myriad thoughts of futility that were beginning to plague me. And just like my thinking shifted about conflict time and meal time, another shift took place regarding substances. At first, they "presented" themselves to me at weekend parties and other places where my peers gathered, but over time, I began to "present myself" to them to take advantage of the pain killing qualities they possessed.

By my early 20's I was addicted to cocaine and marijuana, with my eating disorder lying dormant for the time being. By the time I realized what was happening, it was too late, and I didn't care to stop because they played such an important role comforting me. I had submitted to the slavery of sin and had ushered in death. I was cut off from hope, dreams, goals, and other people. I had adopted a slave mentality and came to believe that I was essentially powerless in the face of external forces that could not be resisted.

Aside from actual slavery, there are very few human experiences that are more emblematic of slavery than the phenomenon of addiction. People who become addicted at first willingly "present themselves" to a substance or activity that offers enhanced pleasure of life, relief from tedium, and freedom from a wide assortment of unpleasant emotions and sensations. But the addicted wind up slaves of the most merciless taskmaster known to man. Addiction never takes a day off, never gets tired of punishing the afflicted, never thinks twice about its commitment to destroying lives, and never relents in its mission to feed on the life of the addict until there is nothing left.

It is nearly impossible for someone who has not been addicted to understand the intensity of the drive behind it and the actions that addicts take to satisfy their urges. When presented with the choice of parenting their children, remaining healthy, maintaining their physical freedom, or continuing in the addiction, the addicted regularly pause for only a short while before choosing the substance over their health, freedom, or family.

My circumstances growing up, combined with my particular genetic and personality profiles, led pretty directly to the slavery of addiction. I was a daily marijuana smoker by age 17 and a daily cocaine user by 23. By the time I was 25 I met most of the clinical criteria for substance use disorder, and I was beginning to become troubled by the loss of freedom I was experiencing. The most restraint I could show was only purchasing enough for one days use at a time; if I bought more, I could not stop using it until it was gone and I would come close to overdosing.

It was also during this time I came up against the limits of what I could do in my own strength. After I decided I wanted to stop using, I promised myself for over a year that "today is the last day" I would use coke, but somehow, before the end of the next day I was placing the same phone call and making the trip to pick up more. My promises, and they were very earnest, were of no value when trying to overcome the momentum of my compulsions. Drugs, like any other slave master, told me where I would be at appointed times, who I would spend time with, how I would spend my money, and what my priorities would be. As my freedom slipped away, I began to despair that I could ever regain it. I also despaired that I would ever find what I was really looking for – a reason to live. I had no idea I was about to find both in the same amazing day!

CHRISTIANITY

It was for freedom that Christ set us free; therefore keep standing firm and do not be subject again to a yoke of slavery. (Galatians 5:1)

When I first started to think about writing a book like this, I debated about whether to make it explicitly Christian or not. During the time I have worked in recovery, most of those I've counseled have not shared my spiritual beliefs, and many have been opposed to them to some degree. But, almost without exception, when I have been able to translate biblical principles into common language and apply them to the lives of others, they appreciate their wisdom and usefulness, even though they don't know their origin. The concepts of forgiveness, grace, and gratitude are foundational to the Christian life but are also indispensable when trying to make difficult change. Proverbs like "If you rescue an angry man, you will only have to do it again" (19:19) capture certain psychological principles as well as anything written since, maybe better.

Not long after I started writing, I realized that to try to write an entire book that was spiritually vague would require obscuring the true source of all the healing I'm trying to describe. I would be talking about miracles without the miracle maker. Because the truth is that, without the relationship that God has initiated with me, I would have nothing important to say about any of the topics in this book. That relationship has unfolded over the second half of my life in some unusual ways. He has revealed Himself to me in every way that was necessary exactly when I needed it. Of course, I didn't always see it that way. But He was playing the long game to my short one.

We are talking about the power of stories to influence our thoughts and actions, and there is a reason why the Gospel is called *The Greatest Story Ever Told*. There has never been, and never will be, a more heroic character than Jesus of Nazareth. He battled the fiercest opposition imaginable as He faced Satan's temptations in the desert as well as the desire to avoid the cross on the Mount of Olives. The battle that He took on was against the strongest possible foe (the Devil) and for the highest stakes possible (the souls of all mankind). His narrative is the template that all others are measured by and His encouragement to "Believe in Me..." is really a call to enter into the story that He has been unfolding since creation began. And, there is nothing more healing to a troubled mind than finding one's particular place in that story. This chapter is the account of how I was ushered into that realization and the transforming power that becomes available when we meet the true Hero.

I grew up in a spiritual vacuum. My parents were both from families with some sort of faint religious tradition, but, by the time I was born, had largely abandoned whatever faith they had been exposed to growing up. God was very rarely mentioned in my house growing up. Not because of hostility, but more because of an inability to see any usefulness of believing in Him. We attended a Mormon church one time because my parents liked the idea of a weekly "family home evening" that is traditional in that religion. My parents must have thought that it would help us bond somehow. I can remember being quite bored during the service we attended and was relieved when I found out I wouldn't have to go again.

As I mentioned, I had questions about existence from an early age that increasingly frustrated me as I got older. Because I sensed that the limits on what humans can intuit about God required me to take some things on faith, I adopted what I called a pernicious agnosticism.

In other words, my doubt and skepticism acted as corrosive elements that gradually ate away at all the reasons people commonly use to add meaning, purpose, and enjoyment to life.

Because of this, one of my intellectual pursuits was the study of religion and the world views that come along with various faiths. Whenever I met someone with conviction about their belief system, I would pick their brains for as long as they would let me. I wasn't doing it to demonstrate their error, I did it because I desperately needed a reason to live and I knew that what I was looking for was not of this world. And because I had no good reason for why anything had purpose, I had difficulty finding a good reason for why I should go to college, get a job, or start a family. But, more importantly, I had no good reason for why I should even draw another breath. If I was honest, I believed that there was no purpose that could possibly be discovered and, because of that, the only purpose to anything was one I made up as necessary. And this contrived meaning to live was wholly insufficient to roll back the depression that was swallowing me as my addiction progressed.

When we were around 25, my friend Charlie Sheen got engaged to Kelly Preston (who later married John Travolta) and bought a house in the hills behind Malibu. It turned out that the house had numerous building code violations and had to be nearly gutted before it could be remodeled to comply with the local ordinances. Because I enjoyed working in the garden growing up and I had opted to forego college, I decided to start working for a local landscaper in Malibu just after high school. I became quite good at it during this time and had started my own landscape contracting business in my early twenties. Because he trusted me to oversee this part of the project, Charlie asked me to manage the landscaping aspect of the remodel.

As it happened, there was a guy about my age (mid-twenties) named Mark who worked for the general contractor and who was responsible for various handyman duties throughout the project.

Mark was a simple kid from Minnesota who I quickly found out was a committed Christian. Mark and I became friends and, over the course of the year or so we were working on the project, ate many lunches together by the pool.

Surrounded by waterfalls pouring over enormous, quartz-streaked boulders imported from Northern California and a life-sized bronze tiger, we would discuss our various points of view about what we thought was important about life. Of course, the topic of discussion frequently turned to his chosen faith, and my curiosity generated many questions about the Bible and how he had made the mental leap from not believing to believing. He did his best to answer my questions, but, because he likely had not encountered many of the objections I had before, his ability to answer my questions was limited.

But his attitude always mystified me. When we got to a subject he did not have an answer for, he was never embarrassed or taken aback. He just honestly admitted he did not know the answer and we continued on another topic. I was mystified because I thought I was asking the questions that were going to enable him to see how shaky his faith really was. But he never wavered, never got angry, never showed one moment of doubt that this person we were discussing was real. And I remember being struck that Mark was convinced he was having an actual relationship with Jesus.

Charlie had hired a family friend named Karen to handle the interior decorating purchases and coordination. Karen was married to Two Blue Jays, who I was told was a Native American shaman. I spent some time with both of them in the years before Charlie bought the house and had heard of several unusual occurrences. Take these stories for what they are worth – I discounted them completely at the time.

One mutual friend swore to me she had seen the spirit of a deceased friend appear at the dinner table when she was eating at their house.

Another night, Charlie and I were smoking weed in his car on an undeveloped piece of land just above the Malibu Pier. An interesting side note is this parcel of land would one day become the estate of the son of Equatorial Guinea's corrupt dictator president. It would also eventually be seized by the U.S. Justice Department after it was determined that the money used to buy it ($35 million) had been plundered from that country's people by means of insider deals involving natural resources.

While Charlie and I were sitting blowing smoke out the sunroof, we were startled by a large owl flying within just a few feet of the open roof. It hooted loudly as it passed directly overhead and we looked at each other with a look that only two people stoned out of their minds could exchange. We returned to Charlie's house an hour or two later and Charlie pulled me aside a short while later in a very agitated state. He told me that Two Jays (as we called him) had asked if there was anything unusual about our evening. Charlie didn't remember the owl flying over, but was blown away when Two Jays asked about us seeing an owl. He then told Charlie that he "was the owl" and then described in detail the area where we had parked. As I said, I was dismissive of this at the time, but Charlie periodically brought it up in the way a person would if they thought they'd seen a ghost.

Toward the end of the project, it somehow became known that Karen was padding the expenses for Charlie's interior furnishings. Charlie quickly fired her, but, because the house was filled with all sorts of valuables (samurai swords, baseball memorabilia, expensive original artwork), he was worried that she would come that evening and steal them. I heard discussions about hiring a security service to come immediately, but, because I was already there, I offered to stay the evening to keep watch on the house. Charlie was relieved and thanked me.

I should backtrack slightly at this point to add a wrinkle to the story. You see, I was actually very relieved that Charlie had agreed to let me stay because I had just had my driver's license suspended for thirty days due to numerous prior speeding tickets. It is embarrassing to admit but I was easily angered on the road and I frequently drove 15-20 miles over the speed limit. To this day, my pet peeve is inconsiderateness and I had a gift for noticing every bit on the road. Ironically, watching someone be rude to another driver would irritate me as much as somebody doing it to me. I would often find myself speeding to catch up to drivers who had cut me or someone else off just to glare at them (or worse). So, spending the night at Charlie's was a welcome development because I was too ashamed to say anything about losing my license to anyone; I was planning on driving without one.

It was a pleasant June day (the 25th), and as the day wound down, all the various tradesmen left for home and I found myself alone. I should also say that this was at the height of my cocaine addiction and I had been unable to get any for the past few days; I was definitely uncomfortable, but I had plenty of weed to take the edge off. To my surprise, someone rang the gate bell and when I answered, Mark told me he had come back to get some tools. He hadn't expected anyone to be there but was glad that I could let him in. He was blown away as I told him the story about why I was there and when he realized that I was staying, excused himself to go get the 12-pack out of his truck. Yes, you heard that right! The Christian guy went and got the 12-pack out of his truck.

It was around dinner time, and I was preparing something to grill in the kitchen when something very unusual took place. As I was prepping the food I experienced a wave of fear that I had never felt before. Not anxiety or panic, but a totally alien, bone-chilling dread that seemed to wash over me and I immediately thought, "I hope Mark doesn't leave." Now, if you knew me at the time, you would know how out of character that statement was for me. In my addiction, I wanted nothing more than to be alone with my drugs and I was not scared in the slightest of being by myself. This fear lasted several minutes and passed as I finished working in the kitchen. Needless to say, I was relieved but also a bit unsettled, as if there was still an unpleasant residue left on my skin.

Not long after, as Mark and I spoke in the living room, the fear revisited me and I realized that having Mark stay would not be enough to quell this feeling. To my own amazement, and almost as if it were not me, I found myself saying "Mark, I have to leave!" He looked at me quizzically as if I was intending to go to the market or liquor store. But, when he realized what I meant, he looked at me like I was the biggest idiot on the planet. We were two young guys in the most lavishly appointed bachelor pad this side of the Playboy Mansion. We had a swimming pool and Jacuzzi, pool table, arcade games, huge screen TV's, a professional batting cage, and an underground shooting range at our disposal. There were very few people who wouldn't die to be in our shoes, and here I was telling him that I had to go!

But what happened next shocked both of us even more. I did something as uncharacteristic as either of us could imagine. Without thinking about what I was saying I asked, "Mark, do you have a Bible?" He looked at me like I was playing some sort of practical joke on him for a second or two. I mean, I was the guy who had spent the past year doubting his answers to my questions enough for both of us. But then he got a look that seemed to understand that something important must be happening if I would seriously ask for a Bible. It would be hard to overstate how strongly I would have protested had you told me that morning I would be asking someone if they had a Bible with them that evening. I most certainly would have laughed in your face and probably cursed at you as well. I had already decided that all the so-called "holy books" contradicted each other so radically that they should all be discounted entirely.

I don't know why I thought that a Bible would help at that moment, but Mark simply said that he didn't have one and then followed it up immediately with something very odd. He said, "But if you have the faith of a mustard seed, you can say to that mountain, 'Be thou removed and cast into the sea,' and it will be!" To explain, the house was situated to take advantage of the view of a large mountain across the lake from us, and that was the mountain Mark pointed to when he spoke.

There are a few profound events in my life that I remember in a dissociated way. In other words, the memory I have is as if I am watching the event happening to me rather than a first-person point of view. This is one of those events. In hindsight, it is kind of comical that Mark would choose to say that to me. To someone with no background in the Bible it is an absurd thing to say - casting a mountain into the sea if my faith is the size of a mustard seed. What does that even mean? I didn't know it at the time, but he was quoting a passage to me from the Bible. Actually, he was confused and mixed two different Scriptures together (Matt. 17:20 and Luke 17:6). Well, it was certainly not the profundity of what he said, but the power of those words did not rest on my ability to understand them.

I didn't have time to reflect on what he said and think, "That sounds really good - I think I'll build my life around throwing a mountain into the sea with faith like a seed." I wouldn't have been able to figure out the application of what he said if I had thought about it the rest of the night! As soon as he spoke them, and I mean at that instant, something entered my body through the crown of my head and pushed something down through my body until it was in the ground below me.

And the memory I have is of being able to see what was happening from the outside. I was watching myself have the experience, and it is quite different than what I would have seen with just my natural eyes. You see, when I looked I saw myself as I really was, but in my current spiritual state. I was a slave, and I saw myself bound in chain like a thick jacket around my torso and shoulders. And there was a lock placed behind me holding all the chain in place. Because my arms were swathed in chain I had very limited range of motion and the lock behind my back was frustratingly just out of reach; even if I had the key I would not have been able to unlock myself.

As I stood there helpless Jesus approached me from behind, inserted the key and sprung open the lock. And then the chain began to slip off of me, slowly at first, and then quickly like anchor chain off the bow of a ship. After several seconds I saw myself standing in the center of a ring of chain about a foot high. It seemed only natural to step outside the ring, and as I did I intuitively knew something had changed in me. I somehow knew I would never have to do cocaine again! It was as if God had handed me back the freedom to choose and left it up to me what I wanted to do with it. I could do cocaine if I wanted to, or I could choose not to if that seemed preferable.

And, even though a miracle had just taken place, Mark and I had no idea what had happened, we only knew that we both felt like celebrating. So he drank his beer and I smoked some weed, and I fell asleep peacefully after he left later in the evening. The next day we didn't discuss the previous evening much, but I had begun to talk myself out of the idea that anything out of the ordinary had taken place. And I could sense Mark was doing the same thing. And then, in the early afternoon, as Mark and I were doing something in the driveway, Charlie drove up, jumped out of his car, and with a beaming smile exclaimed, "Gentlemen, the demon is gone!" Mark and I looked at each other in mild shock; something about his choice of words drove off the doubt that was creeping in.

I was able to arrange to stay overnight at the jobsite until my driver's license suspension was completed. It was a very pleasant month and I reveled in my ability to stay away from cocaine so effortlessly. I also realized that I was smoking very much less marijuana than I had been previously. Before this happened I would smoke 4-5 times a day, but afterward only once or twice every few days. There were some changes in how I felt as well. Previously, I had a very bitter view of humanity and its potential, but somehow I found myself with a very deep and surprising love of mankind that seemed to come out of nowhere. And, I can remember feeling an amazement that was something like what one would experience if, after looking at the world in only black and white for 26 years, one suddenly could see the full range of the colors of nature.

And it was obvious to everyone who knew me that something had changed. One by one, each of my friends approached me and wanted to hear the story of what had taken place. So I told them what had happened as best as I could describe. They listened politely, and even though I knew they were skeptical, they certainly could not argue with the fact that *something* inexplicable had happened. They usually shook their heads and expressed congratulations about my being able to quit cocaine.

It was not until about a month had gone by that I realized that the change in me was lasting longer than I expected. And I was continuing to change. Marijuana had never made me anxious or paranoid in the past - quite the contrary, in fact. I smoked from morning until night and always felt relaxed after I did. But, I was finding myself increasingly uncomfortable when I smoked. After a few weeks, I was so paranoid when I got high that I decided to stop altogether.

About that time, I went to visit my parents at their home. I was in my dad's room and saw a Bible that had been given to him as a gift. Even though I had had a profound life change as a result of asking Mark for a Bible, I had not bothered to find out more about it in the days afterward. I had attempted to read the Bible at times in the previous several years, but always found myself baffled at why anyone would think there was anything relevant in it. It seemed bound in time, and not a time I cared much about. But I picked up my dad's Bible out of curiosity and randomly opened it to see if anything had changed.

I first turned to John chapter 15 and read these words of Jesus "I am the true vine, and My Father is the vinedresser" (v.1). This interested me. As a landscaper, I knew quite a bit about vines and I was impressed that this guy Jesus was using an analogy that made sense to me. As I read, I found myself deeply moved when I read Jesus saying "Greater love has no one than this, that one lay down his life for his friends," (v.13) and began to tear up as He spoke about being a friend to mankind.

I flipped forward a short distance to Romans 8 and my eyes widened when I read "For you have not received a spirit of slavery leading to fear again, but you have received a spirit of adoption as sons by which we cry out, "Abba! Father!" The Spirit Himself bears witness with our spirit that we are children of God…" (vs. 15, 16). I nodded as I identified with the "spirit of slavery leading to fear" part; that described the fear I felt in Charlie's kitchen perfectly, but I was unprepared for what would happen when I got to the "bears witness with our spirit" part.

When I read that, the best way to describe what happened was as if I was pregnant with a full term baby that suddenly leaped inside of me! I felt my insides turn over with great force. Needless to say, I continued reading for several more minutes and found myself in the 3rd chapter of John and read "Jesus answered and said to him, 'Truly, truly, I say to you, unless one is born again he cannot see the kingdom of God" (v.3). I quickly closed the book and became troubled as I considered the implications of what I had just read. You see, at that moment it was clear to me that, without ever meaning to, I had become something I swore I never would – a "born again" Christian.

I suddenly understood that all of my "prayers" about finding some sort of meaning and purpose to existence had been answered in the least desirable way I would have chosen. I was now one of those people I had scoffed at for so long, and I was not looking forward to telling people the full extent of what happened that night at Charlie's house. Despite being mortified at first, I quickly came to see that I had found much more than I bargained for. God had demonstrated such undeniable power in setting me free that I could never doubt His reality again, which provided me with something I never believed I would have – something so true it was worth dying for. And, as a result of that realization, I suddenly had something worth living for as well.

One might expect that everything went happily ever after that. But anyone who believes that does not know what lengths God will go to in order to see us "conformed to the image of His Son." (Romans 8:29). And I had some conforming to do! I spent the next several months devouring the Bible, and everything I could get my hands on that would help me better understand this new relationship God had begun with me.

Unfortunately, that was not all I was devouring. I found myself gaining weight at an alarming pace as the eating disorder that started when I was 6 suddenly became fully inflamed again. I had been quite thin as a result of the stimulant use, but I gained almost 90 lbs. in the first year I was sober. It became clear that God had granted me freedom in regards to chemical dependence, but all the same character issues that were driving that behavior were now driving my overeating. So began a long process of coming to grips with those character shortcomings and rooting them out as best I could.

Whenever I tell people struggling with an addiction about my miraculous deliverance from cocaine, they always wish they could have the same experience. It is understandable that one would want instant relief, but I always caution them that, without doing the hard work of gaining maturity, they will be just as miserable as they were before. And instantly granting the maturity that is necessary to live an enjoyable life is a miracle that God will never do. Nobody ever grows up overnight!

I describe this event as God's "room entry" into my life. Up until the moment I asked Mark for that Bible, I had no inclination to believe that there was anything that existed in the supernatural realm that could provide solutions for human problems. On the contrary, I was one of those that thought religion had brought much more strife than peace to the world. But, just like a S.W.A.T. team picks the perfect moment to burst through the door to set things right, God had picked the time and place for my story to intersect with His. All I did was crack the door the slightest possible amount and He stormed in, drove out the unwelcome guest that had become my slave-driver, and opened my eyes to the reality that there is a higher narrative unfolding alongside the dreary day to day events you read in the newspaper.

Although it would be some time before I could properly see my place in that higher story, God had sowed the seeds of my eventual breakthrough by showing me something so powerful I would never be able to doubt it again. I've never doubted His power since that day He set me free from cocaine; I've doubted His willingness, but never His ability. It's been 26 years, and I have not had one desire to use cocaine or one thought of missing it; knowing what I do now about addiction means that He must have literally changed my brain chemistry to undo the craving in my brain.

This radical and sudden change has also made possible the flexibility of mind that I mentioned earlier. When I was just starting out in pursuit of healing, I had to console myself with very small incremental changes. As I said earlier, depression is the outworking of the belief that the future cannot be influenced with any action one can take in this moment. During this time, I stumbled onto the realization that doing something (anything) that could remind me that I had the power to influence the future (even a tiny bit) could lift my depression for a short while. I had to remind myself frequently that if one little action could produce one little benefit, then, in theory at least, making a bigger step could produce a bigger benefit. And that, if I could string together enough positive actions, I just might be able to overcome the downward pull of my depressed mindset.

Practicing these small actions began to produce reliable results over time. My depression could be lessened by being proactive with creditors, going to the gym, or showing interest in my friendships. As I began to do this more frequently, it produced a more flexible mindset even though I still spent most of the time "below the line." But God had a day in mind to honor my attempts to renew my mind; that moment in front of the roulette table was the ordained time for me to finally get escape velocity from the futility I battled for many years.

The flexibility we're after is described in the Bible this way, "...if anyone is in Christ, he is a new creature; the old things passed away; behold, new things have come" (2 Corinthians 5:17). What we sometimes miss is that the newness mentioned here is not a one-time event that happens when we first believe and then we're stuck after that. It happens as often and as deeply as we need. The old is constantly passing away and the new is constantly coming!

This area of mindset is where the idea of 'taking every thought captive" (2 Corinthians 10:5) becomes the arena for this newness to play out. But be prepared for some intense fighting before it the old thoughts finally surrender to the new ones! With practice, we can subdue the old mindset (and the narrative that goes with it) whenever it makes an attempt to return and instead call on the "mind of Christ" that we have been given in its place (1 Corinthians 2:16). And I can assure you that the narrative that Jesus allows to unfold in His mind has nothing in common with the loser, victim, or villain we may be familiar with. Now that is something worth celebrating!

RECOVERY

When I was a child, I talked like a child, I thought like a child, I reasoned like a child. When I became a man, I put the ways of childhood behind me. (1 Corinthians 13:11)

His divine power has granted to us everything pertaining to life and godliness...For...He has granted to us His precious and magnificent promises, so that by them you may become partakers of the divine nature, having escaped the corruption that is in the world by lust.

Now for this very reason also, applying all diligence, in your faith supply moral excellence, and in your moral excellence, knowledge, and in your knowledge, self-control, and in your self-control, perseverance, and in your perseverance, godliness, and in your godliness, brotherly kindness, and in your brotherly kindness, love...for as long as you practice these things, you will never stumble...(2 Peter 1:3-10)

I wish I could say that, after being granted such a marvelous miracle, all the issues contributing to my vulnerability to substance abuse cleared up in one quick, steady growth spurt. But that would be a lie. Instead, God took me on a very roundabout journey that has unfolded over the past 26 years. It's only in hindsight that I can see the wisdom and necessity of what, at the time, seemed like devastating detours in my attempts to get well. Despite intense focus, my eating disorder continued to frustrate me for much of that time. From about

170 lbs. at the time I stopped doing cocaine, my weight eventually topped out at close to 400 lbs. I don't know exactly how much I weighed at my highest because I didn't have a scale that went past 350, so I estimated once the needle went past that point. The relapse cycle repeated itself numerous times along the way. I've lost the same 20lbs. at least 15 times. But, by God's grace, and the help of many people who assisted me as I struggled to recover, I've been able to maintain my goal weight at a healthy 200 lbs. for the past five years.

I'm a big supporter of the various community-based support programs (Alcoholics Anonymous, Narcotics Anonymous, Celebrate Recovery, etc.) and I think they are indispensable for providing an environment where people who are addicted can heal. I have attended them at times throughout my recovery process to deal with codependence and overeating behaviors and have gotten significant help from fellow attendees of these programs. But, I do have some differences that I've come by as a result of what I've found useful in my own recovery. These differences are relatively minor, and I will explain them as they arise.

I believe the concepts and recommendations in this section will help anyone who is trying to change, even if they do not consider themselves addicted. It might also provide some clarity to those who are struggling to help someone who is addicted find relief. And I'll warn you in advance that this is a longer chapter!

When I consider my own addiction background (or counsel addicts), I generally don't view it as a disease (or try to impress on others that they have the "disease of addiction"). It's not that I disagree with that particular model (called the medical model), it's just that I don't think the disease concept allows us to fully take advantage of what addiction is capable of teaching us about ourselves. Addiction and recovery have so much more potential to inform us about our inner nature than just the idea that "my brain is now different from 'normal' people's brains." I realize that there are many who will take issue with this, particularly those who have gotten sober through the 12-step programs. These programs stress the disease (medical) model of addiction, which certainly is helpful in reinforcing the necessity of specialized treatment for the addict.

Many people believe that the only alternative to the disease model is the moral model of addiction, which holds to the idea that addiction is a moral failing and that addicts are simply weak-willed or morally compromised people. This either/or understanding is needlessly limiting, and one does not have to embrace the idea of blaming addiction on the moral depravity of the addict if one does not ascribe to the disease model. I have no intention of entering this ongoing debate, only to present my own personal perspective that I believe will have some appeal to those looking for practical answers.

One of the things that has struck me when thinking about addiction is how cleanly the language of relationship applies to explain it. Users grow to "love" their substances and rely on them to provide the same sorts of comfort that non-addicts get from healthy relationships with people and their environment. These love affairs with substances invariably become abusive in nature, and addicts struggle to leave them in the same way a battered spouse vacillates about leaving even in the face of extraordinary violence. There are some underlying observations that are commonly seen when looking at addiction from this relational perspective:

1. *Addicts get legitimate emotional (and physical) needs met by their relationship with the substance or behavior.*

2. *Addiction inflames, and then empowers, the immaturities already present in the addict before substance use or compulsive behavior began.*

3. *Recovery is the process of identifying the particular emotional (and physical) needs being met by the substance or behavior and finding alternate ways to meet these needs.*

4. *Left unchecked, the addictive relationship becomes so intense it crowds out all competing relationships.*

Let's look at these one by one. First, *addicts get legitimate emotional (and physical) needs met by their relationship with the substance or behavior.* I sometimes begin group sessions by asking the question, "So why is change hard?" Usually, within 2 or 3 minutes two answers have emerged. The consensus of the group is that change is hard because it is uncomfortable – it puts us outside of our comfort zones. And change is hard because we are dealing with habits. Ironically, these two answers are really two sides of the same coin, because habits are meant to increase our comfort, not make us slaves to our various appetites. All habits are attempts to reduce the stress of having to solve the same problems over and over; what can be made habitual relieves us from that stress and frees up mental processes to handle more important demands of life. Habits are meant to reduce anxiety by making life as predictable and automatic as we can get it.

One of the things I enjoy teaching in groups is about something called *habit loops*. Habits are formed in response to the *reward system* of the brain being activated. When we stumble on an activity that triggers activity in the reward center of the brain, the release of the neurotransmitter dopamine is meant to sear the experience in our memory so that we are more likely to repeat the behavior in the future. Activities that release dopamine are associated with things that tend to increase the survivability of our species – sex, calorie-rich foods, and pleasurable interaction with other people are notable examples.

Unfortunately, we share the planet with some highly addictive chemicals that are small enough to pass through the blood-brain barrier and trigger the release of dopamine in large quantities. The real tragedy is that these chemicals have no survival value at all, but end up tricking the brain into thinking that they do. So, when addiction is fully ingrained, the brain ends up sending the same strength of signal for the substance as if it was literally dying of thirst. That's why it is so hard to deny the urges to use these addictive substances or stay away from compulsive activities that can also release dopamine (gambling, shopping, video gaming, etc.). Addictive drugs and pleasurable activities like eating or sex affect the dopamine-sensitive areas in our brain in strong ways and motivate us to pursue these activities again and again.

Habit loops consist of three basic parts: *reminders* (sometimes called triggers), *routines*, and *rewards*. All habits can be reduced to these elements. When I'm teaching this in a group, I will ask what triggers to use drugs group members have identified. They usually have no trouble identifying numerous triggers – anxiety-producing events, interpersonal conflict, white powders, certain places associated with using, the sound of ice tumbling in a glass, Friday afternoons, or getting a paycheck can all be the start of a habit loop that initiates craving. Many times people will say that physical pain is a strong trigger to find relief. After several minutes spent considering the dozens of ways habit loops are triggered, the group moves on to examine the "routines" they would engage in to obtain, and use, the substance. The group members compare stories about the lengths they went to in order to obtain their drug of choice, and many times they amaze themselves when they recount how determined they were to get high or otherwise escape reality.

But the interesting part is when we talk about the reward aspect of the habit loop. People will recall fondly the relief from anxiety and stress they get from using. Others talk about feeling like a "better version of myself," who doesn't struggle with social awkwardness. Still others talk about the relief from worry or the feeling of power that the substance would provide. Most people can usually talk for quite a while about the good things that using a substance can immediately provide. I say this is the interesting part because, at this point, I will ask "Which of the triggers we talked about are bad?" Sometimes they will say "All of them! They make me want to use!" But when we look objectively at the triggers they have talked about, none of them are inherently "bad." Getting a paycheck, ice tumbling in a glass, feeling nervous, Friday's, and certain parts of town are neither good nor bad. Triggers "just are"- it is that they have become able to influence behavior so strongly that is troublesome. Even depression (a common trigger to drink or use drugs), when broken down into its constituent parts, sadness and hopelessness, is not an inherently bad thing. Sadness is an appropriate response to loss, and it is actually wise to be hopeless in some circumstances; giving up on a lost cause is better if done sooner rather than later. Then I ask, "And which of the rewards that you all talked about are bad?" Again, sometimes the group will conclude they are all bad because of how much freedom they have surrendered in the process of pursuing them. But, after further discussion, the group usually recognizes that there is nothing wrong with wanting relief from anxiety, worry, pain, and feelings of not fitting in socially.

Since we have methodically determined that neither the triggers nor the rewards are the problem, by this time the group can see the problem lies in the actions (routines) that are carried out to get the rewards. All of these learned routines have been reinforced over time until they are literally second nature. And it should be remembered that the reward is the release of brain chemicals that produce the desired calming (or exciting) effects. Maybe it makes more sense now why the disease model misses something? What disease ever provided such rich rewards to those suffering from it? Right now, the pharmaceutical industry is spending billions trying to find drugs that will provide these same rewards without the destructive side effects that drugs of abuse have. In some cognitive-behavioral based recovery groups (SMART Recovery, etc.) time is spent on creating cost-benefit analyses of continuing or discontinuing substance abuse or compulsive behaviors. For what disease would we ever dream of weighing the pros and cons of staying sick or getting well?

In his book *The Power of Habit,* author Charles Duhigg examines some fascinating research done on the topic of habit formation. One of the most relevant phenomenon in addiction is something called *expectation of reward.* This was discovered by examining the brain activity of rats placed in a simple T-shaped maze with a reward placed at the end of one of the arms. A small gate is opened, and a rat is released into the maze while its brain activity is monitored. In the first few trials, brain activity is seen spiking at the start of the maze, remaining high throughout the test as the rat sniffs, scratches, and nibbles his way through the novel environment and spiking again as he stumbles onto the reward at the end. This last spike is associated with the release of dopamine and other pleasure-reinforcing neurotransmitters. But interesting changes are seen as the rat becomes more familiar with the maze.

After several trials, there are spikes seen at the onset (when the gate is opened) and when the reward is obtained, but the brain activity during the time the rat spends between those two experiences looks similar to him being asleep. He has learned the maze so well that he can go on autopilot while he runs to get the reward. This is because his brain has moved what used to require attention in primary processing areas to secondary areas. In the same way, our brains are constantly trying to take what is learned and make it routine (habitual) so that mental energy can be spent on more important tasks. This is what you are seeing when you watch two musicians speak to each other on stage while they are playing a complex piece of music. You can bet that, until they had sufficient practice, they needed all their concentration just to play the music. When you arrive at home after work, but can't remember the drive, you are in the same sort of state the rat is experiencing in that maze.

But, after many trials through the maze, something extraordinary happens. Rather than just the two spikes at the beginning and end of the maze, a third spike is seen just after the rat enters the maze. It is as if the rat suddenly remembers, "Aha, I'm going to get that reward!" This is important because this spike ends up being the largest, and most powerful, of the three. This is the dopamine release (spike) associated with *expectation of reward*. When I teach this in a group setting I usually ask at this point, "Are there any other rats in the room with me?" Almost every hand will go up, because most addicts identify strongly with the experience of this thrill that occurs when they set up a deal and are on the way to pick up drugs. Or the excitement that happens when means, motive, and opportunity all line up to allow one to indulge in their particular habit. In almost every group, an opioid user will recall the times when they were quite sick in withdrawal, but suddenly had a remission of symptoms after they were able to contact their dealer and arrange to pick up; they didn't even need to use the drug to get the release of the neurotransmitter. The chemical release associated with expectation of reward is so potent that, for many people, the final reward of actually using the substance is somewhat anti-climactic when compared with it.

Another important observation about expectation of reward is the single-mindedness that is seen after it enters the learning experience. Before expectation of reward is in place, the animal can be diverted with social experiences or other pleasurable stimuli. But afterward, there is nothing that the animal will allow to divert him until the reward is obtained. This sounds a lot like addiction! The really insidious part of addiction is its ability to make triggers out of every conceivable thing in our lives. I've seen people who have conditioned themselves to begin craving at the sight of a particular shade of red that their beer of choice had on its label.

As the group winds down, some of the members become quiet and pensive. I can tell they are getting troubled. They are confronting in a very visceral way the reality of what they will be lacking if they stay sober. They know they will have to tolerate all sorts of pain when they forsake their relationship with the substance. And the part that is crushing them at that moment is this thought dawning on them – "There is nothing on earth that can ever provide me with the same level of comfort that I've become accustomed to!" They intuitively know that they will probably never be able to feel as good as they now know how to make themselves feel at a moment's notice. What a sad goodbye!

At this point, I will normally put words on what they are thinking, and I tell them I am sorry to inform them that they will never be able to get the "slam" again. This term is not as common as it used to be, but intravenous drug users are generally familiar with it. Slamming is the injection of a substance directly into the bloodstream. It is a very quick acting and powerful way to ingest a drug. Drinkers also sometimes use the word *slam* when they mean they downed a drink very quickly. The idea I am trying to communicate is that they will almost certainly never again experience the sudden, overwhelming flood of brain chemicals that they have become accustomed to. They might stumble on to some very rewarding activity, but it will likely be very hard to plan and/or recreate.

But I don't leave them in despair. Once I remind them that chasing the slam is a recipe for death, I tell them that the alternative is that they must "hook up to an IV drip." What do I mean by this? The idea here is that the same rewards are available to them, just in a more "time released" fashion. Rather than wringing the desirable chemicals out of their brain like a soaked kitchen sponge, they will have to settle for one little drip at a time. Instead of playing mad scientist in their brain and exposing it haphazardly to toxic substances, they will now have to become benevolent scientists and explore the world for experiences that they can rely on to consistently provide a drip or two. These drips can come in an endless variety of ways: walking on the beach, playing with your kids, working out, gardening, surfing, or maybe some as yet undiscovered activity or hobby that will prompt the brain to release something good.

This is also when I introduce the idea that "craving can be your friend" to the group. Because craving is just the brain's response to an uncompleted habit loop. If I spend the time necessary to set up expectation of reward in positive habits, I will not have to fight against the power of my habits - the power will be working in my favor. The problem, obviously, is that it takes a significant number of trips through the maze before you will crave that workout, healthy food, or opportunity to share your feelings at your favorite recovery group meeting. And also that the strength of the habit loop is proportional to the amount of dopamine released; activities that produce only a mild release of dopamine take longer to produce habit loops and require more frequent reinforcing before they become habitual.

Habits are meant to reduce anxiety by making behavior automatic and saving us the trouble of having to make simple decisions over and over. Whatever is habitual requires no willpower to do; very few people have ongoing internal debates about whether to brush their teeth. When something is a habit, it has become a non-negotiable aspect of our schedule and lifestyle. But the opposite also holds true; willpower is required to do anything that is not a habit, and addiction makes simple things like when to wake up or whether to go to work subject to negotiation. And when you find yourself debating internally about whether to do the uncomfortable new routine or the familiar old one, which side usually wins? It's usually not the side advocating for doing what's uncomfortable, that's for sure! Some people spend large amounts of willpower on things that should be habits but, because of inconsistent effort, are still open for debate. When you've spent the time necessary to ingrain good habits, you won't be annoyed by having to go to the gym, eat a healthy meal, or attend a support group meeting - you will be annoyed when something gets in your way of doing those things.

Once the realization sinks in that the old ways of obtaining rewards are forever off limits, the challenge of recovery becomes putting in the consistent, daily effort to chase down enough drips to roughly balance out the loss of what the slam used to provide. This effort, over time, will establish new habit loops that provide measured and sustainable releases of desirable brain chemicals; craving will work in our favor. But here is another area where addicts meet a large hurdle. In early recovery, due to the imbalances they have created in their brains, addicts are almost certain to be in a deficit state in regards to brain chemistry. Because they have used foreign substances to flood the brain with dopamine and other neurotransmitters, the brain "downregulates," or decides to produce less than it would normally to compensate for the imbalance. And, just because substance use is stopped does not mean the brain immediately resumes business as usual. It can take a frustratingly long time for balance to gradually come back. This is just another way that addicts will be out of their comfort zone until balance can be regained.

So it's clear that there are profound emotional and physical needs being met by engaging in substance use or other compulsive behaviors. This also explains why people are so torn about giving up the substance – not only have they discovered a very pleasurable state of being, they have discovered the ultimate shortcut to it as well. What could be better? One of the main hurdles one must confront in recovery is the stubborn tendency to disbelieve that one is truly an addict. So desirable is the reward associated with the substance that people go to great lengths, outlandish lengths, to convince themselves that the costs of continuing to use the substance are worth it.

Many people have asked me how I lost all the weight (close to 200 lbs.). I tell them the same thing. One little, good decision after another for a long time. I left off the cheese and mayo from the sandwich when I desperately wanted it. I had a piece of fruit for dessert rather than the four large cinnamon rolls I was used to. I left myself no option but to go to the gym when I really wanted to stay home and watch TV with some sugary snack and peanut butter. For many months, little deprivations like this could bring me to literal tears.

Because I couldn't trust myself, I steadfastly refused to sit down at the negotiating table with the part of me that wanted to avoid discomforts like exercise and sacrificing fatty foods. I called my accountability partners, friends, and other supportive people even though I had nothing I thought was important to say. I discovered activities, hobbies, and ways to pass the time that distracted me from obsessive thoughts about food. So how is recovery accomplished? One drip at a time!

2) *Addiction inflames, and then empowers, the immaturities already present in the addict before substance use or compulsive behavior began.*

I've heard many people say "I have no willpower!" and beg anyone who will listen for help getting more of it. This is a greatly misunderstood topic in recovery, and I've seen many people get stuck because of the tendency to over-rely on it. When I teach about this, I start with a thought experiment question that I pose to the group. I begin by asking, "Let's say someone walked in, sat down and said, 'I'm here to get more willpower. I have the will to get clean and sober, but I don't have the power to carry it out. I must need more willpower.' Would you agree with them?" Some people think that statement captures it perfectly and can see no obvious flaw in it. They heartily agree that they are in need of more willpower and lean forward in their seats anticipating that they are going to be given the secret they need to finally harness their will. Others have been around the block a few times and have been let down by their tendency to collapse under pressure even when they desperately wanted to change. They affirm the need for willpower, but they know that just wanting to change is not enough to guarantee it will happen. Another group, the ones who have attended the various 12-step support meetings (AA, NA, etc.) have had it drilled into them that relying on willpower is a recipe for disaster. And they're right, the surest way to find yourself back in the pit is to bank too heavily on your ability to will your way out of it.

This concept is counterintuitive and very hard to understand for those who haven't lived it out first hand. It is exactly what Paul writes about in Romans 7: "...what I am doing, I do not understand; for I am not practicing what I would like to do, but I am doing the very thing I hate...for the willing is present in me, but the doing of the good is not. For the good that I want, I do not do, but I practice the very evil that I do not want" (v. 15,18,19).

Curiously though, the one thing that I've seen few people know is *why* willpower lets them down. It's because as long as they are pursuing more willpower, they are trying to get something they already have a ton of! When I tell the group I can prove this to them, they scoff and deny it. I ask them what lengths they have gone to in order to obtain drugs or whatever else they were craving. They immediately recount tales of driving hours through the night to get to the dealer, rescuing food from the trash, or telling whatever lie was necessary to get money to gamble with. I'll ask, "Was there ever any law that stopped you? Did any threat of lost relationship make you think twice? Any health consequences ever get in the way between you and what you wanted?" They invariably answer no, that when they wanted to get their drug of choice, there was almost no obstacle they couldn't overcome. They are forced to consider that, when they have the will to stay sober, they stay sober, but when they have the will to get loaded, they get loaded. And they are capable of great exploits either way. They have the same amount of willpower as people trying to get sober that they always had when they were so single-minded in their pursuit of drugs.

This is because the problem people run into when trying to make change isn't the quantity of willpower; it is the quantity of *wills*. We all have more than one of them. There is a term that everyone attempting to make change should be familiar with – *ambivalence*. This is defined as the coexistence of positive and negative feelings toward the same action, simultaneously drawing one in opposite directions. So the bad news is this, we don't just have more than one will about making the change, we have wills that are in total opposition to each other. I have a will to lose weight, and a will to eat an entire pizza in one sitting.

Allan is the poster child of ambivalence. He was a successful businessman who checked himself into treatment after he had become addicted to painkillers that were prescribed after a back surgery. He entered treatment of his own free will and even paid cash to get a private room with an ocean view. These rooms cost around $3,000 a day which demonstrates his commitment to change. When clients check into treatment they are thoroughly searched for contraband, and it is not unusual to find drugs in their luggage or personal effects that they "forgot" they had with them. Allan had pills squirreled away in several areas of his belongings and pretended that he was surprised when his stashes were found one after the other.

A few days later, while we were in a group session, I noticed Allan "nodding off" as is common with opioid users. I had him leave the group to be drug tested, and he tested positive for Oxycodone, a powerful painkiller. His room was searched again and pills were found in a shaving cream can that had a false bottom on it. I sat down and talked with him about it when he sobered up and his explanation for why he brought drugs with him was classic. He simply said, "I didn't know if I was going to need them or not." That is ambivalence! Somebody willingly checking into treatment, paying top dollar to give themselves the best possible chance to quit using drugs, *and* bringing along enough pills to last almost the entire time he was there.

One of the main reasons people like to believe the answer to compulsive behavior lies in getting more willpower is that it puts the solution to the problem entirely inside of them. If more willpower is all that is necessary, then all one needs to do is ramp up the quality of the promise never to do *that* again one more notch and the problem magically goes away. There is no need for ongoing treatment, therapy, support, accountability, or any other thing that lies outside of the self. Just finally keep the promises you've never been able to keep before and it will be as if the whole sordid episode never happened.

Willpower is just the sum total energy (will) available to an individual to accomplish a desired goal. The problem is that humans have a poor track record at whole-heartedly pursuing goals that require sacrifice or delay of gratification. Our hearts are divided, and we switch back and forth between pursuit of the goal and renunciation of the goal due to the presence of ambivalence. So, if getting more willpower is not the answer, what is?

Assuming one already possesses enough will to accomplish whatever reasonable goal is desired, the key then becomes learning the skill necessary to consistently determine which way one's willpower will express itself - whether for the furtherance of the positive goals of abstinence and recovery or to continue in the futility of the problematic behaviors. This skill is called *self-control*. When one has self-control, one by definition has the ability to decide which way their willpower will be used. As an adult, to lack self-control means to carry out activities that are harmful or in opposition to our stated goals despite the knowledge that there are negative consequences to the behavior.

I started by saying that addiction inflames immaturity that is already present in the addict. How did this word immaturity come into the mix? If you think about it, there is really only one benchmark we use to determine someone's level of maturity – it's whether or not they possess self-control. Can they control their appetites? Their tongue? Their use of time? These are all hallmarks of maturity, and we would not say someone is mature if they could not reliably do these things.

When I teach this in a group setting I'll say, "So, there is a sizable class of people on the planet who have very little patience and tend to have a hard time delaying gratification. They usually have a lower than average frustration tolerance and are provoked to anger more easily than most people. They are prone to deny being responsible even when they are caught red-handed, tend to be manipulative, and are known to lie, even to loved ones, to get what they want. They many times do not respect the boundaries of other's and will take what they want without asking. Who am I talking about?" They roll their eyes as if I'm reminding them of all their shortcomings and say, "Yeah, yeah, we know! Addicts are terrible people right?" They assume I'm talking about them because all those behaviors are exhibited by most addicts to one degree or another. And most of them can readily see that list in their recent histories.

But occasionally (and it's usually an elementary school teacher) someone will intuit where we are going and say "You're talking about children!" And it's true, I am. But I'm doing it to point out an odd side effect of addiction of any sort. Addiction stokes up the childish (immature) parts of us and then - and this is the really destructive part - it empowers these childish parts to hop into the driver's seat and begin making important life decisions. The damage done to an addict's life is done because the part that lacks self-control, the immature part, has been granted near-total say-so in how a person will spend their time, who they will associate with, which financial priorities will be addressed, and which will be put off.

Any family member who has close contact with an addict will tell you it is the traits associated with immaturity that are the most frustrating. The selfishness, self-centeredness, tantrums, entitlement, and denial that one would expect in a small child become extraordinarily off-putting when seen in an adult who should be able to control themselves better. This should not be a surprise because it has been demonstrated that addiction compromises the addict's ability to use the pre-frontal cortex portion of the brain. This is the part right behind the forehead and is responsible for executive decision making such as longer-term planning and initiative. In other words, the most adult part of the brain is cut out of the loop when the addict is trying to decide which course of action to take.

Sometimes, people will ask if it's true that addiction freezes the maturity of someone at the age they began using the substance. For example, if someone starts using at age fifteen, do they stop maturing at that time? My experience is that it does not matter what age someone starts drinking or using for this immaturity to become evident. I've seen people who didn't start using until later in life exhibit all the same immature behaviors that lifelong users do. It is also crucial to understand that this is not just an addiction problem. We all know "sober" people who are very capable and accomplished in life, but when a certain type of pressure is applied they respond in a much younger way. We all tend to *regress*, or resort to earlier ways of coping, when under pressure. Mature people have gone through a process that allows them to examine a range of responses to that pressure and to choose the one that has the best chance of succeeding in managing the stress while not hurting themselves, hurting others, or causing themselves greater problems in the future.

Well, the dilemma is now sufficiently outlined. No matter how good the environment we grew up in, we all come out of childhood incompletely prepared for the challenges of life to one degree or other. And we've examined the uncanny similarities between people struggling with addiction and children; both of these groups are defined by their low self-control. So where can we go from here? What kind of help can we offer to people who are lacking self-control? A lot, it turns out! You see, throughout every culture for as long as humans have been alive we have been gaining experience about how to take low self-control people, expose them to a process, and reasonably expect them to come out on the other side with enough self-control to be a benefit to themselves and society. It's called *structure*.

The first structure we come into contact with is a parental or familial structure. The parenting process is designed to instill self-control into people who start out with literally none. When I ask group members what kind of things are commonly associated with good parenting and what a child can expect to receive from good parents they say things like these: they will be loved, they will get taught, they will be accepted, etc. They usually start with the warm and comforting parts of the parenting process before someone in the group realizes that something has been left out. "They will get disciplined," someone will finally say, almost apologetically.

It's important to have a well-rounded understanding of what causes self-control to grow inside someone who is currently lacking it. Love, coaching, encouragement, acceptance, boundaries, and much more go into making a sufficient *structure* that will support the kind of growth good parents want for their kids. Parents are responsible for clearly conveying the kind of behavior that is allowed inside the structure and the consequences for engaging in behavior outside the structure. They then are responsible for providing all the necessary teaching, encouragement, and feedback that will assist the child in fitting into the structure.

And when the child fails to choose the behavior that he knows is required by the structure, the parents are obligated to impose appropriate consequences in a consistent manner. These consistent and pre-arranged consequences are in the child's best interest and are not meant to get even with the child - they are meant to assist him in the process of adopting positive habits. Many of us know the problems that result from inconsistent or harsh boundaries. Children become very anxious when they cannot depend on parents to be consistent with them. A consistent structure is actually very comforting for a child even though it demands things from him he doesn't like at times.

Society is so convinced that structure is good for low self-control people that it provides multiple layers as the child ages. Children are provided a school structure that picks up where parents leave off. Young people are provided a new set of rules about how to fit into this new structure and what consequences will be imposed if they choose not to. Some children are given a spiritual structure about how to live within the boundaries that God has provided and the consequences of living as if there is no God. And, in extreme cases, when someone demonstrates sustained unwillingness to submit to authority (in the form of laws), we provide a very different sort of structure – jail or prison.

One thing can be counted on in any structure that is able to foster self-control - it will feel confining to those in it at times. It will allow freedom of self-expression only to the limits of the structure. And it will chafe us every time we stand at the threshold and feel the temptation to engage in behavior we know is "out of bounds." We will resent it at times for the overt control it exerts on us. And we know that ambivalence will be right there with us. We will feel the desire to engage in healthy behavior that will earn us approval and reinforce our integrity while simultaneously wanting to gratify ourselves with the forbidden behavior in that very instant!

It is worth remembering that it is expected that no child will be able to live inside a structure flawlessly from the start; it's a given that consequences will have to be imposed at some point. It's also worth remembering that no child ever suffers these consequences without protest. No child ever said, "Congratulations mom, for holding to that rule about taking a shower! It's the best thing you could have done for me. Thank you for showing me such love." Or, "You know dad, you really nailed it by grounding me this weekend for lying to you. You just hit a home run as a parent. I'm so grateful for you!" No, they will go to great lengths to convince parents that they are doing the child a disservice and that it's the parents who are out of line.

But, over time, a certain kind of magic starts to happen. When confronted with the temptation of submitting to the structure or gratifying themselves in some "out of bounds" way, they have an internal conversation that goes something like this. "You know, whenever I get shady and do *that*, I never enjoy the consequences. If I get caught the consequences suck, and even if I don't get caught, I don't feel good about who I am. So, you know what, I'm just not going to do it." At that moment, the child is not thinking like a child anymore. And all the chafing that has happened as he rubbed, over and over again, against the structure that was imposed on him has done its job. The structure no longer exists just on the outside of him - it now is present on the inside. The control that the structure used to impose on him from the outside has now become self-control on the inside of him.

When this happens and the structure becomes *internalized*, the external structure become unnecessary in the same way that training wheels are unnecessary when one has learned to ride a bike. The person can be counted on to exercise his willpower in ways that conform to the values that the structure has instilled in him over time. And he has developed ways to manage the stress caused when ambivalence tries to express itself in him. The takeaway is this, that self-control is a learned skill that is a result of submission to external structure (control) for long enough that it changes us on the inside. There are numerous structures that have been created to help people make difficult changes. All the assorted kinds of support meetings and shared experience groups are essentially structures that are available for people to make use of. People looking to make changes show up to a meeting and find a group of people who are willing to play a role in helping them become a more mature (self-controlled) version of themselves.

Now, another difficulty presents itself at this point. When the low self-control child is born, he gets a family whether he wants one or not, gets a school whether he thinks it's a good idea or not, and has all sorts of structure imposed on him without anyone consulting him. It is not optional. But with fully grown adults there is very little that can happen that will force them to submit to the control of a structure. Some people, those who have had difficulty staying within the confines of the law, may have a legal system imposing structure on them. But, aside from that, whether or not one submits to a structure is purely voluntary. And what person who is already low self-control would choose to put that leash on himself and keep it there? Obviously, it is only a small minority of the people who really could use the help these structures provide who actually take full advantage of them.

When I was working in residential treatment, I was struck by how obvious this principle was. People of all ages, from all walks of life, and all socioeconomic strata, essentially volunteered to have the staff at the treatment center assume parental roles in their lives. They submitted to being told what time to wake up, how they would spend much of their time during the day, whether or not they could leave the facility, and who they could associate with from the outside. Many times they had to surrender their phone due to infractions of the rules or because they could not be trusted with it. Those in treatment willingly surrendered many of the freedoms they took for granted on the outside. And they did this for one reason - to regain self-control.

That is the unspoken exchange everyone who goes into treatment is bargaining for. They are willing to be treated as if they cannot be trusted with their freedom (like children) on one condition - that they leave with the ability to use their freedom in the way they wish. Unfortunately, most people want this transaction to take place in an unreasonably short time – 30 days, tops. Anyone who has raised children knows that this process is painstakingly slow and kids are always surprising us with behavior we were certain they had outgrown.

It is also fascinating to watch how people respond to this sort of environment. There is a whiteboard placed in a central location in the house so that clients can see what the schedule is for the entire day. It has information about group meetings, as well as daily activities and appointments written on it. Some people are immediately comforted by the rules that are imposed and welcome the restraint it fosters in them. Others, however, protest strongly against the boundaries of the structure and have difficulty adapting to the new lifestyle they find themselves in.

An interesting change takes place though after a few weeks. Invariably, there are changes that have to be made to the daily schedule at times. And it is always telling when the clients who used to chafe at the structure and resisted getting up or arriving anywhere on time are suddenly angered when trivial changes are made to the board. After responding like young children and sometimes literally having a tantrum when forced to comply with existing rules, they suddenly are outraged when there are relatively minor changes made to the daily schedule. They have come to rely on the predictability of the structure and, even though they still do not enjoy being "controlled," they sense the protection it gives them from the harm they would do to themselves without it.

One of the things I found myself saying to encourage clients who were struggling with the process was, "You won't need a sober living on the outside when you have a sober life on the inside." A sober (restrained) life on the inside gets there by repeated, consistent, and frequent acts of submission to external structure over time. There is no other way to grow up. Another saying I use to describe what we are talking about in this section is, "If you can't trust the mature part of you to make the decision, you have to outsource the decision." This means that, until the structure has worked its way to the inside, we will be vulnerable to the immature part of us that demands to be gratified immediately. The only remedy we have until then is submission to trusted others who we have decided we will consult and, if necessary, yield to when we are facing the hard decisions required to change.

3) *Recovery is the process of identifying the particular emotional (and physical) needs being met by the substance or behavior and finding alternate ways to meet these needs.*

"Diets don't work! It's all about lifestyle change." Heard that before? It's become a cliché in the weight loss industry. And, like most clichés, we've become so used to it that we fail to take it seriously anymore. But, there is a reason that saying became so commonplace. It's because it's true! Diets don't work. They don't work because the way we use the term implies that we are doing something different from our norm *for a period of time.* And everybody who has been on a diet has a similar story of what happened when they stopped it. Their old behaviors and habits quickly re-emerged, and they gained the weight back plus a few pounds.

And, no matter what you're trying to change, a "diet" will never get you the lasting success you want to have. The "no alcohol diet" and the "no heroin diet" don't work just like the "no carb diet" doesn't work. Because they don't take into account the relationship we've come to form with the behavior and what we will be missing when we give it up. We've already talked about the many reasons why people gravitate to addictive behaviors – and they are all good things to desire. There is nothing wrong with wanting to lift depression, calm anxiety, or relax more fully.

So the terms we need to start thinking in is of a "no binge eating lifestyle" or a "no crack cocaine lifestyle." And in our context, the term *lifestyle* is defined by the importance assigned to the various relationships we have formed and incorporated into our structure of daily life. We have a relationship not just with the people at work, but with work itself. Some of us enjoy our work and take great pleasure knowing that other people gain benefit from our effort. Some of us have a different relationship with work and try to avoid it whenever possible. We may have trouble holding a job or finding passion in the kind of work available to us.

In the same way, we have relationships with recreation, friends, family, food, drugs and alcohol, sex, exercise, etc. All of these activities are devoted time and energy to the degree we value them being in our lives. Addiction and compulsive behaviors invariably distort the relative importance of these things and compel us to devote excessive time and energy to the addictive relationships and neglect others in the attempt to relieve stress and maximize pleasure. Imbalance is the end result of these distorted pursuits.

So what kind of lifestyle changes are we talking about? The good news is that only one thing has to change. The daunting news is that the one thing that has to change is *everything*! This is true because changing the relationship with one element of our structure will force us to alter our relationships with the remaining elements. If we decide to start going to the gym every morning it may force us to wake up earlier than we used to which, in turn, might mean we need to go to bed earlier than we normally would. So, in order to change our relationship with exercise, it may require changing our current relationship with sleep and evening leisure time as well. This is also one of the reasons why New Year's resolutions almost never work - because people don't anticipate the amount of change they are signing up for.

We already examined how attempting to make these difficult changes forces us outside of our comfort zones. And an organism (or person) outside their comfort zone is *under stress* as it attempts to find balance again. When we are able to manage this stress effectively with actions that are beneficial to ourselves and others we have what are called *coping skills*. These coping skills are the "drips" I mentioned earlier: exercise, fellowship, spirituality, remaining accountable and connected to others, and other various self-soothing techniques are just a few of the available activities we can take part in to discharge the stress we are feeling.

One of the things I hear addicts commonly say is "I have no coping skills!" But, just as in the case of thinking they have no willpower, they are mistaken. They are constantly using coping skills to comfort themselves and relieve stress. The problem is the immaturity we mentioned earlier. You see, people start getting imbalance in life because they are relying too heavily on coping skills that they learned as children.

When children try to cope with stress they soothe themselves in a variety of ways, both good and bad. They may seek out people they are attached to and cling to them for comfort. Some kids have a security blanket or other object that can remind them they are safe. Children have a marvelous ability to use their imaginations to escape reality, deny that anything is wrong, find humor to calm a situation, or otherwise pretend that they are not feeling sad, anxious, or unsafe. Expressions of anger and rage are actually attempts to get needs met, as is avoidance and minimization of needs.

We all start out using these ways of coping, and these skills might have worked when the demands of the world were less weighty, but once the adult world starts requiring more of us, relying only on these more childish skills ends up causing as many problems as they solve. And if our structure growing up was not able to teach us enough positive skills we are at a serious disadvantage when trying to manage the demands of adulthood. I once had a client capture this perfectly when he said, "I'm not running from my problems, I'm running from how I think about my problems." He realized that it wasn't the size of his problems that was the issue, it was that he perceived himself to be so small (young) in comparison. The only coping skill that he felt was available to him was the avoidance a child would use, even if it meant his situation worsened as a result.

If I want to lose weight, I must change my relationship to food by eating within certain parameters that will help me achieve my goal. And when I change that relationship by eating fewer high fat or processed foods, replacing refined sugar with fruit or other substitutes, or reducing snacking between meals, I can anticipate feeling a sense of loss at the times when I would normally be eating those foods. I will miss the comfort provided by the kinds and amounts of foods that I have decided to limit, and will have to seek out sources of comfort that will make up the difference.

Unfortunately, there will be a period of time where I will be without the comfort I'm used to and *also* without sufficient alternatives to provide it. This is because it takes time to discover these alternate sources. It's also because the quality of comfort provided by new sources is something like the difference between the feelings of comfort one has with a trusted old friend versus what is available from a brand new relationship that has not had time to form deep intimacy. Newer, unfamiliar sources of comfort have a limited effect until they are practiced enough. We will be in something I call relationship deficit; we are not able to draw enough satisfaction from newly cultivated relationships and skills to compensate for the one(s) we have left behind.

There is a word that I've tried to find a way around in this process of change, but when I try to answer people's questions about what it takes to regain freedom from addictive behaviors I find myself eventually having to introduce it into the discussion. It is the word *suffering*. Because anyone who has tried to leave behind a deeply ingrained relationship (whether with a substance, behavior, or person) will attest to how much it hurts to deny oneself the comfort that one knows is readily available. Combined with the discomfort of the organic brain imbalance mentioned earlier is the torment of knowing that total relief is just one forbidden phone call or trip to the liquor store away. And to have to put up with such discomfort while knowing exactly how to get out of it is among the hardest things a human can be asked to do. It doesn't just require delay of gratification.

Because the addict has no idea (or experience) how to replace the comfort and relief he gets from substances, it requires acceptance of the fact that gratification might *never* arrive. This is when the process crosses from pain into suffering. Pain is the intense discomfort associated with abandoning the relationship with the substance or behavior. Suffering is having to live moment by moment with the realization that this pain could end tomorrow or, in theory, never. Suffering is not knowing when, or even if, the pain will ever go away. One of the critical aspects of successful recovery is to normalize this suffering and to cultivate multiple sources of support that can alleviate all or part of it when it is necessary.

Addiction's great attraction is that it holds out the promise of a non-suffering existence. Unfortunately, because evil has entered into the world, there is no way to escape suffering. We are surrounded by it and, although we spend great amounts of money on tall gates and security guards to keep it at a distance, it cannot be filtered out; it is in the very air we breathe. One of the old-fashioned definitions of this word is *to put up with*. That is a large part of the suffering I'm talking about here. We have to put up with others (and our own) shortcomings. We have to put up with injustice, racism, and intolerance that are deeply woven into our culture. We have to put up with physical and mental challenges and disabilities. We put up with a huge host of things that we would wish out of existence in a second if we could. And most people agree that, if they were told the exact time and day that their pain would end, even if it lay in the distant future, their suffering would be greatly alleviated. Suffering's torment lies in the not knowing how long one has to "put up with" the discomfort they are in.

When I talk about the reality of suffering, I am clear to distinguish between two varieties. One can suffer poorly or suffer well. Suffering poorly is the attempt to deny its presence and to avoid the difficult process of reconciling one's desire for an ideal, safe, and secure world while still staying positive and engaged living in the world we have. People who attempt to cheat the system and avoid suffering always end up with one thing – more suffering! Escaping reality cannot be done for long, and the reality that eventually catches up is always harsher than the one we tried to escape. Always!

Because addicts incessantly try to escape the intolerability of the suffering that is in the present, they end up pushing it to the only place available – the future. When addicts try repeatedly to make this escape they fool themselves into thinking they are letting suffering pass quietly by them into their past. But all they ever do is push today's "putting up with" into tomorrow, then the next day, and so on. Before too long the heap in front of them is so large that they are using just to escape thinking about what is waiting for them.

Suffering well is having the courage and willingness to dive into the healing process that God has made available to us. It is called grieving. People who suffer well allow this process to take place on its timetable. It is the psychological "bowel system" that allows us to take in all of the toxic experiences of this world, strain out the valuable lessons, and excrete the pain, remorse, and regret so that we can live fulfilling lives. This is what is meant by "letting go." When someone lets the grief process work the end result is the letting go of pain, bitterness, and resentment about the circumstances of the loss. In its place one has the ability to receive peace of mind, forgive others, and keep one's heart open to experience the whole range of what God has planned for the future.

Elizabeth Kubler-Ross, in her work with terminally ill patients at the University of Chicago in the 1960s, identified five distinct "stages" in the grief process. They are shock/denial, anger, bargaining, depression, and acceptance. There is some controversy about the validity of her model of grief, and Kubler-Ross herself regretted the misunderstanding some have about her writings. But, the five stages remain a valuable descriptive model when examining the kind of suffering commonly seen in addiction recovery. The stages are not a linear progression that one can use to predict what the letting go process will have in store next for us. It is common to move back and forth between the stages in rapid and unanticipated ways. And, just like the physical bowel system can seize up and stop moving, the grief process can stall at any point on the way to acceptance.

When saying goodbye to a problem relationship with a substance, compulsive behavior, or codependent friendship/romance, the initial stage is likely to be denial of some kind. There is commonly a reflexive tendency to want to believe that facing the complete letting go of the "other," whatever it may be, is not actually necessary. People cling to the idea that the disordered aspect of the relationship can be isolated and removed so that an utter loss can be avoided. People in this stage deny that they are addicted even when presented with clear evidence that they meet many of the criteria required to diagnose substance abuse disorders. When someone is in the denial stage, they will go to absurd lengths to defend the toxic relationship they are attached to. And, almost without exception, the more forceful one is in arguing that the addict has a problem, the more certain they can be counted on to protect (defend) the substance, behavior, or toxic person they are in relationship with.

When the shock of facing that one has become snared in one of these toxic relationships wears off and people see that denial is unsustainable, anger is a natural reaction. "Why did *I* have to become an addict?" or "Why can't *I* drink like everybody else!" are frequently heard complaints. The underlying frustration is because they have come to realize that they cannot have their cake and eat it too. The destruction that the relationship is bringing them has overtaken anything good it used to bring. The necessity of having to say goodbye to the substance or behavior is infuriating because, more than anything, addicts want to have a "manageable" relationship that will allow them to continue getting the comfort they have come to expect without the negative side effects. They loudly protest the "unfairness" of other people getting to indulge in the behavior that they must now swear off of.

At some point, when denial can no longer be maintained, and when protest has become recognized as futile, bargaining will commonly be seen. In denial, people avoid facing the necessity of letting the problem relationship go in any way. People who are in the bargaining stage try to convince themselves that the relationship can be maintained if certain aspects of it are changed or modified. Alcoholics try switching to beer instead of hard liquor. Heroin addicts agree that opioids have to be cut off, but insist on keeping a relationship with marijuana. Other factors that people alter in an attempt to avoid total loss of the substance or behavior are times and/or days of allowable use – "I'm OK if I don't drink before noon (or not on workdays, etc.). This stage is usually when promises are made that "this time it will be different."

This is also the stage where many addicts attempt new "experiments" designed to test whether they are correct in their calculations about how to preserve the relationship in some form.

Because they "never had a problem" with alcohol, they replace cocaine with beer, or Vicodin with marijuana. These experiments fail almost without exception. The impairment of judgment that occurs when the supposedly milder intoxicant is consumed usually leads to the reintroduction of the more destructive one. It may take several iterations of experimentation, but they will eventually arrive at the inevitable conclusion - it is the entire relationship with intoxication that has to be let go of. The reason why they get loaded (to escape suffering) is the same reason why they must not get loaded. Instead, they will have to do the hard work of cultivating other sources of comfort in their "letting go" process.

At some point, one recognizes that no protest will change the reality that letting go completely is necessary, and that no bargain can be struck to prevent that necessity. When that sinks in, the experience of profound sadness is almost unavoidable. Something is happening to them that they cannot drive away with anger or manipulate with clever deal making. This is the same sort of sadness felt when one faces divorce or death of a loved one. There is a gaping hole in one's life and filling it seems next to impossible. Just like someone who loses a long time life partner will doubt that they could ever be replaced, those leaving behind an addiction often feel like they have to resign themselves to a dull and dreary future without the substance they are missing.

When the process has run its course, and the one grieving remains in an environment where healing can happen, we can expect resolution of the loss and the acceptance of a new normal. Rather than being preoccupied with reminders of what we can never have again, we open up to new possibilities and welcome the freedom that letting go can bring. "Time heals all wounds," is something that people say to try to comfort others when they're grieving, but this is not the case. Just like rubbing contaminated dirt in an open wound will prevent it from healing well no matter how much time goes by, the same is true for the letting go process. Time alone does not assure that the process will progress as designed. Only time in the right environment will assure that the healing properties that God has built into us will work as they are meant to.

I knew Sarah from the outrigger canoe club I paddled with several years ago. She was a typical mid-thirties woman in most ways and we both enjoyed the fellowship and friendly competition that the club provided. One day, while we were waiting for our race to begin, she mentioned the fact that she wanted to lose a few pounds before the big season-ending race that was coming up in a few weeks. I asked her if she knew how she was going to achieve her goal and if there was anything obvious she needed to do to get there. She sighed humorously and admitted that she already knew she would have to let go of the 2-3 scoops of ice cream she had come to enjoy for dessert every night. I commiserated with her and teasingly asked how she was going to deal with that excruciating moment when she would want to go to the freezer as usual but ran into the leash she had put on herself. We both laughed knowingly about it and went our separate ways on the beach to handle getting the boats ready to race.

A couple of hours later, I saw her approaching me with some urgency and, as she got closer, I could see she was in tears! She came up to me and told me she finally knew why that ice cream was so important each night. She had lost her father about a year before and, after spending a few months in the grief process, had discovered that she could numb herself just enough with those scoops of ice cream to keep the remaining grief from expressing itself. And now that she was imagining how she would feel without that small comfort, she came back in contact with the remaining sadness of the loss that was still waiting for her to deal with. Because she thought she "should be over it by now," she had pulled away from family, friends and caring others and stopped talking about her loss. But time alone had done nothing to lessen the pain of losing the relationship with her father. Her pain drove her to discover another relationship (with ice cream) that could provide just enough comfort to not have to face what losing her father really meant to her.

It's important to remember that, if we are staying in a given relationship, even if it is problematic, it is because there is something positive about it that we are reluctant to lose. One of the ways people try to lessen the impact of losing something is to *devalue* its meaning to them. When I ask people what the upside of their addiction might be, they many times look at me like I'm crazy. "Are you kidding?" they ask, "There's nothing good about heroin. It's killing me!" I understand the temptation to make the substance or behavior "all-bad" due to the anguish and frustration it has caused. I've done it myself. But, as I mentioned earlier, if we dismiss it as a disease we miss opportunities to recognize the meaning the substance or behavior provides in our lives. And, until we realize the positive aspects of its role in our life, we will not have a clear idea of what needs we must become more proactive in meeting.

That is what Sarah had done when she lost her dad. Rather than honoring her feelings of deep loss, she decided to act like losing him was no big deal. It was then that she discovered ice cream had painkilling qualities that could take the sting out of her loss. And the tears she shed that first day were not about losing her father (those would come later), they were about losing the ability to escape the pain of her loss. The grief process had stalled when she minimized her loss and avoided the deeper realization of what she was missing without her father. When she decided to forgo the ice cream, her pain began to remind her that she was still in need of comfort and reassurance that she had relied on her father for previously. Now her challenge would be finding new relationships that could somehow make up the difference. In the same way, the pain of letting go of a substance or toxic relationship provides clues about exactly what kind of comfort we need to seek out from healthy sources.

We can learn some important things by paying attention to the kind of escape we get from our chosen substance or activity. Whether it is relief from anxiety, loneliness, or pain, our compulsions point directly to where we are not using adult coping skills. These areas are where we've become reliant on dangerous or toxic relationships to manage stress. In some recovery settings, you will hear people say they are "grateful" for their addiction. They don't mean they are fond of looking back at all the time they spent in a fog. They're grateful because, without the crisis the addiction generated, they never would have been forced to grow and find the more fulfilling relationships they can now enjoy. But, I guarantee they didn't feel that way when they started the process; the letting go of the "easier and softer way" that they were leaning on caused them much grief for a significant amount of time.

One of the things I've seen numerous times in recovery is the reactivation of the grief process. Many people start off their sobriety knowing they have unresolved losses or trauma, but they feel frustratingly numb to it. They describe the tears coming right up into their eyes and then receding back down to the depths even though they want them to come pouring out. They instinctively protect themselves from pain that they desperately want to be free of. And they try to make the process resolve as an act of will, always to no avail.

But something happens about a month into their treatment. The process begins to move unexpectedly and they find themselves deep in the process of letting go. What happened? They put themselves in an environment where they had the support of other caring people who they had come to rely on as "painkillers" in a good sense. When they had begun to trust the love and support of their peers and counselors, the grief process began to do what God designed it to - rid them of their toxic, emotional "waste."

This decision to bring themselves out of isolation is the necessary factor that allows facing what was placed on hold in the past. Terri was furious in group when she discussed her rat of an ex-husband. She seethed as she detailed his betrayal and refusal to pay child support. She reacted strongly to any group member's suggestion that she might need to address her anger toward him. "What he did was unforgivable!' she'd maintain, even while admitting that her anger was a strong trigger for her drinking.

Her anger was so palpable, and his behavior so frequently discussed, I assumed that this was a fairly recent event that had happened no longer than a year ago. She began to detail such an elaborate history of mistreatment I suddenly got curious about when this had happened. I was saddened when I heard her response, "I've been dealing with this for 12 years!" This poor woman had been frozen in protest over what her ex had done to her over a decade earlier. Time alone had not done one ounce of healing. Her ritual now was to invite alcohol in as her sole source of comfort in her rage.

But, after the group had let her pour this out on them, and after enough time had gone by for her to get comfort from their support, she was able to see that ruminating in her anger was part of what was killing her. She began to work on acceptance and letting go and was able to leave treatment significantly improved. She was able to talk about more of what was in her heart beyond her anger toward her ex. A major victory!

4) *Left unchecked, the addictive relationship becomes so intense it crowds out all competing relationships.*

That this is true hardly needs to be explained. One of the sadder things about watching the television series *Intervention* is listening to family members recount what the addicted person used to be like before addiction took hold. Over and over, these are people described as happy, energetic, artistic, talented, kind, and lovable. But, as the substance demands more and more time, devotion, and mental energy, all other relationships that will not accommodate the addiction are sacrificed. Only relationships that will overlook the dysfunction brought on by the addiction are maintained.

And because this can happen so gradually, loved ones many times have come to accept things that they never would have if the change were sudden. Like the story of the frog who quickly jumped out when placed in the already boiling water, but died when placed in the cool water that was gradually heated to boiling, they take on little pieces of responsibility that don't belong to them until they are managing nearly all the adult responsibilities of the addict.

Frustration and resentment are common in those supporting the addict. They are invariably mystified by the behavior their loved one exhibits and the poor choices they make as a result of the addiction. If they have gotten some help for themselves, they know that it is not a matter of appealing to their loved ones ability to reason or live up to the promises they swear to keep. Sometimes there is confusion about what they are feeling as well. They have been told not to take it personally, but there is often a feeling present that does not make sense until relational terms are applied to describe what they are feeling. Spouses who have tried to hang in with the addict through the ordeal will identify strongly with the feeling of being cheated on. Their mate is in another love affair that always seems to take priority over the marriage. This is when they say things like, "If you really loved me you would stop drinking!" And the sad thing that I mentioned is how long they will allow themselves to be betrayed in the attempt to be a good partner.

Jesse's husband was an alcoholic who had started a successful contracting business at the start of their marriage. He had begun the relationship as an active, outdoorsy sort of guy who had a strong group of friends, hobbies, and love of motorcycles. Over the 20 plus years they were married, his drinking periodically interfered with their relationship and Jesse tried everything she could think of to make it clear to her husband that he had a problem with alcohol. She begged, pleaded, cajoled, nagged, and threatened him at various times, to no avail. She had gradually taken on many of his previous responsibilities at his job and, over the years, had also assumed total control of the parenting and household duties. She described being so angry at him that it was worrying her. "I'm becoming someone I don't recognize!" she said through tears one day. She felt as if her anger was so intense it could not be justified, and she felt guilty about the strength of the hatred his behavior could generate in her.

I asked her to imagine if every time he ditched work to drink he had instead ditched to be with another woman. Or that every time he brought home a 12-pack, it was really another woman he was inviting home with him. Or that the reason why he sacrificed all the activities they used to do together was so that he could spend time with another woman. Then I asked her to imagine how angry she would be if all those scenarios were actually true. Finally, I asked her how she would feel if he blamed her for his cheating just as he blamed her for his drinking. She broke down sobbing and realized that she was *exactly* as angry as if he had been cheating on her *and* blaming her for it throughout the marriage. Her anger finally made sense. And, after she granted the validity of her anger, she was able to see it as a guide that would allow her to set appropriate boundaries with her husband. She would never in a million years put up with him having the kind of long-term affair he had been having with alcohol if he had been having it with another woman. So, rather than empty threats and broken promises about the consequences she was going to impose on him, she began to make changes to protect herself from his "affair."

There is a period of time in early recovery that I've come to call the "unthinkable stage." I first noticed this when discussing enjoyable things that people might do for recreation or hobbies that could take the place of substance use or problem behaviors. Sometimes they will mention how they like to go to the river or play cards, etc. But then they further consider that they will have to do these previously enjoyable activities *without* the substance. And the most common response is despair that they will not be able to engage in the activity again, almost as if it has been spoiled due to the presence of the substance. Going to the river with friends could never be as rewarding without alcohol, so they figure they will never go to the river again. Going out to eat without a glass of wine could never provide the same pleasure again so why do it? It is literally unthinkable that they could have an enjoyable, fulfilling life without the substance or behavior. That is how totally the relationship has insinuated itself into the person's life; unless the substance comes along there is no point in doing the activity.

Not only does this relationship with the substance demand inclusion in all activities, it demands the exclusion of all other relationships that threaten it. Loved ones who try to aid the addict are shunned, previously enjoyable activities are sloughed off, and the relationship with work will eventually be renounced if the relationship with the substance is not addressed. This is what is meant by "hitting rock bottom" in recovery. It is when the addict realizes how totally the relationship with the substance has cut him off from supportive and rewarding relationships that would be available otherwise. But, as any addict will tell you, there is always a bottom below the one where you stand right now. Unless action is taken, the addiction will force someone to sacrifice their relationship with life itself.

One of the phrases that is common in 12-step based recovery has to do with "character defects." This terminology refers mainly to the addict's maladaptive (faulty) responses to stress, self-seeking motives, and exaggerated emotional expressions. Participants in these groups do the necessary work of examining how their addiction has led them to exhibit "defective" tendencies like chronic lying, denial, avoidance, acute selfishness, and manipulation.

But, I don't like the term character defects because it doesn't do a good job of capturing what kind of problem we are up against. When something is defective, we usually don't spend much time trying to repair or otherwise improve it. We ship it back to the manufacturer and request a new one. Now, I do wish that it was possible to get a brand new character from the factory in exchange for the one I have, but my experience is that growth in character is a painstaking process requiring persistent attention and sustained effort. Some changes happen faster than others, but very few are instantaneous or accidental.

For this reason, I prefer to talk about character immaturities rather than defects. Because if something is immature, I'm much more inclined to put in the effort necessary to nurture it until it reaches maturity. Especially with something I value as much as my own character and integrity. As we discussed, all the defective behaviors addicts are known for are commonplace, even expected, from young people. The problem is that a tantrum that is typical, and maybe even cute, in a 3-year-old, is extremely distasteful in a 33-year-old.

It is an amusing cliché that kids ask, "Are we there yet?" so impatiently, but seeing an adult with that sort of impatience is troubling. So the defect is not the presence of intense anger, paralyzing fear, or rampant dishonesty. The "defect" is never having learned methods of coping with frustration, fear, or anxiety that adults need to manage these, and other, difficult emotions. And the kind of relief provided by substances or compulsive behaviors is so gratifying that it is an enormous effort to tolerate the presence of these "defective" tendencies while we painstakingly practice the more mature methods of coping. It is so much easier to escape by indulging in the compulsive behavior.

Another benefit of looking at it as a maturity issue (rather than a defect) is that the idea of being in a process is inherently included in the discussion. For something to come to maturity implies that the environmental elements and factors that are required for growth to occur have been present as the process has progressed. For example, if a fruit tree is to produce mature, healthy fruit it is understood that the tree will have been properly pruned, pollinated, watered, fertilized, and tended. A significant amount of effort will have been put into ensuring that nothing that can disrupt the process is allowed to remain in the tree's environment. But people are much more complicated than trees. Is it possible to know what elements are necessary to ensure that people grow into maturity and become fruitful? I believe it is.

SPIRITUALITY

Make a tree good and its fruit will be good, or make a tree bad and its fruit will be bad, for a tree is recognized by its fruit. (Matthew 12:33)

"What does it mean to be spiritual and what does it have to do with recovery?" is a question I love to ask in a group setting. I love it because of how quickly it escalates the passions of the people in the room. It is not uncommon for there to be more opinions than there are people in the group, as some people will augment their previous answers as they listen to others' definitions. And if I don't manage the discussion well, it can quickly turn ugly with people discounting other perspectives and belittling those they think are naïve. There are also many people who see it as a nonsense word that has no place in recovery or even life in general. Some people identify themselves as very spiritual and some resist the label entirely.

After we spend a few minutes discussing how different all the opinions present are, and face the potential for conflict, I announce that I believe I can get everyone present to agree that they are, indeed, spiritual people. I also tell them that there is a way to think about spirituality that identifies the elements that are common to all, from hardcore fundamentalist to committed atheist. Without exception, some will say it's impossible, but, despite their misgivings, I almost always get them to see these commonalities before we are done. Now, in full disclosure, I am as Christian as it gets. I believe Jesus was who he claimed to be and that following him is still as necessary as he claimed 2,000 years ago. My relationship with God colors everything else in the world – it is the lens I see everything through. But, I also believe that, because all people have a spiritual nature, there are certain things that they all have in common, and certain things that work for everyone, whether they agree with each other's worldviews or not.

Whenever I raise this topic in the group, a significant segment will admit to wanting to become "more spiritual." I always ask them how they will know if they achieve that goal. Common answers are "I will have more peace," or "I will forgive more easily." But, after we discuss the various motives of group members, it becomes obvious that at the heart of all spiritual pursuit is the desire to *change*. Nobody ever says they want to become more spiritual so they can remain the same. And, without exception, all the world's religions are concerned with *growing* into a different sort of person to one degree or another. This is the first thing we all have in common if we are honest, because no one with any self-knowledge ever says they want to remain exactly as they are. Even if things are going well, it is always possible that they could go better.

As I mentioned, some people are frustrated by any inclusion of spirituality in the discussion of recovery. They see no reason why the two should be considered together. There are at least two reasons that I'm aware of so far that make spirituality relevant in recovery. The first has to do with meaning. If there is any transcendent meaning to life, it cannot be found in the things that relate only to our physical existence. There are a million things our instruments can tell us about the universe we inhabit, but there will never be an instrument that can tell us why the universe exists. Or why we should obey the law. Or why we should stay sober. These are all spiritual questions that require spiritual answers. And, at least for people like me, having an answer to these questions makes it easier to choose to face the suffering that recovery generates rather than run from it. As Nietzsche said, "He who has a why can bear almost any how."

Earlier, I mentioned Dr. Philip Zimbardo's concept of time perspective bias toward the past (past-negative vs. past-positive). But, we also have a bias toward the future. The spectrum used when viewing the future is mundane (worldly) on one end and transcendent (spiritual) on the other. We all fall somewhere between thinking that the amazingly complex interactions of atoms only appears to have purpose, or that absolutely everything happens due to the influence of an organizing mind that most people call God. And where we fall on this spectrum has implications that affect our experience of life.

A certain amount of the mundane perspective is helpful when making plans for the future. People who are focused on the worldly aspects of the future tend to delay gratification in the present so their future can be more satisfying. But too much emphasis on the mundane is what lies underneath workaholism as people forget to enjoy the present in order to protect their future. The sacrifices that the purely mundane perspective requires are things like fewer vacations, longer hours at work, and scrimping on expenses. The irony is that the overly mundane view means people never let the future arrive and instead postpone their pleasure indefinitely. Too strong a bias toward the mundane leaves one with only the rat race to look forward to. On this view, history is not moving toward any culmination or climax, and there is no ultimate difference between success or failure, war or peace, sobriety or drunkenness.

A transcendent (spiritual) bias toward the future, on the other hand, adds something intangible to the mix – it adds meaning, and beyond that, great importance. Because the spiritual bias assumes that there is a purpose in even trivial events, what seems random in the mundane view is laden with importance far above what is detected only by our five senses. This importance is carried down to the smallest degree; there are no rogue atoms in the universe that have broken free of the purpose they were created for. This concrete certainty makes possible what Viktor Frankl put this way, "There is nothing in the world, I venture to say, that would so effectively help one to survive even the worst conditions as the knowledge that there is a meaning in one's life." If you could prove to me that there was no purpose or meaning in creation, I would be the first to buy us both a drink!

There is a downside in too strong a spiritual bias, though. These are the people who are, in Oliver Wendell Holmes Sr.'s words, "so heavenly minded that they are no earthly good." This means that too much time and energy is spent on discerning signs from heaven before action is taken, or a distorted view that concludes that, because someone is suffering, it must be God's punishment for their past sins. This is the dark side of karma. These people anguish over whether they should assist the one suffering because they feel they are undoing the will of God.

The other reason why spirituality is important to the discussion is that spiritual growth drains the power of addiction to drive us toward the behaviors we are trying to stop. It is common for certain emotional states to generate craving and trigger the desire to use. Strong anger, anxiety, or sadness can all trigger the desire to escape by using drugs or engaging in a compulsive behavior. It follows then, that if I can reduce the intensity of these difficult emotions, I can also reduce the intensity of the cravings that they can trigger. It should also be remembered that the Bible describes self-control as a fruit of the Spirit (Galatians 5:22), which means that we can count on getting more of it as we pursue spiritual growth.

To better understand the similarities that we all share spiritually it helps if we begin by looking first at our physical similarities. Because the one thing that both of these natures (spiritual and physical) share is the ability to grow or shrink depending on the kind of nourishment we take in. Let's look first at our physical makeup to get an idea of what I mean. By manipulating our environment and taking in different amounts of energy (in the form of food), we can influence the kind of physical growth we want to take place. We can grow (or shrink) as a result of exposure to our environment. If I want to lower my cholesterol I can alter the amounts and kinds of animal fats I consume or eat oatmeal to help rid my body of it. If I want to lose weight I can reduce caloric intake and add more activity. If I want to reduce my blood pressure I can limit the sodium I put in my body and bring it down. There is a wide variety of environmental change I can make that can directly influence the kind of growth I want to take place. And one thing that these physical changes have in common is that *they can all be measured by human tools*. I can get blood tests to measure cholesterol, get on a scale to see if my weight has changed, and have my blood pressure checked by a sphygmomanometer (just in case you wondered what that cuff was really called!).

But what about spiritual growth? What can we agree on when we talk about this sort of change? A lot it turns out! Just like we can alter our physical environments to induce desired change, the same can be done for our spiritual qualities. "OK, great" I can hear you say, "but what *are* those?" Simply put, our spiritual qualities are the ones that grow or shrink in response to our environment but *cannot be measured by human tools*. Our environment either promotes or hinders our attempts to become more loving, kind, courageous, or forgiving, and we can demonstrate more or less of these qualities depending on the kind of (emotional) energy we are "ingesting." And no doctor ever cut someone open and remarked, "Jeez, no wonder this guy is so angry! He's got 4 lbs. of it sitting in his gut."

These qualities are hard to trace, and while their presence may be detected by certain tools (a brain scan can tell if I'm relaxed or tense, etc.), there is no tool yet devised that can measure calmness itself. It's also interesting to note that these spiritual qualities are no less descriptive of us than our physical ones, perhaps even more so. When we want to identify someone we talk about their purely physical characteristics (6 feet tall, blond hair, blue eyes, etc.), but when we want to describe what it's like to actually know a person we talk about their spiritual qualities (nice, funny, bitter, angry, etc.). In the past, it would have been very much more informative to describe me as sad or negative than to say anything about how I looked on the outside.

Alright, so our working definition of spirituality to this point is "the part of us that grows or shrinks in response to our environment but cannot be measured by human tools." It means that everyone has a spiritual nature, and is responsible for its well-being, whether they recognize it or not. Some of you might be starting to wonder, "OK, then what is this environment you're talking about? Because I want to grow in some areas and it's not as fast as I'd like."

At this point, we need to talk about macronutrients and micronutrients. Macronutrients in our diet are proteins, carbohydrates, and fats. All the food in the world falls under these three umbrellas. Micronutrients are things like vitamins, trace minerals, and phytochemicals that are provided by ingesting macronutrients. When we want to effect change in our bodies, we alter the ratio or quantities of these things to get the desired results. And there are always diet books being written about the benefits (or dangers) of the amount of protein, carbohydrate, or fat that we take in. Our physical nature will always respond to the diet we eat whether we believe in the science of nutrition or not. I can deny the existence of fat, but if I eat too much of it, I will still change the makeup of my body.

We all eat these things according to our preferences and their availability, and their effect on our bodies has very little to do with what we believe about them. They nourish us because it is in our physical nature to grow and respond to the energy we take in as food. We are built the same way in our spiritual natures. There is an environment that, when ingested, will improve our condition whether we believe in a million gods or none. And, just like there are dietary macro and micronutrients, there are also spiritual "nutrients" that will nourish us and foster growth in the emotional realm. Dr. Henry Cloud, in his book *Changes That Heal*, identifies three broad elements that are necessary for humans to thrive and reach their full potential: *grace*, *truth*, and *time*. These elements are what I will describe as spiritual "macronutrients." When these things are present in sufficient quantity, people who are intentional about taking them in will become better versions of themselves.

Grace is a frequently misunderstood concept; many people think it has something to do with praying before a meal or the way a ballerina moves. It is misunderstood because it goes against so much of the relational scorekeeping that comes naturally to humans. Grace is receiving what we have not earned and have no right to demand. You might have heard of a *grace period* that a creditor will give a customer. Parking structures sometimes provide a short grace period when you take your slip out of the machine at the entrance. A credit card company might give you a grace period of several days after the bill is due. The idea is this – that even if you miss the deadline and are technically liable to receive the penalty, you will be treated as if you are completely innocent. Not because you're a "good person" or deserve a break today, but because someone decided to overlook your true guilt. In psychology, Carl Rogers introduced this same concept and called it "unconditional positive regard." In other words, no matter what horror story you bring to me about what you have done or are capable of doing, I will choose not to define you by that and will instead put acceptance of you as a person as the most important aspect of our relationship.

Because it suspends the natural tendency to judge and punish, grace allows people to fully express their wrongs and shortcomings without fear of losing love. And deep healing cannot happen as long as confession is too risky to undertake. When someone goes to an Alcoholics Anonymous meeting and introduces himself as an alcoholic, the others present don't stand up as a group and walk out in disgust. They actually welcome the person who has just made a potentially alienating admission. That is grace. In some other places, the reception would not be nearly as warm or welcoming and may even be met with outright rejection. But the AA meeting is an environment where grace can (hopefully) be counted on to be shown consistently. In fact, the 12-step meetings have a saying, "We're only as sick as our secrets!" Without grace, it would be wise to keep our sins secret.

We all have stories about a parent, teacher, or significant figure in our life who was particularly good at showing grace. These people are sought out because of the warmth they exude, and rightly so. But there is a downside to grace. If all I'm receiving is unconditional positive regard from people who are affirming how wonderful I am, I may be tempted to adopt a skewed opinion of myself and come to rely on having my sin overlooked. I may even begin to presume on the grace offered to me and begin to think I have *license* to behave badly. Grace alone will not prompt me to grow. Some of you may have grown up in homes where your specialness was affirmed above everything else. Some of you may be married to this person – I'm so sorry! People who have grown up with grace alone usually have a hard time being confronted with negative aspects of their behavior. That's why we need the second macronutrient of *truth*.

Truth is necessary if we are going to make any difficult change. It holds up a mirror to us as we are and pulls no punches. Because it can be so painful to face the truth about who we really are, we become experts at deceiving ourselves and others. Who wouldn't avoid facing the dysfunction inside themselves if they could? When I was spending time with Charlie in my early twenties, we frequently were in situations where he could expect to be scrutinized because of his celebrity. And, because we were snorting cocaine in some of these situations, he was concerned that someone would see cocaine residue in his nostrils. He had a ritual where he would wipe his nose and clean it as best he could and then would face me, lean his head back, and ask "Dude, am I hangin'?" He needed someone to check to make sure that there would be no photo of him with something hanging out of his nose. It sounds funny, but we all need people who we can ask that kind of question. We all have blind spots and need to be told the truth when we're "hangin'."

But truth without grace is also inadequate for spiritual growth. This is the demoralizing state of *legalism*, where our intentions to become better people are meaningless and only our ability to follow the rules is considered. Progress toward the goal of growth is discounted and only our ability to conform perfectly matters. Rather than the unconditional worth granted to us by grace, legalism is focused solely on the condition of performance to a standard. Whether this is a family that holds impossibly high standards or some distorted view of God that lacks grace, legalism crushes people with burdens they cannot, and were never meant to, carry. Those of you who grew up in these environments know the frustration and longing for escape that they create.

As any sort of addiction or relational dysfunction progresses, we tend to get these two nutrients, grace and truth, from two wildly different sets of people. When we are in our addiction/dysfunction it is usually our using friends, drinking buddies, or codependent family members who are the ones thinking well of us (showing us grace). I've heard people who gravitated toward isolation say that it was the substance itself that was giving them the approval they craved. Talk about a warped relationship! This is the "grace" of one drunk wrapping his arm around another and slurring out, "I love you, maaaan!" when he really means "Thank you for keeping me company in my misery and not reminding me that I'm neglecting my responsibilities."

And because these sorts of friends don't want to be confronted themselves, they can rarely be counted on to provide the kind of truth necessary to stimulate personal growth. This is usually left for the healthy family and friends who actually love us enough to tell us that we've lost ourselves to the addiction. These people are put in the position of having to draw hard boundaries with us and risk losing the relationship rather than participate in our self-destruction. But an interesting thing happens when healing starts to take hold. Rather than instinctively setting up two (or more) groups that each know only part of us so that we can live the double life of addiction, we begin to cultivate the kinds of relationships where we are getting grace and truth from the same group of people. The same friends and family that are showing us unconditional acceptance are also telling us when we're hangin' and don't know it.

This brings us to the third macronutrient – time. Many people get tripped up here because impatience is a hallmark of the kind of immaturity we've already examined. I've had people tell me that AA doesn't work because they've attended a single support group meeting and they got no help from it. Just like it is not reasonable to expect to lose 10lbs. in a week or measurably reduce my cholesterol in a month, we are setting ourselves up for defeat if our expectations are too high. Very few of us got into the pit we're in overnight, and it will take a serious time commitment to get out. That is the essence of "lifestyle change" because it throws out any time constraints and assumes that this is the way it will be *from now on*. Then, we can relax and trust that the change will take place because we know we are in a process that has been proven reliable over and over again.

If lasting change is going to occur, it is because we make the intentional decision to place ourselves in an environment where healing can occur. Everyone who has struggled with addiction can tell you they've discovered a spiritually toxic environment. As long as drugs or alcohol were in the mix, we became less and less the person we wanted to be. We draw up the elements available through our "roots" until what we are feeding ourselves with affects our "fruits." If we are rooted in lies, manipulation, shame, and self-centeredness, we will bear the fruit those things produce. We will have conflict, depression, alienation, anxiety, and hopelessness. And we need to account for the time it takes for us to change as a result of what we are nourishing ourselves with. Just like we didn't decline until we had been ingesting toxic substances for some time, it will also take time for grace and truth to work their way up through our roots until we are bearing different fruit.

People who have struggled with compulsive behaviors can almost always be counted on to have large amounts of guilt and shame. Because of the troublesome behaviors that tend to accompany addiction, this is a common topic in recovery groups. It is always a painful discussion with frequent tears. These feelings are so toxic that I like to frame the solution as finding an antidote for them. And many people have difficulty imagining where they might possibly find an antidote for these things.

Let's look at these a little deeper. First, is there a difference between guilt and shame? Because, if there is, there will be different antidotes to seek out. The dictionary defines guilt as *a feeling of responsibility or remorse for some offense, crime, or wrong.* Guilt is simply the awareness that we are without defense against an accusation. We did it, and it's undeniable. If that's true, then the only thing that can act as an antidote is pardon. To pardon is to erase guilt from the wrong committed. When we talk about this in a relational way, we use the word forgiveness. There is a ton of misunderstanding about what it means to forgive and there is a reason Alexander Pope wrote, "To err is human; to forgive divine." It's because forgiveness is really hard to do and is unnatural for our species. We are master scorekeepers and retaliators.

The hurdles people face in forgiving are huge. Some are hindered because they think that forgiving means the same as saying what happened was OK. Some think that if they let it go the other person will "get away with it" and the injustice will stand forever. Others believe that they will have to like the person again or spend time with them periodically. Forgiveness is none of those things. It is merely the cancellation of a debt that cannot be repaid even if the offending person had the desire to repay it. The reputation that was lost because of the slander cannot be restored. The safety that we were robbed of growing up because of the irresponsibility of the adults in the house can never be paid back. And the innocence lost because someone violated us physically is gone forever.

The problem we face is that we are owed a debt that, no matter how much energy we put into getting "paid back," the offender can never make good on. We have every right to pursue them around the world with our hand out demanding repayment. Forgiveness is just realizing that the energy it takes to keep reminding ourselves (and others) of what we are owed is robbing us of the ability to live a full life. When I write the loss off as unrecoverable, and decide to no longer keep mental track of what is owed me, *I'm* the one who goes free. I get my mind back.

And, if I'm the one who needs to be forgiven, taking the action necessary for this sort of transaction to occur means that I'm valuing others' emotional well-being at least as much as my own. It also means that I'm letting guilt do the only thing it was meant to do. Guilt exists only to drive us back to the offended party and attempt, to the best of our ability, to restore what we have cost the other person, establishment, or institution. Once we have taken that action, guilt has served its purpose and put us in a position where pardon can happen. And if the offended party chooses not to forgive, then they will have the misfortune of trying to hunt us down for a debt we cannot ever repay. Good luck!

There is sometimes a flaw in the system, though. It is not unusual for people to continue to feel guilty even after they have listened to their guilt and made the approach to the other party. Sometimes guilty feelings persist even after they have received forgiveness from the other party and the transaction remains incomplete despite doing all the right things. It is as if some people feel the need to continue punishing themselves for the mistakes they've made even after they've been let off the hook. Or, because the other party remains bitter, they must continue to refresh their guilty feelings whenever they recall what they did.

When we insist on holding on to guilt despite being forgiven it is a backhanded insult to the person doing the forgiving. It's like saying, "I know you say you're letting go of this offense I committed, but I know you're nowhere near as bighearted as someone would have to be to do that!" I've even seen people say they need to hold on to their guilt so that they will be less likely to make the same mistake again. Both of these groups completely miss the power of forgiveness to clean the slate and allow us to go forward with a clean conscience. And both groups almost certainly struggle with totally forgiving others. They also unwittingly set themselves up for relapse, because guilt is so unpleasant that it acts as a potent trigger to escape by any means possible; whether or not the other party chooses to forgive, finding a way to leave the guilty feelings behind is a necessary aspect of healthy spirituality.

Shame is related to guilt, but has more to do with what we (and others) believe our thoughts or actions say about us as people. We can carry shame about misdeeds we have done, but there may not be any misdeeds at all. And these don't even have to be actions that are illegal; intense shame can come from seemingly trivial occurrences such as wearing the wrong clothes to an event or making a minor social faux pas. It can also come from the actions of others that we think affects how we are seen by others. A spouse that has been cheated on may feel shame even though it was their partner who strayed.

Many people can intuit that guilt needs pardon to neutralize it, but when I ask what the antidote for shame is people rarely have a clear idea of what its opposite is. One of the synonyms of shame is disgrace. When we look at shame as disgrace, it becomes pretty obvious what the antidote might be - grace. The only good thing (and I mean only good thing!) about shame is that it points out the areas where we lack grace. And think about this through that lens of acceptance *despite* what we have done or how we think others feel about us. If we are struggling with shame, we are being reminded that the environment we are living in needs more sources where grace can come to us. It's also important to remember that without us taking the risks involved with being vulnerable and honest about our shortcomings, grace will be stunted.

Grace only becomes fully realized when our sins are completely out on the table. When we hide and minimize our flaws and fears, we create the perfect breeding ground for shame to grow in. King David learned this the hard way after his adultery with Bathsheba and murdering her husband to cover it up (2 Samuel 11). After he was confronted and forced to confess by the prophet Nathan, he found the relief that God has made possible through truth and grace. This was when he wrote, "Blessed is the one whose sin the LORD does not count against them and in whose spirit is no deceit. When I kept silent, my bones wasted away through my groaning all day long. For day and night your hand was heavy on me; my strength was sapped as in the heat of summer." (Psalm 32:2-4) When David got honest about what he'd done he put himself in a position to receive grace – not having his sin count against him. Even though David was guilty of some terrible things, he was still able to find his way back to blessing after guilt and shame had done their work. The same experience is available today to everyone who makes the effort to cultivate grace and truth in their life.

We've talked about the spiritual macronutrients of grace, truth, and time and our need to seek them out. But the analogy to nutrition extends to the micronutrients I touched on earlier as well. In our physical diet, micronutrients are all of the various vitamins, minerals, and phytochemicals that we get from ingesting carbohydrates, fats, and proteins. In our spiritual diet, these micronutrients equate to things like church attendance, meditation, prayer, fellowship with likeminded people who are trying to grow, or reading spiritual books. In short, any activity or pursuit that acts as a conduit for grace and truth to reach us in a consistent way over time.

Some people may gravitate to a spiritual diet that contains more or less of these spiritual elements just like some people may gravitate to a physical diet higher in antioxidants or pantothenic acid. The point is there is room for personal preference and taste in both our physical and spiritual diets. One person might swear by a "diet" high in prayer and solitude while another might find spiritual music and mindfulness more able to nourish them. There is no right answer about how to get grace and truth over time, only that they are irreplaceable in the effort to change.

OK, so the point I want to leave you with is that we have two natures – a physical nature and a spiritual nature, and that each is influenced by our external circumstances. Scientists have devised a checklist to determine if something meets the definition of being alive. These "characteristics of life" are seven factors that scientists look for in living things, but we will touch on three in particular: *living things use energy, living things grow,* and *living things respond to their environment.*

Living things use energy – we take in energy as food (calories are actually a measure of heat) and, as we metabolize it, break it down into the elements we need to keep bodily processes functioning. Spiritually, the energy we take in is provided by other humans and from God, if we believe in one. We are living in a spiritual environment where others are inputting all sorts of "energy" into us. A bad boss may be inputting anger or frustration, a bitter spouse inputting blame or resentment, and a faithful friend might provide encouragement and remind us of our purpose. Just like I am responsible for the results of my physical diet, I'm equally responsible for the fruit that I bear as a result of the spiritual environment I create for myself.

Living things grow – Physically, if I am not careful about providing the right mix of foods, I will cause growth in ways that will have negative side effects (weight gain, hypertension, diabetes, etc.). It is the same for our spiritual natures. If my "diet" lacks grace and truth, or if I only get them periodically, I can be sure that I will exhibit growth toward becoming less of someone I would like to be.

Living things respond to their environment – Just as it is impossible to exercise enough to overcome poor dietary habits, it is equally unlikely that we can overcome a bad spiritual environment by trying harder. What we draw up into our bodies, and our spirits, will inevitably produce the corresponding fruit in our lives. If I'm irresponsible and dismissive of what my body needs to operate optimally, I will reap the health consequences of those decisions. In the same way, if I neglect the spiritual environment I'm connected to, and choose to live in guilt, shame, isolation, and deceit, I will harvest a bitter crop if I harvest anything at all.

There is another aspect of nourishment that should be remembered. It is not the presence of food that ensures proper health. And it is not the presence of grace and truth that nourishes spiritually. It is the conscious act of *taking them in over time* that produces the results we are relying on. It is not enough to just attend support group meetings, just like it is not enough to attend the supermarket. It is not enough to just eat on weekends, just like it is not enough to attend to my spiritual needs on two religious holidays a year. It is not enough to cultivate friendships if there is no intention of actual intimacy taking place. We all gasp in surprise when one of our heroes is suddenly exposed as having a double life. But, when we lack the spiritual nourishment of grace and truth, creating a double life is unavoidable. Shame dictates that we hide our sin with lies and pretend that we are not in need of grace. When we do that, we will certainly relive what King David said his experience was – heaviness of heart, sapped strength, and the feeling that we are being opposed by God rather than loved by Him.

There is no way to get ourselves spiritually fed without effort and risk. Grace only comes to us after we make ourselves vulnerable by telling the truth about the unpleasant things we've done and what goes on in our heads. We risk rejection and disapproval, but without that risk, these things will never be available in the measure that we need to thrive. In order to get sufficient truth, we must let others know that we value their honest, and sometimes stinging, feedback about our blind spots.

As young people, we may have found ourselves in an environment that lacked sufficient nourishment, and, if so, we will for certain enter adulthood with some doubts about whether vulnerability is a wise to position to be in. As long as we act according to that doubt, we crimp off many of the ways grace and truth can flow into our lives and heal our emotional wounds. As adults, we are given the opportunity (and responsibility) of creating an environment where people of good will can play healing roles in our lives. We also have the responsibility of becoming people who love grace and truth so that we can maintain successful relationships with others.

I started this section by affirming my belief that anyone who *takes in* grace and truth will get the spiritual benefits they provide regardless of whether they actually believe in anything "spiritual." That's because it is in our spiritual DNA to grow in the right environment just like it is in our physical DNA to grow in response to our physical environment. Some people will stop there and rule out the possibility of a relationship with a "higher power" that is talked about in many 12-step groups. For those of you who do desire a relationship with a higher power, my hope is that you choose one that provides the same sort of spiritual nourishment that we identified in this chapter. Because a higher power that lacks grace will be terrifying, a higher power that lacks truth will be impotent, and a higher power that is not willing to invest the time necessary to see the process through will be unavailable when we need help the most.

"And the Word became flesh, and dwelt among us, and we saw His glory, glory as of the only begotten from the Father, full of grace and truth. For the Law was given through Moses; grace and truth were realized through Jesus Christ." (John 1:14,17)

"For I am confident of this very thing, that He who began a good work in you will perfect it until the day of Christ Jesus." (Philippians 1:6)

SECURITY

Let your conduct be without covetousness; be content with such things as you have. For He Himself has said, "I will never leave you nor forsake you." So we may boldly say: "The Lord is my helper; I will not fear. What can man do to me?" (Hebrews 13:5-6)

What do you think of when someone is described to you as being "insecure?" You might think this person is overly concerned with getting credit for their accomplishments or their appearance. Maybe you have experience with someone whose insecurity led them to take subtle (or not) jabs at others in order to elevate themselves. It's possible that you've had someone in your life who was threatened by your success or the accomplishments of others and always seemed to be a critical voice of discouragement rather than uplift. All these things are hallmarks of insecure people and, if we're honest, we're all tempted to exhibit behavior like this from time to time.

There are many more characteristics that could be listed, but the thing insecure people all have in common is a lack of confidence in the worth that they currently possess. Insecure people are worried they are not attractive enough, smart enough, alluring enough, or capable enough as they are, and they are constantly trying to compensate for what they think they lack. So they exaggerate their victories, blame their shortcomings on others, use social media to foster jealousy if they can, and avoid situations where their shortcomings are likely to be exposed. And the important thing to notice is that insecure people are always trying to manage other people's perceptions of them.

As I said, we all lack confidence in some areas or under certain circumstances and attempt to cover it up in a variety of ways. Insecurity and self-esteem are negatively correlated. That means the more insecure someone is, the lower their self-esteem will be. It also means that if someone's self-esteem can be raised, they will be less insecure as a result. Self-esteem is a function of what we think we are worth, and because insecure people are riddled with doubt about their worth, they struggle to think well of themselves consistently. Their worth fluctuates wildly depending on a variety of factors.

I sometimes bring this topic up in groups by posing an imaginary scenario. I ask, "If someone you knew and loved came into the room, sat down and confessed that they had terrible self-esteem and always felt like a worthless pretender in life, what would you say to them to build them up?" Usually, people will say things like, "I would tell them they are a good person and that they make me laugh" or "I would remind them of how much their family loves them and that they are a good mom or dad." Some people say they would offer compliments about certain characteristics or personality traits that they admire in the one with low self-esteem. A few say they would just listen supportively. As the group mentions the qualities that they think should boost self-esteem and worth, I make a mental list to refer to as we progress.

Once the group has come up with what they think is a sufficient amount of compliments and affirmations I commend them and ask, "Some of you said you wanted to remind your friend that they should feel like they had worth because they were good at their job or they were a good parent. If they were to lose that job or their role as a parent, would they have less worth?" They think for a moment before answering, "No, they would have the same worth." Then I say, "Some of you said you would try to boost their sense of worth by telling them you like their personality or sense of humor. But, if they were to have a stroke and lose the qualities that you mentioned, would they lose any worth?" The group will usually affirm that under those conditions someone would not lose any worth as a person. One by one, I ask if losing the things they said were of value in their loved one makes them of less worth, and the group is always reluctant to say that losing any one, or even all, of those qualities would affect their value and worth in the slightest. I then ask the obvious question, "So if losing these admirable qualities can't make the person of any less value, how does possessing them give them more value? Doesn't that mean that their worth was always based on something other than their skill at work, how good a parent they are, or whether they are a nice person?"

One of the big problems people have when assessing their worth is that they base it on things that can be *lost or removed*. I can lose my job no matter how good I am at it. I can lose my kids to divorce or some tragic accident and no longer have that role to draw a sense of worth from. I can suffer illness or accident and lose that winning personality or even literally forget who I am, and if my self-esteem is based on possessing these things, it will obviously evaporate when they are removed. And it follows that the more my worth is built on things that can be lost the more insecure I will be. When we use the word insecure to describe someone, it is because the things they have based their worth on are subject to rapid change or loss. And the more vulnerable to loss those things are, the more insecure someone will be.

So then, where does self-esteem come from and how can it be increased? The short answer is by basing it on something that itself has great worth as well as great stability. And there are only three "foundations" that self-esteem and worth can be built on. When we start out in life, we are dependent on our parents or caregivers to provide feedback to us about our value. We are not born giving ourselves positive affirmations in the mirror. The adults in our life give us clues about how to behave in order to get more of this positive feedback. In a typical family, the more we please the adults with our compliance and obedience the more esteem building feedback we receive.

It's here that we need to introduce the word *contingent,* because no discussion of self-esteem can get far without it. If one thing is contingent on another, it means that the occurrence of one thing hinges on the occurrence of the other. To get dessert, you have to clean your room. Dessert is contingent on the room being cleaned. In the context we are using the word, esteem-building acceptance is contingent on pleasing behavior in the home. Young children generally delight in learning how to please their parents - until they learn the word "no," that is.

We all start off with our esteem needs being met primarily by our caregivers and contingent upon our willingness to fit into the structure we find ourselves in. We naturally gauge our worth by how we are received and thought of by our family. This continues until a dramatic change happens in the young teen years. Suddenly, kids are much less concerned with the acceptance and feedback they get from their parents, and instead look to their peers for this feedback. They no longer care as much if they fit into the structure at home and instead become consumed with fitting in the structure at school. They still have a contingent self-esteem, it is just based on the acceptance and approval of a different set of people. As long as they are using the right slang, listening to the right music, wearing the right clothes, and performing any other expected behaviors, they can count on the affirmation and acceptance of their chosen peer group.

Sadly, many people never progress much from here, and choose to base their worth on how well they are received by the people they admire, how financially successful they are, or the quality of the mate they have been able to attract. We used to call it "keeping up with the Joneses," but now it's probably more apt to say "keeping up with the Kardashians!" This sort of contingent self-esteem relies on staying relatively equal with our peers in achievement, ability, and performance. I say sadly because when people choose to build their worth on how they are perceived in the eyes of others, they sentence themselves to become the most self-conscious version of themselves possible. When I rely on the approval of others to maintain good feelings about myself, I have to scrutinize myself constantly in order to judge whether I am living up to the necessary standard of performance.

And not only that! If I'm concerned about being looked at favorably by a certain group, I also have to scrutinize the performance of everyone in the group I want to be approved by. How else would I know if my behavior is "good enough?" This is extremely tiring over time, and most people who are living this way spend huge amounts of energy determining where they stand in relation to their group. Many people go to great lengths in this pursuit because if they lose the approval of the group, they lose the source of their worth and are faced with finding a new identity. They spend money they don't have, join clubs they don't care about, and have surgeries they don't need to continue fitting in.

Some people see through the emptiness of that sort of pursuit and decide to base their worth not on their performance, but on their existence. They will say, "Everyone is of equal value because they were born that way!" Rather than affirm their worth on what other's see in them, or the level of status in their peer group, they base their worth on the idea that humans are born with it. And this is a stronger foundation than the first one we talked about. But, it is lacking in its own way. My worth may not be contingent on what others feel about me anymore, but now it is contingent on how I feel about myself. And that can change quite a bit depending on my circumstances. Under certain conditions, it may be easy to maintain that I have value because I exist, but there are situations that can just as easily lead me to conclude I was fooling myself.

It also can give no account for its assumption that everyone is of equal value. If someone were to approach them and declare that certain types of people should be removed from the gene pool, they could muster nothing beyond a horrified outrage that someone would say that. This foundation of worth can make no appeal to an outside arbiter to settle the argument. The best it can hope for is that someone who thinks that Jews should be exterminated would never get into the majority position. And, when an objective standard to guide behavior and moral obligation is ruled out, you will see people advocating for the euthanization of "inferior" minorities, the mentally ill, or physically disabled. Oh wait, that is happening already. At the time I'm writing this there is ethnic cleansing happening in Myanmar, systematic starvation of children in Yemen, and extra-judicial killing of drug addicts in the Philippines. All these persecuted groups have been deemed unworthy to continue their lives by people who disagree that everyone is of equal value just by virtue of being born.

So far, we've looked at the foundations of, "What other people think of me," and "What I think about myself" when building self-esteem. The last foundation can be stated as, "What God thinks about me," and there can be no firmer ground to build on. I used to think that this was the only non-contingent kind of self-esteem, but I do think it is contingent on something – my faith. It takes faith to believe that God exists, that He loves all humans equally, and that He has created everyone and everything for a good purpose. If I have the faith to believe those things, I have the firmest foundation possible to settle the issue of what value I (and others) have. If one is convinced that he was created by God for a particular purpose, then whether or not he is celebrated, rewarded, or even welcomed, he can fall back on the affirmation that "people didn't grant my worth, and people can't take it away!" It is the only foundation that can make an appeal in the face of genocide or human trafficking and declare that it is objectively wrong to treat people created in the image of God in that way. It is no longer about "might makes right" between two factions who disagree about the value of people.

There is a saying that is fairly common in recovery circles that implies self-esteem comes through "esteemable acts." This sounds logical and attractive on the surface, but it is actually backwards. And, if you look closely, you may be able to see a contingent basis for self-worth trying to creep back in. I can hear someone who believes this saying, "If I perform enough self-less and admirable actions, I will be able to overcome all the wrong actions of the past that are making me feel worthless." One problem with this is, if you base your worth on your accomplishments and works, the unavoidable consequence is that you must factor in *all* your works, esteemable or not. You then put yourself in the difficult position of having to determine which works count for how much credit or demerit. And unfortunately, people with already low self-esteem will tend to undervalue the positive things they accomplish just like they undervalue themselves.

Most people have difficulty thinking well of themselves precisely because they have made it contingent on performance. This is also where narrative and time perspective bias can come in to play again. People who have loser narratives struggle to feel pride about even their good works and past-negative people look at their deeds and accomplishments through a lens that devalues the good they have done.

And just ask the same question we started with, "If I lost my ability to do esteemable acts, would I lose my self-esteem?" If that's true, then we are really just on the same treadmill of works-based human value that we are left with when we reject grace. Remember, grace is the idea that you're loved and valued despite your performance, not because of it. You don't have to perform one shred of work to be valued in the highest degree by God. And God has no interest in creating an environment where we have to strive, worry, and wonder how many good acts it will take to earn and keep His acceptance and love or how many bad ones will tip the scales against us. A loving God would not subject us to that kind of anxiety.

God's answer is that accomplishments are irrelevant in the determination of human value; we are granted value by virtue of the worth of who created us. We have the firmest possible foundation for self-esteem because we were created by the One who creates nothing unless it is a necessary expression of His wisdom, goodness, and eternal purpose.

The reality is that your worth does not flow from your works. Your works flow out of your worth. When you can put that idea at the forefront, there will be a liberty that will make your efforts a pleasure rather than a drain. If you can utterly renounce the idea of your worth as a person depending even slightly on your ability to perform any sort of acts at a certain level, you will enjoy the works you do like never before. Rather than pressure to excel, you will feel gratitude that God has gifted you to do your job well and given you a platform to do it. So self-esteem does not come through doing good deeds, good deeds naturally flow from you when you base your worth on the truth that God has made you exactly as was intended, for the right reason, and at the right time.

STABILITY

*Be to me a rock of habitation to which I may continually
come; You have given commandment to save me, For You
are my rock and my fortress. (Ps. 71:3)*

There is another aspect of security that is rooted in something
called *attachment theory*. This sort of research began in the 1950s and
focused on children's interactions with their primary caregivers
(usually mothers) and how these interactions affected later
development. Since this research began, the theory behind it has been
validated repeatedly, and the validity holds across every culture it has
been tested in. There is something very foundational to our species
need and ability to attach, and there are very predictable
consequences if that need is unmet.

As I write this, there is a growing furor over the practice of
separating children of illegal immigrants from their parents when they
are caught at the border. Aside from the political arguments being
had, there is also much more in the news about the effects that these
types of separations have been known to have on many children. In
fact, the original research was undertaken to examine the impact of
the many separations seen as a result of World War II.

Attachment begins at birth (and possibly before) as a young child
learns to depend on its caregiver (or caregivers in some cultures) to
provide comfort and calming feedback when the child is alarmed,
anxious, or fearful. Children come into the world with no ability to
comfort themselves or regulate their own emotions; they rely entirely
on their early caregivers to convey safety and calmness when they are

distressed. Think of this like the child being an almost naked bundle of nerves and the caregiver as a sort of blanket that can soothe the child and convey the calmness they need almost by osmosis.

As attachment forms, when the child experiences these distressing emotions, they learn to seek out the physical proximity of the caregiver in an attempt to find safety. As this process is repeated, and the child learns to trust the caregiver's responses, the child gains what is known as a "secure base." This secure base becomes the firm footing that the child will end up using to push off from into more and more complex and challenging situations. Most children are fixated on their mother's (caregiver's) face while this secure base is taking shape. Babies love to gaze into the comforting eyes of their mom. As they learn to walk, the mom is usually seeing much more of their read end.

But, an interesting thing can be observed at this time. The child will be actively exploring its environment and almost seem to lose track of the caregiver, until, at one point, he will suddenly seem to become aware of her absence and whirl around to look for her. The mom will wave and reassure the child that everything is fine and the child will relax, turn around, and continue exploring as before. This is a good example of "secure base" behavior. The child experienced mild anxiety or distress from the separation from the caregiver and sought out the reassurance necessary for him to continue exploring his environment. That word reassurance is probably the single most important word in attachment theory. It is what that child is seeking when he makes attempts to reconnect with the calmness and soothing love that his caregiver represents.

Over time, the child begins to hold memories of the soothing his caregiver provides, and gradually begins to *internalize* the comfort that she symbolizes. Because he has an abiding memory of his secure base, the child can go for longer and longer stretches before distress sets in. The child can tolerate greater discomfort due to his increasing ability to call on internal resources to soothe himself.

During this time, between complete reliance on the caregiver to provide relief from anxious feelings, and the ability to soothe himself when necessary, the child will commonly use something called a *transitional object*. This could be a blanket, teddy bear, stuffed animal, etc. that the child uses to satisfy and soothe himself when the caregiver is unavailable. As most parents know, the importance of the transitional (security) object can be profound, and a misplaced blanket or teddy bear can be a small-scale disaster!

As the internalization process continues, the child will eventually possess the skill to effectively soothe himself and will no longer constantly require the object to provide comfort – he will have it inside. External comfort is internalized in the same way that external structure is – gradually over time as the child is exposed to generally predictable responses from the people around him. This doesn't mean that he will not need his caregiver anymore, but he will have a general confidence that, when he is anxious or overwhelmed, reaching out to his attachment figures will have a positive result.

As this attachment forms in the first years of life, the child creates an internal *working model* of what to expect from his environment and the people he shares it with. If the process goes well enough, his working model will be that his relationships with loved ones are useful to provide relief from anxiety, stress, sadness, and various kinds of emotional pain. He will have something called a *secure attachment style*, which means that he can easily trust his caregivers to provide the emotional support that he needs. He learns that asking for what he needs gets a generally positive response and that he can handle challenging situations better with the involvement of his caregiver(s).

Unfortunately, that is only about 40% of the population, and recent studies are pointing to this number shrinking. The rest of us come out of these years with some degree of dysfunction in our working models and attachment styles. Even good parents miss many opportunities to respond positively to a child's need for reassurance, and, if there is addiction, mental illness, high conflict, or other circumstances that distract the caregiver(s), the chances that the parent's availability will align with the child's needs are slim. The parent's own attachment styles are also a large factor when considering what is being transmitted from their nervous system to the child's nervous system.

There is an assessment tool called the Strange Situation Protocol that is used to determine what sort of attachment style a child has adopted. The child (aged 11-17 months) is exposed to an unfamiliar environment and subjected to a predetermined sequence of separations and reunions with the mother both in the presence of a stranger and alone. The child's reaction to these separations can be used to reliably assess what sort of attachment style the child is using. Some children are easily soothed by the return of the mother and protest only briefly before allowing the mother to comfort them. Others remain agitated when the mother returns - some will ignore or punish the mother, while others will demonstrate that they have no use for her when she does return. Some other children appear to be unaffected by either the separation or reunion with the mother.

Along with the secure attachment style, the remaining 60% of us are roughly divided equally between *anxious* and *avoidant* (either ambivalent or fearful subtypes) attachment styles. These can be further broken down into more detailed subcategories, but, for our discussion, these three are sufficient. One way to visualize this concept is as a seesaw with secure attachment style in the middle with anxious attachers on one side and avoidant attachers on the other. And, just like the seesaw is more still the closer to the center you sit, and more turbulent the farther away from center, those with the most anxious or avoidant styles generally experience more turmoil in their relationships.

What is interesting about this aspect of our development is that the attachment style that is in place by about 18 months is the one that we, in most cases, are likely to use as adults as well. The preferences and assumptions about relationships associated with these styles are expressed by the following statements:

Secure attachment - "It is relatively easy for me to become emotionally close to others. I am comfortable depending on others and having others depend on me. I don't worry about being alone or having others not accept me."

Anxious attachment - "I want to be completely emotionally intimate with others, but I often find that others are reluctant to get as close as I would like. I am uncomfortable being without close relationships, but I sometimes worry that others don't value me as much as I value them."

Avoidant attachment (ambivalent subtype) - "I am comfortable without close emotional relationships. It is very important to me to feel independent and self-sufficient, and I prefer not to depend on others or have others depend on me."

Avoidant attachment (fearful subtype) - "I am somewhat uncomfortable getting close to others. I want emotionally close relationships, but I find it difficult to trust others completely, or to depend on them. I sometimes worry that I will be hurt if I allow myself to become too close to others."

As you can see, attachment style has a great deal to say about who we end up being in relationship with as well as the tenor that relationship will take. Another point to consider is the overlap between these operative statements about attachment and the overall narrative that we ascribe to our lives. These simple statements reveal a great deal about how trustworthy, reliable, and good-willed we believe other people to be. It is not a great leap from any of the anxious or avoidant styles to a loser, victim, or villain narrative.

There is also something noteworthy in how early in life attachment styles can be identified. If something this basic can be detected by 18 months old it is very deeply seated in one's personality.

This also means that these internal working models are conceived in us *before* we even have words to describe the feelings that created them. If a child's working model is that care is unreliably provided, and that his caregiver is disinterested, distracted, or withholding, when words do become available to the child it will not be a surprise if that victimization is part of the early narrative. Or, if the child's needs for soothing are burdensome to the mother for some reason (due to depression, addiction, etc.), and the child subtly learns that he is not important enough to merit attention, a loser narrative is only a short distance away.

This early and deep-seated anxiety, avoidance, and fear also explains part of why it is so difficult to change narratives mid-stream as adults. Because the "current" of the working model runs quite a bit deeper than the words used to describe it (which came later), trying to apply a new narrative over it can feel inauthentic. I can say I'm worthwhile, capable of success and an asset to society, but the feelings underneath make it ring hollow. Anyone who has tried to adopt positive affirmations about themselves in place of negative ones knows how ridiculous it can feel to believe (or even say) nice things about yourself. The underlying attachment-generated messages require quite a bit more attention and healing than just some shiny, new phrases we stick on our bathroom mirror.

There are some other reasons why paying attention to attachment issues is important. Who we choose to relate to has much to do with our style of attachment. Secure people tend to wind up with other secure types, while anxious and avoidant types seem to gravitate to each other. That sounds logical because avoidant types tend to avoid each other and anxious types accentuate each other's discomfort, driving them apart. And it is important to note that ambivalent in this context doesn't mean disinterested, it means simultaneously wanting attachment and separateness; ambivalent attachers are torn between getting their closeness needs met and getting their need to preserve their freedom and autonomy met.

It is also possible to see people rapidly switch styles to accommodate the person they are in relationship with at the time. When an avoidant attacher finds himself in relationship with someone more avoidant than they are, it is not unusual to see them assume the anxious role to balance the "seesaw" I mentioned earlier. This is also true on the anxious side of the seesaw - the less anxious one will adopt a more aloof stance to counter the anxiety of their partner. And, let's remember why humans make attempts to attach in the first place – to get calmness and soothing on the inside that they currently do not have.

People with more anxiety and avoidance about attaching to others are at a disadvantage when it comes to employing relationship with other people to reduce stress and maximize coping and this has profound drawbacks when attempting to make difficult change. Remember, change puts us outside of our comfort zone and, if we lack trust or vulnerability with others, we will have limited ability to draw on the assistance of other people to withstand the temptation to fall back on our negative habits. Trying to make that sort of change requires a wide variety of coping skills, and the ability to soothe ourselves with rewarding social interaction is indispensable.

Securely attached people are more likely to use *problem-focused coping strategies* which have to do with more proactive and externally focused solutions such as time-management and enlisting social support to solve problems. Secure attachers are more likely to use social support as part of their problem-solving attempts, while insecure attachers tend to perceive fewer available social supports and, in a cruel twist, are likely to report less satisfaction with the support they do get. Insecurely attached people carry a deep sense of being on their own that has ripple effects when they are faced with challenging circumstances. Insecure attachers use more *emotion-*

based coping strategies, meaning they try harder to manage stress and anxiety internally. Some of these strategies, such as prayer, meditation, and mindfulness are useful when dealing with stress that is out of one's control, but others such as denial, suppression, and use of drugs or alcohol are doomed to fail.

In general, anxious attachers have an elevated need for reassurance that can be frustrating to the ones they are in relationship with. Because they are worried about whether their loved one values them, and they are conflicted about asking for reassurance as much as they would like, they use mind-reading and rumination as their primary coping skills. Close attention is paid to relational cues that will let them gauge how the relationship is going, and they may scour social media for tidbits of information that will bring them the reassurance they are craving.

They are many times described as "clingy" or "needy" by those close to them, and these types have been known to send dozens, or even hundreds, of texts to their partners when their uncertainty is peaking. This nagging uncertainty and doubt can become obsessive; the most anxious sorts of attachers become quite jealous, controlling, and, in the worst cases, stalk they ones they "love." For the anxious attacher, the lack of internalized comfort fuels a frantic internal experience that generates a strong desire to find someone to be close to, regardless of suitability.

It's a sad irony that anxious and avoidant attachers gravitate easily to each other. At the start, the avoidant one will appreciate the energy and desire for closeness that the anxious one provides. And the anxious partner will appreciate the (usually) calmer demeanor of the avoidant one. But, before long, the avoidant one will withdraw slightly to avoid feeling smothered. This, of course, triggers the anxious partner's fears of abandonment and prompts them to pursue more aggressively, causing the avoidant partner to withdraw further. And this cycle will repeat itself forever if left unchecked; the anxious will require more reassurance and closeness than the avoidant can consistently provide, leading to frequent conflict and finding stability only for short periods when each is getting their needs met.

I first became aware of my avoidance of attachment not long after high school. Whenever I would run into old friends or acquaintances that I hadn't seen in a while, I was always surprised at the difference in excitement between their response and mine. Usually, they would be able to recall shared experiences with a great deal of exuberance while I would have a more muted emotional recollection. I had the same memories, but I wasn't able to recall them with the same sort of pleasure that my friend would have. And I wished I could; they seemed to be having a fuller experience than I was. Many times, I remember thinking, "Hmmh, I must have made a bigger impression on you than you did on me."

And the impression I'm talking about didn't have anything to do with the quality of my character, but rather it was the sort of impression, or lasting mark, that an object would make if it were pressed into wet clay. It was as if the person I was talking with could reach inside and feel the outline of the impression I had left on them and could take pleasure in reuniting the impression on the inside with the one who had made it (me). When I reached inside, it was as if my "clay" was harder and I couldn't find where they had "left their mark" on me, which limited my emotional response to the reunion.

As I've met more people with my attachment style, I've come to recognize some things that many of us have in common. Besides this ho-hum attitude about reunions, avoidant attachers tend not to be very nostalgic about scrapbooks or old photographs, and tend to let long distance or high-conflict relationships die. They tend to identify themselves based on qualities they possess as individuals, rather than as members of a family, association, or nation. Avoidant attachers can surprise themselves with how little they "miss" important people in their lives when separated.

It's not uncommon that they have heard themselves described as "abandoning," "distant," or "aloof." Avoidant attachers seem to realize that they only have a limited amount of time and energy to draw nourishment from their relationships and, when distance or conflict interfere with their ability to get that nourishment, they cut them loose to be more present to the other relationships that are working for them. In short, avoidant attachers have a hard time drawing on historical experience in order to get calmness or stress relief in the present.

Another thing that is tell-tale about insecure attachment is the reaction that is typically seen when an insecure person makes an attempt to get reassurance that is ignored or rebuffed. It is then that the attachment style will fully react to the unmet need. Anxious attachers will usually redouble their effort and pursue even at the risk of alienating their partner; they may call or text dozens, or even hundreds, of times in a relatively short time span to get the peace of mind they crave. And, when neglected, an avoidant or ambivalent attacher quickly accesses their internal working model that it is unwise to rely on people to meet their emotional needs and will commonly shut down or divest from the relationship. They need very little evidence to conclude that they were right all along about remaining aloof in the first place.

Because of the inadequate internalization of security and comfort in childhood, people with attachment problems are more focused on what is *at hand* to soothe themselves. They are not well able to conjure up memories of comfort that they can console themselves with and instead put most of their effort into attempts to use what is readily available to gain relief. This can be a source of great pain and anguish. I've seen mothers who were certain that they were evil because they didn't miss their children even after prolonged absence, and decent people judge themselves harshly because they gradually let relationships that used to be very important to them go extinct because their friend moved 500 miles away.

For many years, I carried a nagging sense of missing something inside that could not be replaced. It is hard to convey the sense of haunting aloneness that many people feel due to the lack of internalized comfort they came out of childhood with. This gnawing sense of emptiness is also what underlies much of the compulsion seen in addictive behaviors; addiction is the attempt to finally get "full" of the peace, love, and safety that people need to effectively handle the stress of adult life.

Substances of abuse, or codependent relationships, offer the false promise of finally getting the comfort we need on the inside of us where we lack it; the greedy hunger seen in addiction is the desire to never have to trust that tomorrow's love, peace, provision, or satisfaction will meet us there tomorrow. The addictive desire is for enough of those things on the inside right now that will eliminate the need for faith that God will provide those things at the time we need them. The story of manna in the wilderness is the model of our hunger for security. God provided enough manna for one day no more (except for the Sabbath) to emphasize the need to live "one day at a time."

In my case, I had an internal working model that care may or may not be provided or that asking for care might occasionally get the opposite. This was due to my mother's depression, negative narrative, and dissatisfaction with her marriage. I have an early memory of attempting to engage with her and hearing her say, "I don't care if I ever see you again!" This was a total shock, and no doubt helped me create the narrative I did. I also have a memory of me sitting in the back seat of the car and hearing my mom and dad briefly argue in the front. After they exchanged some words, my mom got out, opened the back door, and suddenly took my security blanket out of my hands. That was that. I never saw it again, but, at that moment, a sense that I didn't have what I needed to handle the world crept into me. Even many years later, I had an unshakeable feeling that I was always just a little younger than I needed to be to handle what I was up against - like I was pretending to be the adult that I seemed on the outside.

An unexpected bonus of my roulette table experience was the ability to look at my attachment style in an objective way. Before then, I judged myself critically because of the internal deformations I felt. After the experience, because of my change in narrative, I was able to accept this part of me without judgement or blame and see just how it had affected me. While it led me to pick romantic partners similar to my mother (victims), it also created the ability to make strong commitments. Because I could not consistently rely on my feelings to keep me close in a relationship, I compensated for it by making my attachment based mostly on mental commitments. This has at times led me to overcommit, but overall I prefer too much commitment rather than too little. And, like a person who loses their sight and relies more on their hearing, I made up for my hindered ability to attach with an ability to *connect* deeply and quickly.

Although these sound like the same thing, they are not. Attachment has that abiding sense of impression that I mentioned earlier. It is like a meal that, even though eaten years ago, can still be drawn on for sustenance. Connection has no such time implications – it exists for only the time the connection is occurring and then is gone. You can have a connection with someone at a bus bench or in a supermarket line and there will be no expectation that something more will be made of it. But attachment and connection feed the same hunger for social interaction, belonging, and stress reduction, just in different quantities and for different amounts of time.

If attachment is difficult due to previous injury, connection can be used to make up the difference. In fact, most insecure attachers I've met have already become better than average connectors. When I was able to change my narrative and let go of the scathing judgments of myself, I found that connection nourished me sufficiently if I made consistent efforts to go out and get it. Because I cannot always rely on attachment to provide a lasting sense of belonging and feeling loved, I have to make a concerted effort to take in connective experiences in a regular and frequent fashion. And, while the downside is I tend to let relationships drift off, I find myself happily released from jealousy and the painful, unquenchable longing for the closeness of others that used to torment me. As I've come to accept the implications of what my attachment style lacks, I find I'm also able to appreciate the areas that have become more sensitive as a result.

It should also be noted that, just because a person has an insecure attachment style does not mean that they cannot attach – it just means that, when they do attach, it brings alive a measure of anxiety or avoidance along with it. Many professionals believe that it is possible for those with insecure attachment styles to create something called an *earned attachment* that roughly approximates the experience of a securely attached person. When one becomes aware of the problematic internal working models that were adopted in childhood, and consistently works to minimize their influence in current attachments, the insecurely attached person can take steps to ensure that their needs are met by their partners and avoid replaying the dysfunction they witnessed in early relationships. With this in mind, the relational connection I mentioned earlier can be used to ensure that a person with a problematic attachment style can get their needs met.

Another unexpected area that my changed narrative has transformed is that I have finally found a secure base after 48 years of being without – God. Only after I was released from my loser narrative was I able to appreciate all of the attachment statements that He uses to provide a firm and secure foundation for our lives. When He says, "I will never leave you nor forsake you," (Hebrews 13:5), He is using attachment language. David's prayer of, "Be to me a rock of habitation to which I may continually come," speaks to one of the most basic human needs there is - the need for a secure base.

And, because it is God who has created us with this foundational need to attach in order to internalize peace and security, it is not surprising that He has the intention and ability to dwell on the inside of us. James writes, "He jealously desires the Spirit which He has made to dwell in us... (James 4:5)," and Paul adds, "...do you not know that your body is a temple of the Holy Spirit who is in you...?" (1 Cor. 6:19). It is left for John to record some of the more powerful words that anyone craving attachment can hear, "I (Jesus) will ask the Father, and He will give you another Helper, that He may be with you forever... because He abides with you and will be in you. I will not leave you as orphans; I will come to you... [and] because I live, you will live also. In that day you will know that I am in My Father, and you in Me, and I in you." (John 14:16-20)

Stability has to do with the immovability of the foundation we choose to construct our life on. If we are trying to make a "secure base" out of anything that can be shaken, whether it is what people think of us, our ability to earn money, attracting an appealing mate, or any other thing that can be lost, we, to a certain extent, are choosing insecurity. And, like it or not, there is only one firm foundation – God Himself, who says, "I am the Lord—I do not change." (Malachi 3:6)

PRIORITY

Delight yourself in the LORD; *And He will give you the desires of your heart. (Psalm 37:4)*

Not too long after I became a believer, I had my first biblical lesson on the importance of proper priorities. I was still supervising the completion of the landscape project on the house Charlie was building and learning everything I could about this God who had suddenly appeared in my life. I was reading the Bible quite a bit and one morning before work came across this passage in Matthew (6:19), "Do not store up for yourselves treasures on earth, where moth and rust destroy, and where thieves break in and steal." I remember thinking that the application of that was pretty outdated. I mean, my mom used to put mothballs in her closet, but aside from that how many treasures do you hear of losing value due to rust? So I packed up for the day and headed to work.

The house was nearing completion, and I arrived at a beehive of activity. I was present for several discussions about protective measures that needed to be taken for certain items that were to be displayed in the house. After an hour or two, as I realized what topics were being focused on by at least a dozen people, my jaw dropped as I recalled what I had read that morning. All morning I had been included in serious discussions about how all the vintage baseball uniforms must be protected from moths, what could be done to ensure no rust would damage the samurai swords, and exactly how sensitive the alarm system should be calibrated to keep out the thieves!

It is not an accident that God is so explicit about us getting our priorities in order. Without proper priorities, we end up fighting against reality. In recovery meetings, it is common to hear people say they experienced relief only when they accepted "life on life's terms" rather than demanding life accept their terms. They have learned firsthand that trying to force life to yield to their selfish priorities is a recipe for discontent and disaster. It is in our nature to elevate our own agendas above God's, and when we do, we complicate our attempts to change. In fact, we end up changing in the wrong direction! One of the things we get when we renew our minds is the ability to see the value in things that we previously dismissed. Qualities like humility, selflessness, generosity, and vulnerability become more appealing, and their opposites are seen as progressively more distasteful. Recovery from addiction requires a near total shifting of priorities from hiding our double life to exposing it to trusted others who can give us the grace and truth we need to take in.

One of the topics that relates directly to our priorities is the degree of willingness one has to take necessary actions that will support the change they want to make. Are you willing to put the desired change above the desire to see friends who will eventually offer you drugs? Are you willing to cut certain foods out of your diet entirely if you have demonstrated you cannot eat them moderately? Are you willing to reach out for support from others instead of isolating when you are struggling with obsessive thoughts of using or indulging in the compulsive behavior you want to stop?

I have heard many people declare (after several failed attempts at sobriety) that they are finally "done" with using drugs and I'm always curious why they are so certain that it's true this time. In hindsight, and almost without exception, the ones who do succeed say something about their willingness to prioritize the things that support their desired change above things that don't. They are willing to quit working in the bar even though it may mean less income. They are willing to set appropriate boundaries with unsupportive family members even though they know it may mean seeing other family members less. They are willing to attend support group meetings and put energy into engaging with the group rather than just showing up late and bolting out the door the minute it's over. They get their priorities right.

No discussion about priorities can get far without assigning value to whatever factors are involved in the area being addressed. It is impossible to effectively prioritize unless one has a clear idea of the respective importance of the elements being considered. Identifying value allows us to define our goals and provides clarity when confronted with the ambivalence we discussed earlier. For certain, if you are attempting to change, you will find yourself at numerous forks in the road where both paths will have something you want at the end - this is the ambivalent dilemma. One path has short-term discomfort and promises gratification at some unspecified point in the future. The other will have certain, immediate satisfaction but the end of the path will deliver you right back to where you started - facing the same fork. Addiction and compulsion, over time, make it seem like there is only one path to take, and the demoralized frustration of winding up at the same decision over and over is difficult for a non-addict to understand.

When value has been assigned, and goals have been made clear, decisions about which path to take are easier to see. Notice I didn't say easier to make! Let me explain. Unless goals are specific, it is difficult to see exactly which path to take at that fork I mentioned. If I have no clear destination, then there is no way to know if a certain decision at any fork in the road will get me closer or not. When my goal was just "lose weight," I found myself capitulating to short-term gratification frequently because I rationalized that I could make up for treating myself this time by depriving myself at another time. It allowed me to indulge myself while still believing I was making progress toward my goal to weigh less. My success was limited, and I spent a lot of time losing the same 5, 10, or 20 lbs.

At some point, I got tired of this and realized I had to hold myself to a more stringent level of accountability if I was going to get where I wanted. So I made my goals more specific. I would lose 6 pounds this month. I would not bring cheese, ice cream, or salami into my house. I would exercise for 45 minutes at least four times per week. I knew I was setting myself up for more discomfort in the short term, but the value I put on succeeding was now clearly expressed in the goals I set. And an interesting thing happened. Whenever that temptation to eat unnecessarily arose, I had a much clearer idea of what the proper decision would be. In the past, I was a little hazy as I stood at the fork in the road and debated with myself about which way to go. But now, with clear goals, I could examine each decision in light of the value of the goals I had set. If I wanted to lose 1.5 lbs. this week, would mayonnaise on the sandwich get me closer or farther away from my goal? Would ordering steamed vegetables as the side dish rather than macaroni and cheese get me closer or farther away from my goal? As I said, it suddenly became easier to see the right decision.

Making that decision was something else entirely though! This is where every self-gratifying fiber in my body would scream at me for depriving myself. Many times, I would literally curl up in a fetal position and cry when I decided I would not return to the grocery store for another meal after I had already finished dinner. This was also when I learned the value of support in a deeper way. One of the practices I cultivated to distract myself was making phone calls to people I had met at the support groups I was attending. And I would make a point of spending time with other group members who were fellowshipping after the group would end so that I wouldn't be tempted to return home and overeat.

This season became the one where I would learn the importance of suffering well. And, as we already discussed, suffering well always includes other people in the process. Over time, as I began to confront the bad habits I had formed around food, I found ways to compensate for the pleasure I was missing from eating. I found satisfaction in the feeling of warm exhaustion after vigorous aerobic exercise around people at the gym, eating with other people rather than always alone, and having meaningful phone conversations during times when I knew I would be tempted to overeat.

Another unfortunate side effect of the loser narrative I was stuck in was the difficulty it added to establishing even simple goals. I chuckled derisively when I heard people talk about goals they had for the next five years. I couldn't believe how much arrogance someone would have to have to think they had the power to influence the future to that extent. I also couldn't see how my own perspective played into my reluctance to set goals that would make me accountable.

We discussed Dr. Philip Zimbardo's research on the topic of *time perspective bias* toward the past and the future in earlier chapters (past positive vs. past negative and mundane future vs. transcendent future), but there is also a spectrum of bias in how we perceive the present. Dr. Zimbardo has labeled these two poles as hedonistic vs. fatalistic. When I bring this up in a group setting, most people assume that both of these poles are negative. They know that unbridled pleasure seeking (hedonism) is what has gotten them into so much trouble. And there is nothing about fatalism that sounds good in the slightest!

People with a hedonistic bias elevate pleasure seeking above all other factors. They seek excitement and sensation while trying to maximize fun and enjoyment of life. Obviously, at the extreme end of this spectrum is where addiction and compulsion thrive as pleasure is sought on a near constant timetable. On the other end of the spectrum is the fatalistic resignation I was exhibiting about goals and goal setting. These people are convinced that there is a way that reality will unfold and that very little can be done about it in the present.

Just as there are benefits and costs to how we think about the past, the same is true for hedonism and fatalism in the present. Hedonism is important because, without it, we would quickly give up on trying to improve our lives at all. The most important factor surrounding our decisions is usually whether it will bring us pleasure. Without pleasure, we would lose vigor and eventually stall because all decisions would have the same value to us – none. We need the energy that pleasure-seeking adds to our lives; without it, we would have no incentive to make progress at all. But what good can come from fatalism, this sense that nothing can be done to affect change? Well, without a measure of fatalism, we would be at a disadvantage when considering when to abandon a certain course of action. Fatalism assists us in deciding when to quit adding energy into a given circumstance. This is what the AA Serenity Prayer is getting at when we ask for the "wisdom to know the difference" between the "things we cannot change" and the things we can. Fatalism saves us from pouring out more and more effort on a lost cause.

Obviously, time perspective bias toward the present has a lot of influence on our relationship to goals and goal setting. People too far toward hedonism will cheat their future for a bit of pleasure today. This is the story of Esau sacrificing his birthright as the firstborn for a meal of lentils because he was hungry after a day of hunting (Genesis 25:31-34). Those on the other end (toward fatalism), scoff at the notion that they have enough power to stand up to the full force of the world and fight their way to accomplish even simple goals. They give up preemptively to avoid the futility they are certain is waiting for them.

Another area where assigning value can go haywire has to do with our ability to experience gratitude. In recovery settings, every year around Thanksgiving there would be a flourish of support group meetings focusing on this topic. So much so, that everyone would groan when the topic was announced. There is a strange connection between recovery and gratitude that is not obvious at first sight. In the various community - based support groups (AA, NA, CR, etc.), much emphasis is placed on creating lists of things that one is grateful for, and participants are encouraged to make a practice of expressing gratitude on a daily basis. And, I can tell you from experience that trying to conjure up gratitude when you are feeling none is a particularly vexing activity. I used to be one of the groaners.

But, I found that in the groups I was leading, rather than try to get to gratitude by brute force, it was a more fruitful discussion to examine areas of life that group members used to value, but no longer did. Because, almost without exception, they all could identify with the idea that, as the substance or activity gained value to them, the value of everything else was drained out. Family and friends that used to be important were sacrificed as the relationship with the substance demanded more attention. People who used to value their physical fitness decided it didn't matter enough to stop drinking. Parents will even elevate the substance over the well-being of their children. The interaction looks like this: our values determine our priorities, our priorities determine our goals, and whatever we value we are grateful for. But the process also works in reverse. If we increase gratitude by reassigning proper value to the relationships we are in (with family, work, friends, romance, etc.), our priorities and goals will shift as a result. Our actions will align with what we say we value and we will protect these things rather than let them deteriorate.

Perhaps the single most important lesson about value was taught to me by my mother. I would love to say that she had her priorities all squared away by the time I was reaching adulthood, but, like all of us, she was still a work in progress. You see, my mother was a compulsive hoarder. And if there's one thing that hoarders have got wrong, it is the value of the things they surround themselves with. As soon as something comes into the possession of a hoarder it becomes treasure, even if it is literal trash. Hoarders cannot bear to part with anything once they have a relationship with it – the anxiety and grief are too great. My mother used assorted possessions to manage her anxiety and depression, and the story of how God addressed this is one that still makes me smile.

While my father was still alive, his presence put a check on my mom's compulsion to acquire goods. I remember his frustration at her tendency to obstruct the stairways in our home with strange things like fire extinguishers or small trash cans. Part of the decision behind him moving into another room in the house was because there was no closet space for him in the master bedroom. It was my job to maintain the yard, but my mother had so much extra crammed into the tool shed it was a nightmare to even get out the lawnmower.

One day, when I decided to remove the trash that was taking the shed over, I was mortified to see my mother literally drape her body over the workbench and threaten to call the police if I touched anything. She finally agreed to get rid of only the trash and allowed me to remove three full garbage cans of used sandpaper, rotten twine, liquids that nobody could identify, etc., and I could have thrown away at least another three, but she would not agree. But, when my father died, my mother began a more rapid pace of collection. After several years she had filled a 3,000 square foot home with assorted goods, usually obtained at the local Malibu thrift store called the Artifact Tree. She was very glad to find a home for all the things her wealthy neighbors were discarding and loved to tell the stories about where certain things in her home came from.

Her compulsion progressed until there was almost no flat surface left uncluttered in her home. The sofas were blanketed with clothes, many of them still with tags on, the dining room table was always covered in boxes or projects, and the kitchen counters were filled with an enormous amount of cleaning supplies and vitamins. Boxes and bins took up the floor space in most of the house, and she had created pathways through them to maintain access to the stuffed closets. As she aged, she needed more and more help to manage all her treasures, so she hired my landscaping crew on the weekends. She would have three or four of my crew help her "go through" all her clutter in order to get rid of some. That was my mom's euphemism for throwing things away – she couldn't bring herself to say that she needed to throw things away so she would "go through" it instead.

So, as they would go through the house from room to room, I assumed that the overall quantity would reduce. I was wrong. The stuff in the house would simply migrate from room to room and, if it was reconfigured at all, it was only to make room for more stuff. And, because so much of it was not able to be moved fast enough, the vermin were just starting to encroach – she had created the perfect rat habitat.

My mom was in her early eighties and was slowly failing to keep up with what was necessary to maintain a home filled with hundreds of boxes and assorted piles of who knows what. As God would have it, I just happened to have found a job at my church in Orange County listing things on eBay. This was a very large church, and they had a good-sized warehouse filled with donated goods that needed to be sold. My job was to peruse the shelves for interesting items, research what their value was, create the description online, and supervise the eBay auction. I became very familiar with the process and did it for several months before my mother first started talking about having a garage sale to get rid of some of her stuff. The idea was daunting for sure. Just sorting through the mountains of stuff filling her house to find what to sell would be a massive chore.

And, even though my mom was convinced she could part with some of it, I knew she would certainly overvalue it and refuse to let much go. So I offered her the perfect solution. I told her I would inventory her home and catalog everything so that she could sell it on eBay. She wouldn't have to drag everything out on the driveway, haggle with people about prices, and bring it all back in again. She could select what she wanted to sell, set the price, and it would quietly vanish from the house. It seemed like the perfect solution. I spent the better part of an entire week opening every box and looking under every pile to get an idea of what was in the house. I was able to determine that my mother loved steam irons (she had eight of them), candles (hundreds of pounds of wax), and Jones New York clothing from Macy's. There were multiples of almost everything she collected, from blenders and pewter collectibles to coins and geodes. The variety and quantity of things was boggling – this would not be easy. It was then that God intervened.

It was November 24th, 2007 when "disaster" struck. I say that in quotes because it was actually the beginning of a season of great blessing for my mother, although it would be some time before that became obvious. I was living in Anaheim, and I got a call at around 6 am from my mother telling me that the embers were raining down on her house and that she was evacuating at that moment. Brush fires are not uncommon in Malibu when the Santa Ana winds blow, and this was the third one of the year. I should also say that my mom's hoarding was not limited to the interior of the home. Much of the ¾ acre property was littered with junk as well. There were old tires, stockpiled wood, and assorted garden-related items. One of the things my mother loved to have on hand was the chipped tree clippings that local tree trimmers would bring by. They loved my mother because they could drop their clippings on her property and avoid a trip to the dump. She would spread the clippings out as a thick mulch to create paths and keep weeds down. But much of this mulch was from eucalyptus trees, which are notoriously flammable.

So the stage was set, a house stuffed to the gills with mostly flammable items, a yard covered with the perfect fuel to sustain an inferno, and embers from a nearby brush fire being whipped in by hot desert winds. It only took a few hours to reduce the home to ashes. The firefighters later said there was so much fuel that all they could do was watch it burn. And did it burn! The entire property was black as coal when the fire ended and, aside from a car that was slightly singed on a neighbor's property, the fire had burned right up to the property lines on three sides and stopped. The embers had blown in from about a mile away, destroyed my mom's property entirely, and left everything around it untouched. God had "gone through" the house in His own way and decided what was worth saving. My mom got some photographs, jewelry, and her dog out. That was it. Everything else was lost, and my mother was in shock.

I need to backtrack a little at this point. Because the story is about much more than just losing a lifetime's worth of possessions in one morning. It is about the goodness of God and His ability to bring, as Isaiah said, "beauty [out of] ashes." At the time, I had no idea that a few months before the fire, my mom's insurance agent had called and told her that he thought she was underinsured based on the policy's current coverage. He suggested increasing her coverage to protect her more fully in case of catastrophic loss. And she agreed. This was the first circumstance that, in hindsight, was not the coincidence it appeared to be.

Ultimately, the task of managing her welfare fell to me after the fire, and it was very sad to see how heartbroken and lost she was in the aftermath of the tragedy. Part of this managing was negotiating with the insurance company about the amount of money it would take to replace the possessions that were lost. Because I had taken an exhaustive inventory of what she had in the house just a few weeks earlier, I was able to create a 700 line spreadsheet cataloging everything that had been lost in the fire. The job I had taken in Irvine just happened to have equipped me perfectly to determine the value of everything my mom had stockpiled for the past thirty years. I had several long discussions with the adjuster who was handling her account explaining how someone could lose dozens, or sometimes hundreds, of items that an ordinary house would have just a few of. I was able to effectively make the case, and she got her policy maximum totaling almost $400,000! And that was just for the contents of the house. This was despite having no receipts or tangible proof for most of the items that were lost.

So God "went through" her house and determined that almost nothing was worth saving. But, He had arranged for her to have a very comfortable landing. In a blink, she had lost a lifetime's worth of accumulated junk that she had been progressively drowning in for years, but it had been transformed into a very substantial financial windfall. Of course, this was of little consolation to her in her grief. She had lost all of the relationships that she had learned to rely on for comfort – the relationships she had formed with her clutter. And, if you remember me saying, my mom had a very ingrained victim narrative, so the fire gave her a whole new body of evidence to support that story.

Before the fire, she had been struggling on a fixed income and was frequently stressed about her cash flow. I had encouraged her to consider selling the house on several occasions, but she could never bear to part with it despite being progressively incapable of the upkeep required. But, after the fire, she had complete liberty to live in luxury that many people would give their right arm for – and all paid for by the insurance company while she decided whether to rebuild or not. She had rented a two-bedroom condominium with an ocean view in Malibu, and, as far as I recall, never could experience relief or gratitude for the entire time she was there (almost a year).

On the contrary, her agony was palpable. She frequently expressed wishing she could just die to escape the pain she was in. I had to stifle my tongue whenever I heard my mother say she would rather have all of her stuff back than the freedom she had to start over. Because of her own anxious attachment style, she alternately begged for, and demanded, my constant physical presence with her during this time. If I'm honest, part of me was rewarded by watching her in pain. Many times growing up, I had encountered her irrational attachments to things that were obsolete or irreparable, and had always come out on the losing end. There were times that it felt like she valued her junk more than her family. And, more than once, I fantasized about employing the "Polynesian fire method" of therapy for cluttering. I wanted to tie her up while I burned her trash in front of her. Forgive me if that sounds cruel, I'm just being honest about it; I felt like any child of an alcoholic would eventually feel about the booze bottles in the house.

But the healing that God had planned would gradually unfold over the next few years. My mom eventually settled on the idea of placing a manufactured home (mobile home) on the burned out property. I was concerned she was trying to recreate the same sort of disaster she had before, but I felt like my position was primarily to help her create as comfortable a life as possible for however much time she had left (she was 82 when the fire happened). The city of Malibu was also accommodating to her situation. They agreed to allow the placement of the home with just temporary permits. As long as she was "in the process" of rebuilding they would essentially look the other way and let her finish out her life on the property she had lived on since the early 1960s.

Another important wrinkle in the story is that, just before the economy crashed in 2007, I had closed my landscaping business due to my own personal meltdown, which meant I had enough free time to supervise the new project for my mother. It turned out she needed every skill I had gotten good at over the course of my life. I acted as her proxy to obtain the necessary permits from the city, something I had experience with due to my background as a contractor. I designed the layout of her new home, factoring in the need for mobility assistance I knew she would need more of soon. I rehired part of my old crew to assist in the installation of the home and landscaped the entire property as low-maintenance as possible. And, as important as anything else to her, acted as her personal pastor, suicide hotline, and consoler for the entire year it took to finish the project.

As my mom went through her grief process, I was gratified to see her begin to rely on friends she had made in the community more and more for fellowship and comfort. Her house had been so cluttered before that she rarely invited anyone over, but now, with her brand new home, she delighted in hosting friends and making the property available for church gatherings on occasion. Aside from filling all the closets up in the house with clothes (many still with tags), she never did get carried away with her old pattern of amassing ridiculous amounts of goods that she would obsess over.

God also allowed some significant healing to take place between her and me as well. I had previously harbored deep-seated anger toward my mother for the way I mentioned she would "rewrite history" as well as some other issues that had remained unresolved for years. But, because of my own "letting go" process, I found the ability to honor her and begin to appropriately value the good things that she had done for me.

This process was difficult to perceive in myself until I noticed the feedback I was getting from people who were observing the interactions between my mom and me. In particular, I had several encounters with people (usually older women) at Costco who would see me pushing my mother in her wheelchair with the special basket on the front and pull me aside to tell me, "You're a good son." On the third or fourth instance of this, I thanked the person, and as I was walking away, felt the whisper of God saying, "You're a good son...to Me." It had taken 45 years, but God had arranged the circumstances that would allow the greatest healing possible to occur.

My mother changed her priorities regarding the value of her clutter, which allowed her to experience friendship and the love of her family in a fuller measure than ever before. And I was set free from a bitter resentment that allowed me to see much greater value in my relationship with my mother than I had previously. She passed away at home on November 15th, 2013 in her sleep at the age of 88.

Throughout the Bible, God is always trying to help us get our priorities right. Every prophet ever sent attempts to get people to reexamine their values and adopt ones that line up with what God values. The conversations that Jesus has with the Pharisees are one long rebuke of their skewed priorities. The Scripture verse we began with is one of the clearest examples of this: "Delight yourself in the Lord, and He will give you the desires of your heart." But what exactly does it mean to "delight [my]self" in the Lord? Does it just mean to consider His character and how he is described in the Bible? I don't think so. It would not be any delight at all to hear of how loving, kind, merciful, and just God is, if there was not anything recorded about how those qualities guide His actions toward us.

A God who sits by passively while feeling those things would not be a delight to us. But, we have an abundant record of how all those traits of God find their outworking in our lives. His mercies are "new every morning." His eyes are moving throughout the earth to "show Himself strong" on behalf of those whose "heart is completely His" (2 Chron. 16:9). He loved the world so much "He gave His only begotten Son" in order to redeem it (John 3:16).

The delight we are meant to take finds fullness when we include all the actions and involvement that His character dictates. A God who did nothing as a result of His love, justness, or mercy would not be a perfect being. When we understand that His attributes generate His active, intimate involvement in His creation, the proper response should be nothing short of delight. A perfect being who has no limitations on how much love He will express to you, no limitations on how much protection to provide for you, and no limitations on the wisdom He will make available to you really does exist. What will your response be? Delight would be a good place to start!

And the most impressive part is what He promises as the result – we get the "desires of our heart." When I hear that phrase I cannot help but hear the word "passion" along with it. The desires of my heart are the things I am passionate about. How sad is it when you see someone who has lost contact with their passions or, maybe worse, is passionate only about satisfying their own lust? Solomon, the world's expert on the pursuit of lust said this: "He who loves money will not be satisfied with money, nor he who loves abundance with its income. This too is vanity" (Ecclesiastes 5:10). This was said by an extremely wealthy man who had 700 wives, 300 concubines, and more possessions than he could personally count.

Solomon had discovered something called the *hedonic treadmill* – the tendency to revert to a previous set point of satisfaction despite an abundance of positive stimulation. It might be better said that he who loves money will never be satisfied with the money *that he currently has*. The pleasure that money provides will always be slipping back to a previous level unless more money is gained. The same thing happens with any sort of pleasurable activity that becomes unduly valued. Our greed becomes stoked, and our appetite is inflamed to such a degree that nothing can satisfy it for long. This is why people get caught cheating on spectacularly beautiful spouses or insider trading deals when they are already multi-millionaires. The treadmill of chasing pleasure applies to anything that we assign improper value to. As Solomon said, it is all in vain.

Connecting more fully with what we are passionate about is one of the great rewards of getting our priorities right. This is something that God wants desperately for us to experience. He is passionate about His creation and wants us to be too. Passion, when properly contained and directed, makes life a great adventure and protects us against the temptation to shrink back when confronted with opposition. A person with passion will not let disappointment stop them for long before they get back into the fight. One of the ways I encourage people who say they are not in touch with their passion is to ask them what kind of help they want to bring to other people. What kind of help are they able to offer others that would bring them satisfaction?

This question brings us straight to the unique abilities that every person is born with; we are each created with certain giftedness that is meant to find its expression in the context of relationship with other people. No master artist is meant to create in solitude for the benefit of only himself. No gifted speaker is meant to talk only to herself in the mirror. And nobody who is skilled with managing numbers is meant only to play internal mental games for fun. Because the theme behind every gift of God is that He gives them to us for one reason only – to help each other.

In Paul's discussion of spiritual gifts, he makes it clear what the purpose of them is: "Now there are varieties of gifts, but the same Spirit. And there are varieties of ministries, and the same Lord. There are varieties of effects, but the same God who works all things in all persons. But to each one is given the manifestation of the Spirit for the common good" (1 Corinthians 12:4-7). Every skill that God has granted human beings is for one ultimate purpose – to be used for the common good. Ask anyone who has discovered their gift how satisfying it is when God arranges ways for it to be expressed. Talk about passion! These people are the ones saying "Don't tell anyone, but I'd do this job for free!"

It shouldn't be a surprise how much success has to do with getting simple priorities right. It's a message that God is always trying to get through to us. Two of the most quoted Scriptures about priority are so familiar that they have become near clichés.

"Trust in the LORD with all your heart and do not lean on your own understanding. In all your ways acknowledge Him, and He will make your paths straight" (Proverbs 3:5-6).

"But seek first His kingdom and His righteousness, and all these things will be added to you. So do not worry about tomorrow; for tomorrow will care for itself. Each day has enough trouble of its own" (Matthew 6:33-34).

Many others could be added to this discussion, but it is safe to say that God is consistent in His desire for us to bring our priorities in line with the only thing that brings meaning to everything else – Him. Changing our values to line up more with God's values is one of the great challenges presented to humankind. We are not generally predisposed to consider others above ourselves, turn the other cheek when wronged, or forgive as generously as God asks of us. It's in our nature to want to lay up treasure that is vulnerable to the elements and needs to be guarded, managed, and insured. He wants us to have the desires of our hearts, but only if those desires have been purged of lust and aligned with His priorities. This frees us up to find our unique God-given gifts and pursue goals that will work in concert with our passions rather than enslave us to them. And as we assign proper value to the things He has granted us, we will find gratitude a constant companion. When we pursue the desires of our heart while lust to sate our various appetites is the top priority, we bring misery and, to borrow Solomon's term, vanity into our lives.

PROPERTY

Lord, you alone are my portion and my cup; you make my lot secure. The boundary lines have fallen for me in pleasant places; surely I have a delightful inheritance. (Psalm 16:5-6)

My mother's relationship with that piece of land in Malibu ended after just over fifty years, but mine had a bit more to go. And if God had done only what I've described to this point, it would be an amazing thing. But there was quite a bit of reprioritizing left to do, and He was not finished yet. After my mother died, I spent a few months settling her estate and examining my options about what to do with the land and manufactured home that had been placed on it. My parents had the foresight to purchase in Malibu at a time (the early '60s) when many people were skeptical of the decision. It was quite a distance from any developed area at the time and it had almost none of the appeal it does now. But, the land they had purchased was now one of the more desirable plots in the whole city. Situated right in the middle of the 27-mile long city and just a short walk to the beach, there were very few pieces of land like it, and even fewer come up for sale each year.

But there was a downside. Because of its proximity to the water, any plans for development had to be approved by the California Coastal Commission as well as all other local entities. This adds significant cost and delays to any development project. As I said, the city had allowed the placement of the home under the same sort of temporary permitting that they would require for a trailer meant to be used as an office while construction of the main residence took place. The power to the property was still being fed from one of those brightly colored wooden poles that you would typically see on a construction site; the power could not be fed underground until the permits were made permanent. For that to happen the home would have to be placed on a permanent foundation, fire sprinklers would have to be installed, and the septic system would have to be updated. I got bids for these and was told the cost could approach $200,000. And there was one other upgrade, unknown at that time, that would soon present itself and turn the next year into a complete fiasco.

The manufactured home was only 1,300 square feet, and developing the property up to the standard of the neighborhood would have cost at least $300 per square foot of new home as well as a significant expense for the landscape. And I did not have nearly enough cash to develop the property. I had inherited just enough to do the upgrades necessary to make the permits permanent for the current home, but it was sorely out of place in a neighborhood filled with much larger, multi-million dollar residences. So I consulted with a trusted local realtor who informed me that, even with the uncertain permit status, the value of the property was at least 1.3 million dollars. Maybe you can imagine my shock. A guy with a mindset that nothing is going to end right for him is told that he is sitting on something worth more money than many people see in a lifetime. And all tax-free due to the laws concerning inheritance. I let myself believe that things might actually be going in my favor at last. But God had a plot twist in mind that was waiting in the not too distant future.

I hired a realtor and put the property on the market in early 2014. It immediately received several offers, and I went into escrow with a buyer for the price mentioned above. There are numerous inspections and disclosures that have to take place in a sale of this sort, and I tried to limit my excitement as the close of escrow neared. The escrow was scheduled to close in the middle of June and, as a sort of pre-celebration, I arranged to take my whole family to Hawaii for the last week in May. One of my mother's last wishes was to have her family together in one place on the beach somewhere. To honor that wish, I brought my mother's ashes with us to Kauai with the intention of finding a beach to scatter them on. We rented a large house across from Poipu beach and had a splendid week. In a strange coincidence, the buyer called me while we were basking on the sand in Hanalei Bay to ask a question about the septic system. When I told her where I was she was astonished. Her son had gotten married at almost the very spot I was standing on the same day a few years before. It seemed a very good omen!

We returned reluctantly and started counting down the days. I had heard many stories of last-minute problems with escrows and I was praying that all the bases were covered. Then D-Day arrived. June 6th was a difficult day. I got a text from my realtor asking me to call him immediately. He began to tell me there had been a problem with the inspection of the water flow out of the fire hydrant closest to the home. It did not supply enough water to satisfy the county's regulations and they would not approve any final permits until it did. The buyer had been quoted a price of $500,000 necessary to fix it and had canceled the sale. The realtor had contacted the other bidders and they had all declined as well. The place was suddenly radioactive!

As I had begun to believe that the sale would go through, I had uncharacteristically allowed myself to plan for the future. My wife and I had plans about where we would live, I had plans about going back to school for a doctoral degree, and I was looking forward to the opportunities that would be available to us after the sale. These were all destroyed in one morning. I was suddenly aimless and stunned. I chided myself for believing that something so good would ever actually take place for me. And, of course, God, in His desire to teach me another sour lesson, would dangle it so close before suddenly yanking it away. Remember, this was before the roulette table had happened; I was still in the loser narrative.

My wife and I tried to figure out a Plan B. Fortunately, I still had a sizable amount of cash from my inheritance, so we were comfortable with the other income we earned. I had not worked regularly while my mom's condition deteriorated and I jokingly described myself as re-TARD during this time. Something slowed down between employed and retired. After the initial shock wore off and I realized that I was going to have to keep the property for a while, I made my top priority figuring out just what I was up against to find a solution.

My contracting background helped me assess where the problems were that kept the water from flowing at the proper rate. The culprit was a portion of the water main feeding the neighborhood that was narrower than it needed to be to comply with code. After months of poring over the various maps and plans I was able to obtain, I got excited when I discovered that, rather than replacing a ¼ mile of pipe at the cost of half a million dollars, I could get the proper flow by replacing just a 400 foot segment of pipe that was narrower than the pipe on both sides of it. This would cost between $200-250,000. But, I was shot down by a county engineer who informed me that, while the water would flow out of the hydrant at the proper rate, it would also flow through a portion of the pipe at a speed that was a fraction over what would be allowed (by about 2 inches per second). He told me this despite the fact that the water currently exceeded the mandated flow rate in the portion that I would replace by a much greater amount. If that doesn't make sense don't worry, it didn't to me either!

My proposed repair would eliminate this problem entirely and, in any world concerned with fairness and decency, would have been approved in a heartbeat. But I needed approval from several different players in the system, all of whom expressed deep sympathy about the unfairness of what I was up against. Each of them promised that they would sign off on their portion of the project - if one of the other players would sign off first. Nobody was willing to put their neck on the line in case something was to happen down the road.

During this time, my marriage was also rapidly failing (for the last time). Blame could be assigned in a number of places, but, at the core, we had two narratives that conflicted deeply and were ultimately irreconcilable. I moved out abruptly in early September (2014) and moved into the home in Malibu. It might be hard to conjure up some sympathy for me about that news, but, if you remember, I had heard from the city that they would no longer turn a blind eye to the fact that there were no plans made to rebuild in the five years my mom had lived there. They had overlooked this as a concession to my mother, who just wanted to die where she had spent the past fifty years. The city threatened to shut off the water and power so that it could not be inhabited; I had to beg them for the sake of the landscape not to do so. If any one of my neighbors (many of whom had put up with my mom's junk piles for years) were inclined to complain about the slightest aspect of my presence there, I would have had another nightmare on top of the two I already had (the water and my marriage).

As I imagined how the situation would play out, I could feel the noose tightening around me. If I had to move out, the city had mentioned I would not be allowed to rent it, and the upkeep on it would be a significant drain while it sat vacant. And, after settling the finances in a possible divorce, I would not have enough money to sustain the upkeep on two residences indefinitely. My mother was always happy that she would be able to pass on the property to me and provide a blessing as she left. But this inheritance was beginning to feel like a great curse. I wasn't allowed to live in the property, couldn't sell it even at a great discount, and I couldn't develop it without spending a fortune installing a new water main for the entire neighborhood.

I tried finding partners who would bankroll it, but no one would take on the complexity of it – my phone calls started to go unanswered. Between all the various permitting authorities, regulations, and potential friction with neighbors as their water service was interfered with, there were just too many possible headaches. As my despair deepened, I seriously considered sitting in the middle of the property and shooting myself in cosmic protest. That last sentence is not an exaggeration, my despair, combined with the feeling that nothing could ever possibly turn in my favor, led me to one of the worst mental states of my life. You might recall me saying that 2014 was not the best year - at least the first 51 weeks of it.

But this was also the year when God met me in front of that roulette table and changed my perspective on everything that had preceded it. And I can say with certainty that not everything that happens in Vegas stays in Vegas. Thank God! I was progressively more astonished as the fallout from that experience began to alter my attitudes about everything that was upsetting to me before it happened. The burden that I felt about being stuck in such an absurd situation with the house was suddenly replaced with a deep-seated gratitude that He had provided such a beautiful place for me to live while the rest of my life went through significant upheaval. The financial anxiety and anger at being so powerless evaporated as I began to finally believe that God had been present with me throughout my life and was carefully managing everything that had previously seemed haphazard. Because of the precise, long-term, orchestration He had demonstrated in the roulette experience, I suddenly trusted that my life was unfolding with His explicit involvement and oversight.

And perhaps the single most remarkable change was how I felt about my estranged wife and kids. Previously, when my wife and I were separated (which was not uncommon), the thought of her being happy with someone else was a great torment. I felt diminished when

I recounted that I had spent most of my life to that point doing the therapy, prayer, and difficult internal work that was necessary to become a better husband. Seeing someone else reap the benefit of that was too much to bear! My distorted attachment style also contributed to a deep-seated longing to be reconciled with her regardless of how ill-suited we were for each other. But to my surprise, I found myself utterly released from the dysfunctional bond that kept me attached to her in ways that only exacerbated the problem. In its place was a sincere feeling that, were I to hear she was happy with someone else, I could actually congratulate her for finding something that is relatively rare. It is a source of satisfaction that, when our relationship finally did end after 21 years, I was able to navigate the divorce from this place of general good-will.

As God became my "secure base," the self-recrimination and blame about the problems that my attachment deficiencies created in my relationships gave way to an understanding about why those close to me sometimes talked about feeling "abandoned" even though nothing of the sort was in my heart. Because I sensed the presence and security of God in a profound way, the truths about me that used to cause great shame and anguish could be faced with a new self-esteem based on His opinion of me and not my own (or others). I was suddenly released from basing my worth on what people thought of me, good or bad.

His intervention was causing me to reevaluate all the assumptions about what I had valued up to that point. I had equated pessimism with wisdom, mistook devotion to dysfunctional relationships as nobility, and considered underachievement a badge of honor signifying my unwillingness to conform to a wicked world system. Now I could see how my fear, depression, and anxiety had led me to adopt these, and other, distortions to maintain a coherent narrative and identity. Suddenly, my tendency to self-sabotage made perfect sense. When my identity as a loser was threatened by the prospect of success, I took whatever action necessary (usually avoidance) that would let opportunity slip past so that I could be saved from the anxiety of trying to adopt a new identity that I didn't believe was authentic.

All of this and more took place in the first few months of 2015 as my new mindset settled in, and I began to see something I had totally missed before. I realized that, rather than any material possession, the most valuable thing I owned was my story. More and more, my eyes were opened to the importance of the words I choose to describe who I am, who God is, and the kind of relationship I am in with Him. Consider these words of Jesus (from Matthew 12:36-37): "But I say to you that for every idle word men may speak, they will give account of it in the Day of Judgment. For by your words you will be justified, and by your words you will be condemned." Every time I cursed myself, begged for death, or complained about how little reward I got from life, I was boldly speaking the idlest of words.

This whole problematic episode with the sale of the home was a necessary part of the experience. You see, if God had allowed me to sell the property before He met me in Las Vegas, I would have been just another depressed Malibu native. And trust me, there is no one more miserable than someone who has everything the world says is valuable, but who can't overcome a negative mindset or find gratitude in his abundance. I've met plenty of them. It was only after He allowed me the freedom to choose happiness, and to see how little it was related to the things I thought previously, that He would allow the sale to go forward.

A little less than a year after the first escrow fell through, my realtor called to tell me the property had gotten "stale" and that I should think about reducing the price slightly to generate some new interest. So we lowered the price and tried again. To our shock, one of the original bidders decided that he wanted the property as-is and made an offer. After a short negotiation, we settled on a price that was "only" $75,000 less than I had originally agreed to take from the first buyer, and I was not liable for any of the repairs necessary to comply with permitting requirements. God had completely redeemed the situation! The blessing that my mother intended was restored and I walked away with something priceless – the knowledge that God never wavers in the least from His goal of loving us in whatever way is required to bring about the greatest good. Even if that means pruning us in ways that push the limits of our ability to understand. I am not being glib when I say that, if it were necessary in order to keep that knowledge, I would gladly sacrifice every dollar gained from the sale of that property.

I had been enjoying my new mindset and narrative for some time before I rediscovered this Scripture in Revelation, "And they overcame him (Satan) because of the blood of the Lamb and because of the word of their testimony, and they did not love their life even when faced with death" (Rev. 12:11). Obviously, the main focus of our testimony will always be of the victory that Jesus (the Lamb) won for us when He shed His blood on our behalf, but I now know our testimony can be so much more than that. My testimony isn't just what He has overcome - it's what He has brought me to overcome as well. The blood of Jesus alone is not sufficient for us to overcome the enemy. If it was, everyone would be saved – even those who despise Him. It is our testimony of what His blood has accomplished that is the catalyst for our salvation. By our words we will be justified! And, if it's our testimony (sworn statement) that we overcome the devil with - can you think of anything more valuable?

VICTORY

*Do you not know that those who run in a race all run,
but only one receives the prize? Run in such a way that you
may win. Everyone who competes in the games exercises
self-control in all things. (1 Cor. 9:24-25)*

It has only been a few years since I was set free from the loser
mindset that defined my first 48 years. And, as wonderful as it is to
finally understand that God is much more involved in the minutia of
my life than I previously thought, there is still a residue of that
narrative that I find at work in me at times. It is the reflexive tendency
to avoid competition. If I'm honest, I have to admit that I don't like
either side of the outcome. If I lose, I have to find a way to let go of the
sting and talk myself back into the game. And if I win, I have to be OK
doing that to someone else. Not only that, but, if I win, I can be sure
there will be another challenger before too long who will want to start
the competition again.

As much as I'd like to think otherwise, this is not the world
where everyone shares generously with everyone else; that is the next
world. This world, because of sin, requires struggle, work, and
competition with others to some degree or other. If I meet an
attractive woman, I can be sure she will be pursued by other men who
find her desirable as well. If I'm attempting to grow a business, there
are others who will want the same customers I am after. Part of many
people's college experience is competing with others for coveted spots
in prestigious schools. In this limited world, there is no way to avoid
competing if we are going to reach our potential. Nobody can

surrender their way to success. Now, to be clear, I do believe that there is an ordained place for each one of us that God has set aside to ensure our needs are met. But, I also believe that we get to that place because we persevere when faced with opposition and run with the intention of winning.

While I embraced the loser narrative, I considered myself more noble because I laid down preemptively when competition arose. I told myself that I was a better type of person because I refused to "play the game" with the same gusto that I saw others exhibit. I see now that it was only fear that stopped me. Actually, there is a stronger word that captures it − cowardice. Cowardice is the lack of courage to face opposition, conflict, or pain. And there is no path to the hero identity without confronting cowardice − it is one of the internal struggles we talked about in an earlier chapter. This is a lesson that God continues to teach me in unusual ways. I seem to have a knack for finding myself in situations where my tendency to want to collapse in the face of opposition can express itself. One such lesson occurred at the end of 2016 and certainly qualifies as unusual.

About midway through the year, I decided to plan some sort of vacation for the winter. I was looking for something more exotic than I was used to, but was reluctant to go anywhere alone. I finally decided that to be true to my new narrative, I should not postpone adventure because I had no company to go along with me. So I began researching options and quickly bogged down in choices. I realized that one of the things I wanted a partner for was so that I could defer to their preference of where we would travel. I didn't know what I wanted. So, after some thought, I settled on the sentence, "I want to eat swordfish the same day it is caught." I have no idea where that thought came from, but it sounded like it would take me someplace interesting.

As I researched this, I stumbled onto a fishing lodge in Costa Rica in a little town not far from the Panama border called Zancudo. The Zancudo Lodge is located on the Pacific side of the country and is one of the world's big game fishing hotspots. It seemed like a good candidate to try to make my operative statement a reality. I then noticed that the lodge was hosting a fishing tournament in the middle of December which seemed a way to heighten the adventure I was seeking. Now, I should say at this point that I am a completely novice fisherman. I had been fishing for marlin only twice before in my life and had been lucky to catch a 200lb. blue marlin my first time out in Mexico with Charlie many years earlier. So, I contacted the owner of the lodge and asked about the tournament to find out whether I was too inexperienced to enter. The owner, Gregg, told me that the competition was not too serious and that he would find me a teammate so I wouldn't be fishing alone. So I booked the trip and waited until the day arrived to head to Central America.

I took a red-eye flight from Los Angeles and arrived in San Jose, Costa Rica early in the morning. Unfortunately, due to some miscommunication between the owner and his wife, I was not booked on the smaller connecting flight from the international airport to the lodge until the day after I arrived. I was in a foreign country with no flight from the capital city to the lodge, and, to make matters worse, I couldn't get my phone to work on the local network even though I had set it up days before I left. This was my first challenge and, while I was relieved that the employees at the airline were knowledgeable and helpful, I was also fighting the temptation to conclude I had made a mistake in coming; this was not the way I had anticipated the adventure beginning! As the airline attempted to figure out what went wrong, it became clear that some other passengers that were there with me were also going to the same lodge. This calmed me somewhat, but, because of my situation, the flight that they were all supposed to take was delayed. Eventually, the problem was solved, but some other passengers had to have their luggage flown to another airport close to our destination because of weight limitations that my presence made necessary and they were not thrilled by that.

So, my introduction to my fellow competitors was not ideal. Making matters more awkward was the fact that they were all long-time friends who frequently took such trips together; I was a complete outsider. On top of this, they were all from an economic strata far above mine. They were very wealthy car dealership owners and auto manufacturers who, besides taking fishing trips together, also owned race cars that they drove in races on the east coast. These guys were all well acquainted with competition and were not conflicted about it in the slightest! I am usually good at appearing calm when under duress and I had to call on this skill as we introduced ourselves and got to know each other better. When I told them that I worked in a residential addiction treatment facility, I was pleasantly surprised to find that a few of them were in recovery for alcohol dependence and were interested to talk to me further about my experience. It was the first glimmer of reassurance that I was in the right place, and I was looking for as many as I could find. After we arrived at the lodge, we ate a meal together and settled in for the afternoon. I had the opportunity to speak privately with another guest about his experience of sobriety and at last began to feel that God had accompanied me to Costa Rica after all.

The next day I shared a boat with two other anglers as we took in a day of fishing before the tournament started. I was impressed by the magnificence of the scenery and the wonderfully languid pace of the area. We rose early and stopped not far from the lodge to fish for bait. This was my first opportunity to demonstrate my complete lack of skill at fishing for anything and I was surprised it had arrived so soon. The captain guided the boat toward schools of smaller bait fish that we caught on unbaited, small hooks that attracted fish solely with their shine. I dropped my line in and attempted to look like I had done something like this at least once before. My fishing partners quickly began pulling 6-8 inch long bait fish into the boat, sometimes three and four at a time because there were multiple hooks on each line. At last, I began to get the hang of what we were doing, but, strangely, I kept catching a certain less desirable species of fish with sharp spines that annoyed the captain as he unhooked the fish from my line. At this point, I was just thrilled that I was catching anything and, before too long, we had enough bait to last for the day.

We sped out of the bay where the lodge was located and headed north, where we began slowly trolling for fish near the shore. This part was easier - just hold the pole while we slowly trolled just outside the surf line. Again, I was struck by how lush and green the jungle was; thick vegetation pushed almost all the way to the water, and the tropical climate was warm and moist. After an hour or so, both my partners had caught a fish or two, and I was again wondering if my lack of experience would become a major hurdle in my ability to enjoy the trip.

I was actively harboring some doubts as Dennis, one of the other anglers, caught his second fish, a large red snapper. He expertly pulled the fish into the boat and handed me the camera to take a picture of him holding it. At that moment, and I mean precisely that moment, my own reel began to scream as something bit it on the other end. After a vigorous fight, I landed a large pompano that amazed me with its bright, silvery skin and prehistoric appearance. At the time, I remarked that the timing of the bite was interesting. I felt as if God was telling me, "I didn't send you here to take photos of other people catching fish!" After that, I held my own for the remainder of the day. I caught two roosterfish over the next few hours, one of them in the 25lb. range. The first day of fishing ended well and I felt a measure of satisfaction that I had made it through the day without seriously embarrassing myself.

That evening, we ate at the lodge's restaurant and went over tournament rules as a group. After dinner, Gregg introduced me to Keith, who would be my fishing partner for the tournament. Keith worked as a mechanic and bartender in Wisconsin when he wasn't in

Costa Rica and had been coming to the lodge for the past twenty years. Keith had arranged to trade his services as a skilled mechanic for the opportunity to spend a good part of the year in Costa Rica. It was his home away from home, and he had caught just about every kind of fish found in local waters. When I told him that I had no appreciable fishing experience and that I worked as a substance abuse counselor in Malibu, he rolled his eyes as if to say, "Oh boy, I can't wait for the headaches you are going to give me!" He had his own experience with alcoholics and probably assumed I would be puritanical or judgmental about the amount of drinking that was taking place as the tournament wore on.

One of the things that was necessary to determine was each team's participation in the Calcutta pool, or jackpots awarded according to type and size of fish caught each of the three days of the tournament. The basic entry fee of $500 per boat would be split between me and my teammate Keith, but the Calcutta was an optional expense beyond that. The tournament was structured so that there were three groups of point scoring fish – billfish such as marlin or sailfish, gamefish including dorado (mahi mahi) and yellowfin tuna, and a separate category for roosterfish. Scoring is done differently for each category; the billfish are awarded points for each species (400 for blue marlin, 200 for striped marlin, and 100 for sailfish), the gamefish are scored by weight (1 point per lb.), and the roosterfish are 100 points each. Each of these three categories had a jackpot for each day, meaning that to go "all-in" the Calcutta would cost a total of $900 per angler ($100 for each category, each day).

Originally, I had planned on sitting out this portion of the action because of my inexperience, but, because my partner wanted to go all-in, it would have been very difficult for me not to. It would have meant conflicts about who should land the fish because of the money at stake. I also noticed that it was assumed that everyone would be going all-in; remember, these are rich guys who love to compete! I had no desire to look like the only timid one in the crowd, so I swallowed hard and came up with the $1,150 cash to cover the entry and Calcutta. I chuckled as I thought how little chance I had to win it back, placed it in the hands of the tournament director, and considered it spent.

The other order of business that evening was to draw lots for boats and captains for each day of the tournament. This was done because three of the boats (called Contenders) were faster than the others, which means that more time can be spent fishing rather than traveling to the fishing grounds. Not all the captains are of equal skill either, and while all are capable, some have significantly more experience in local waters than others. Because Keith was a frequent visitor to the lodge he had knowledge of which captains were preferable, I left the choosing to him. Our draw went very well with our team getting the top 2-3 picks on each day. Keith felt very good about our chances, and I was willing to accept any help I could get. But then something interesting happened. Because there were eight teams in the tournament, and only three Contender boats, it was necessary to draw lots for the use of those boats.

But, on that day of fishing before the tournament, one of the Contenders broke down on its way home. After it arrived, it was determined that it would not be ready to run again for the tournament, which meant that the draw for boats and captains had to be redone in part. To our dismay, we drew the eighth choice for the second day of the tournament – dead last. But, in a major coup, we were able to get one of the Contenders for the final day of the tournament as well as the most expert captain, named Tito. While we were at a disadvantage for the second day of the competition, we had more latitude to take chances on the final day due to the boat and captain we had won.

The first day of fishing was eventful, with Keith hooking up a beautiful sailfish a few hours in. Because the billfish are caught and released, there must be photographic proof that the fish was brought close enough to the boat so that the captain could grab onto the line close to the fishes mouth (called the leader). This meant that the task of being videographer fell to me. Now, I know how to do this, but I'm not well versed on how to determine whether an actual video is being taken or how much memory is left, etc. Maybe you can see where this is going! Because it is hard to know when the fish will be brought close enough to film, I ended up stopping the video at points so that it would not run too long and exhaust the camera's memory. Well, after we released the fish, we reviewed the video to find that the memory had failed at the crucial moment. We had no proof that we had landed the fish. What a way to start!

I apologized to Keith and he was gracious to quickly forgive me, but I again found myself entertaining loser thoughts. Because I was so far out of my comfort zone, and because it was too early to tell how significant my gaffe would be, I was having a difficult time fighting off the temptation to feel ashamed by my failure. And if there is one thing strong enough to take the pleasure out of competition, it is shame!

Later in the afternoon, I caught another sailfish that was very active and jumped repeatedly as I was reeling it in. It was definitely a memorable experience, and, because Keith was using my phone to video the landing, we had more than just a memory to show the tournament director. The day ended with us tied with four other boats that had landed one fish, but one boat had caught two sails that day and had taken the daily billfish jackpot by themselves ($800). We groaned when we realized that we would have split it with them had our video not malfunctioned.

The next day we went out with Popín as our captain. He was an eager guide, but was very young and had limited experience in Costa Rican waters, which is why he was left until last for us to choose that day. It was a bit overcast as we set out to get a roosterfish if we could.

Because of the way the tournament was structured, in order to score maximum points, teams must catch fish from all three categories – billfish, gamefish, and roosterfish. Additional points are awarded if a team can catch from all three categories in the same day. So we wanted to start the day fishing inshore (where the roosterfish are) and then move out to try for bill and game fish. It didn't take long for each of us to catch a roosterfish, and we headed out to the blue water about 15 miles offshore. Around noon, as Keith and I were talking and looking back at the lures trailing the boat, we both saw a large fish rise up out of the water and slam down on one of the lures. We had hooked a big fish! Keith offered to let me take it, but I insisted he go instead. In hindsight, I kind of regret that decision, but I can honestly say it was equally exciting to watch my teammate fight the fish.

And what a fight! We had hooked a large blue marlin that took two hours to even get close to the boat and another hour to finally land. It jumped numerous times, and we were concerned it would be able to dislodge the hook as it thrashed repeatedly. I was pouring water over Keith and his gear to keep him from overheating while trying to document it on film at the same time. Finally, we got it up next to the boat and I got my first close look at a marlin in over twenty years. It was a beautiful fish, with a huge girth, and I was startled as it showed its color near the side of the boat. Magnificent, electric blue flashed along the length of its body as we brought it alongside. We released it after we were sure we had videotaped it well enough, and Popín estimated it to be close to 400lbs. Keith, who had fished for many years, said it was the biggest fish he had ever caught. It was even more fortunate because, when we brought the fish close, we saw that it had been hooked on the side of its head rather than in the mouth, which explained why it was able to resist for so long.

When we got in that afternoon, we were pleased to hear that no other blues were caught that day, which meant that, because of their higher point value, we would almost certainly win the daily jackpot. That was good news - we were crushing the billfish category but, because we were one of the few boats that still had not caught a gamefish (tuna or dorado), we were not getting the bonus points for catching fish from all three categories, and we were in 5th place overall.

Day three began with a meeting to plan our strategy for the day. We had already caught two roosterfish, but other teams had caught many more than we had, so we surrendered that category, hoped our lead would hold in the billfish category, and focused on hunting for tuna in order to get the bonus points we needed to jump up in the standing. After filling up with baitfish as before, we headed straight out for the blue water at top speed. Because Keith had gotten the big marlin the day before, we agreed that I would take the first bite of the day. It didn't take too long for that bite to come! After about a 40 minute ride to the fishing grounds, Tito rigged 6 rods and put our lines in the water. It took another 30 minutes to hook what we thought was a sailfish at first, but, after about 20 minutes of fighting it, I brought a striped marlin that weighed roughly 150 lbs. to the side of the boat.

We were pleased to get the 200 points for that species of fish, but we were now so far ahead in the billfish category that we didn't want any more of them. So Tito began to scour the horizon for any signs of schooling bait fish that would be attracting the larger tuna and dorado. After about another hour, Tito noticed some far away birds that looked as if they were diving for baitfish, a sign that bigger fish would be feeding there as well. So we headed their direction and kept our fingers crossed that we would find our quarry when we got there.

It must have been around 11am when we intersected the birds we had seen earlier. It was unlike anything I had ever seen before. We had arrived at the scene of a feeding frenzy! A large school of spinner dolphins was slowly driving what must have been an enormous amount of smaller baitfish along in front of them. Spinner dolphins get their name from the characteristic spinning jumps they perform and it was possible to see dozens of dolphins making these twisting leaps at any given time. We could see numerous tuna flashing through the dolphins with regularity as well. We had stumbled onto an absolutely ideal situation, and Tito was beaming as he trolled back and forth out in front of the dolphins. Adding to our delight was the fact that, because we were in the faster boat, no one else had arrived yet – we had this all to ourselves.

After an hour had passed with no bites, Tito began to adjust his techniques trying to land a tuna. He tested out various lures and varied the pattern of his trolling passes, all to no avail. Another hour passed and his frustration was becoming more evident. Other teams had also arrived and we began to see our advantage slip away. Our only consolation was that nobody else seemed to be catching much either. The tuna were just not biting. The tournament rules stated that boats had to have their lines out of the water by 4 o'clock in the afternoon, or, if they were currently fighting a fish, it had to be landed by 4:30. As the hours ticked by, I began to entertain the thought that we would not land the fish we needed after all.

In hindsight, I can say that I was trying to let myself down gently. Rather than stay at a high level of hope and let 4 o'clock crush me, I would conclude that defeat was near certain and protect myself from that letdown. It was the same sort of proactive surrender that had characterized so many competitions I had been in before. Whatever had caused my friend to comment on my inability to sustain my level of tennis play, or my wife to notice that I "always seemed to find a way to lose," was evidently still alive and well in me. I was finding a way to make losing tolerable.

We continued to search for the tuna more and more urgently as the day wore on. With about an hour left, Tito abandoned the methods he had been using earlier in favor of live baits and wooden lures known as "poppers." As I fished with live bait off the stern of the boat, Keith casted the popper off the bow and skipped the lure over the top of the water as he reeled it in, causing a popping sound in the water and giving the lure its name. With 15 minutes left, Tito was becoming frantic and was shouting directions at us as we fished. While this was going on, my thoughts were not of the potential still present in the moment, but rather of having given it a good try and having the clock run out on me; 5th place was not so bad. And watching Tito and Keith continuing to escalate their efforts highlighted the internal surrender that I was engaging in. On the outside, I was trying hard, but internally I had already come to a conclusion - loss was inevitable.

Then, at about five minutes to 4:00, and to everyone's surprise, a fish struck Keith's lure and bent his rod nearly straight down. I reeled the other lines in to make sure there would be no tangles, and gave moral support to Keith as he fought what was looking to be a large tuna. Keith battled the fish for some time without gaining much line on it, and we started to get concerned that the fish would outlast the 4:30 time limit and would not count toward our score.

Finally, after about 20 minutes of struggle, the fish tired and rose near the boat. Tito and I both positioned ourselves with gaffs to ensure the fish would not get away. As soon as it came close enough, we quickly gaffed it and lifted it over the rail. It was a hefty yellowtail tuna that we put into the ice cooler immediately, and while Keith and I settled in, Tito sped for home. We arrived last, and were informed that another team had just brought in a 59lb. tuna that had secured them 3rd place in the gamefish category for the tournament. Our fish would have to exceed that in order to leapfrog them into 3rd place. We waited anxiously while the deck crew prepared to weigh the tuna we brought back, and were elated when we saw that it weighed in at 61.6 lbs.!

This had vaulted us into 3rd place in the gamefish category, and it turned out our lead had held in the billfish category, which meant we actually had a good shot at winning the whole tournament! All the teams cleaned up and met for dinner a short time later where winners would be announced. This would also be when all the Calcutta results would be awarded as well. Keith and I were greatly enjoying telling our fish story to the rest of the entrants and we reveled in the drama of it. We were also gratified when we were told we won three out of the nine total jackpot categories: Keith's blue marlin won on day two and his tuna on day three, while my striped marlin won the jackpot for day three. So we split $2,400 for those wins.

Next came the tournament results and it was announced we had tied for second place overall. To determine prize money, a coin was flipped and we won the toss as well, meaning we won additional prize money. All together Keith and I each won close to $1,700 for a net profit of $550! We were within 100 points of first place, but the winning boat had earned the special bonus of catching fish from all three categories in the same day. We were pained when we heard that the gamefish they caught to get the victory was a measly 7 lb. dorado.

As our stunning comeback sunk in, I began to examine my thinking over the past few hours. In much the same way I had chosen a story of defeat at the roulette table, I had adopted a similar story over the course of the afternoon. The closer the deadline got, the more I chose to entertain thoughts of inevitable loss rather than last-minute success. As I mentioned, this is a strategy I adopted years ago to relieve myself of the anxiety of anticipation and to avoid a greater letdown. If I put energy into keeping my level of hope high until the very last minute, the letdown would be much more sudden and steep when loss did happen. I was disappointed in myself for abandoning hope long before the competition ended, but I didn't let my introspection interfere too much with my enjoyment of the experience. After all, I was leaving Costa Rica as the reigning billfish division champion of the Triple Crown Tournament!

In hindsight, I look at this fish story as a sort of bookend to my experience at the roulette table. In both cases, it was the timing of the experience that made the stories remarkable. In order for the roulette table to have the power it did required previous experience with a European table 25 years prior, which, in turn, required me to befriend a particular person (Charlie) at the age of six. And the surrounding events that had to be managed to assure that meeting took place are too numerous to conceive of. Then, I had to walk up to that roulette table at precisely the right moment for all the pieces to add up. The wisdom of God I see in that will forever astonish me. I feel so honored now to be given that story to tell, even though I suffered significant loss and anguish for the 48 years preceding it.

And the timing involved in catching the tuna is equally impressive. After we returned to the dock and compared notes with the other boats, we found that only one other tuna had been caught that whole afternoon when the conditions were as perfect as could be asked for. Ordinarily, those conditions would have seen several, perhaps dozens, of large tuna brought in by the combined boats that were there. And, God could have arranged for us to catch that tuna in the first five minutes of the 1st day rather than the last five minutes of the last day and the outcome would have been the same. We would have been awarded 2nd place overall and won the same prize money. But how exciting a story would that be? Nowhere near as what actually happened! Again, it was the timing of the event that was so illustrative of how He operates.

There are a few lessons that I learned in a fuller measure as a result of my trip to Costa Rica. The first is that what seems to be a great drawback can turn out to be a huge advantage. When we had to redraw for captains and forfeit our good position for the least desired one, it was tempting to conclude that we were at a disadvantage. But, it was our day with Popín that saw us land the only blue marlin of the tournament, which was the single largest fish of the competition. It was also the most exhilarating fish Keith had ever caught, and he had been fishing his whole life. This is pretty basic, but it was good to be reminded that the "limitations" that we come up against cannot thwart the plan of God; in fact, these limitations are the necessary plot points that will eventually allow the hero narrative to express itself most fully.

The second is that God is at work in crafting the course of our lives even down to the most minute details and can be counted on to finish the story well; I like to say, "The devil never gets the last word!" To be honest, the most important part of the experience for me wasn't the thrill of making such a dramatic, last-minute comeback - it was the thrill of being reminded that God is detail-oriented in the best possible way. If we knew how intricately He was orchestrating what, on the surface, seem to be unremarkable details of our lives, and that He was doing it to ensure that our eventual story will be the most triumphant possible, we would celebrate very much more than we currently do!

Above all, this opened my eyes all over again to an idea that I have a hard time holding on to most of the time. Competing well means we do it with the understanding that the competition is supposed to be fun! And this can only happen when we have the deep-seated assurance that He is thoroughly invested in both assuring the outcome to be in our favor and protecting us from any harm loss could bring. Notice I used some squirrely language in that last sentence! I didn't say He would ensure that we win every time, I said the outcome would be in our favor. If we can keep that realization in mind when we find ourselves in any kind of competition, we are released from having a shred of our identity invested in the outcome, whether we win or lose. When fear of losing is present, we ensure that the competition will involve a great deal of frustration and anxiety. And when we are lusting for victory, we will find other distasteful appetites coming alive and tempting us to compromise our integrity in pursuit of it. We are only responsible to run in such a way that we "may win," and when we can let go of the results and instead relish the fact that God is present in the struggle, competition suddenly has the potential to thrill us regardless of the outcome.

And, trust me, I know that not every story includes a comeback win, a miraculous provision, or an unexpected healing. Sometimes cancer can't be stopped, bankruptcy can't be avoided, the overdose is fatal, and the marriage can't be saved. I have seen all of those up close and have held the hands of people dying long before it seemed proper for their lives to end. I've had things happen in my own life that I was certain He would never make me go through - and I was wrong. At some point, if my life is not cut short, I will get a diagnosis that I desperately do not want. That is just reality.

The flexible mindset and positive narrative don't assert that everything that happens is good, they assert that everything that happens is *for my good*. Because God superintends our lives, it is impossible to nullify the reality that even unspeakable events in our past can bring forth unexpected blessing and heroic triumph. This is the promise of Romans 8:28: "And we know that God causes all things to work together for good to those who love God, to those who are called according to His purpose." So, how can we say that the story ends well when those things happen? There is only one way. It is by reaffirming that those circumstances - divorce, disease, destitution, and even death, are not the end of the story.

VOLATILITY

Divide your portion to seven, or even to eight, for you
do not know what misfortune may occur on the earth.
(Ecclesiastes 11:2)

For some reason, I think of Wile E. Coyote whenever I hear the word volatile. I'm not sure if they still show those Coyote and Roadrunner cartoons, but I spent a lot of time watching them when I was a kid. I was always amused at how the coyote's elaborate plans inevitably backfired on him or, literally, blew up in his face. Despite his efforts creating elaborate traps to catch the speedy roadrunner, there would always be one factor he couldn't account for, and he would invariably see his plans self-destruct. Volatility can be like that. If something is volatile it is subject to rapid, even explosive change, and, if not handled carefully, will quickly turn and bite you if you're not prepared. The term is used in chemistry to refer to chemicals that quickly change states. Certain people and relationships can be volatile; anyone who has lived with an addicted or abusive partner understands how quickly things can change to something frightening or even dangerous.

After I sold the property in Malibu, I had to decide what to do with the proceeds of the sale. I'm not saying this to boast, but I literally had more money than I knew what to do with. Because I had always been an under-earner and intimidated by money, I had not put a lot of effort into learning how to manage finances beyond keeping a checkbook balanced. For most of my life up to that point, every dollar I earned was owed to at least one other creditor. And the older I got, the more my loser mindset kept me from asking my peers basic questions about investing because I didn't want to look inept. Before the roulette table experience freed me from the loser narrative, I mistrusted the stock market because it seemed like nothing more than gambling to me. I used to joke that, even if the market was doing well, it would immediately plunge when I put my money into it, but I actually believed that to some extent. If there was a gamble to take, I believed I would be on the wrong side of it no matter how sure a bet it seemed.

I sat on the cash I got from selling the house for about six months before I could bring myself to "put it in play" in a way that I felt was responsible and wise. A team of financial advisors had been referred to me by my bank and, after interviewing several others, decided I would trust them to invest my money how they saw fit. They asked me certain questions about my life and future plans in order to determine how much risk I was comfortable accepting in the pursuit of growing the portfolio. One of the words they frequently used was the word volatility. They explained at length the strategy they would use to limit the effects of volatility in my investments. They would invest in small-cap, mid-cap, and large-cap stocks. They would invest in both foreign and domestic stocks. They would find growth as well as value stocks. They would have established blue-chip stocks as well as emerging market investments to hedge against each other. They would have a portion invested in bonds that would provide steady income if stock prices flattened out. They mentioned all the different sectors of the economy I would be invested in so that, if one sector slowed, another would pick up the slack. And, to this day, I would not be able to explain to you what most of what I just said actually means!

But I did understand that all this diversification was intended to make the sharp, volatile swings the market is capable of much more smooth. Rather than frequent ups and downs in the growth of my investments, they were trying to create one steady, upwardly trending line over time. In short, not only did they "divide my portion" to seven or eight, they divided each of those seven or eight into seven or eight more. And they did that several times over. And all this was done because they didn't know what "misfortune may occur on the earth."

So they did their part to take the worry out of my investments, but the other thing they emphasized repeatedly was the benefit of looking at the long-term trends and not the day to day changes in the market. This was my part of the solution to volatility. I've since learned that a good portion of their job is to reassure clients when the market makes large swings and they know in advance which of their clients are most likely to respond emotionally and need special attention to talk down "off the ledge."

There is abundant potential for volatility in the market when you look at only the short-term ups and downs, and some event that happens across the world can send it sharply in either direction at a moment's notice. And, if you follow the daily news about the stock market for any length of time, it becomes comical how little snippets of news affect the direction of the market so quickly. One day it's "Tech company X reports higher than expected earnings, market is up!" The next day it's "Oil prices take a dive, market is down!" Some companies use services that analyze the "micro-expressions" that treasury or Fed officials make when giving speeches about their plans for the economy to look for clues they can use to guide their investment strategies. And computers are so entwined in the market now that huge sell-offs (flash-crashes) can happen with lightning speed once certain algorithms get triggered. If you have money in the stock market, it can be very anxiety producing to watch the minute to minute activity taking place on Wall Street.

Financial advisors advice to look long term is really about adjusting the scale of your perspective. When you look at events with a small scale, as if they are cut off from the larger context, isolated circumstances appear much bigger and gain inordinate power to create drastic mood swings. One day it's "I got a raise at work, isn't life great?" and the next it's "I had another fight with my wife. What was I thinking? Life sucks!" Looking at life with a small scale means that you will be riding a roller coaster of emotion that will soar and crash based on daily, transient circumstances. And, no matter how much you like roller coasters, if we put you on one long enough you would be begging to get off. Just like staying on the roller coaster too long makes what might otherwise be fun a total nightmare, using too small a scale when looking at life will drain out the measured excitement we are meant to have and replace it with an overstimulated dread.

Looking at life with the proper scale is vital if we are to experience the kind of peace God says is available to us. If my scale is small, it will be impossible to "consider it all joy...when (I) experience various trials (James 1:2)," because I will only be seeing the unpleasantness of my current circumstances. With the proper scale, I will be able to rejoice that the struggle I'm undergoing will produce a faith that allows me to endure the inevitable ups and downs of life with much greater ease and steadiness (James 1:3-4). And, if we are going to shift into the hero narrative, we will certainly need endurance to sustain it. Proper scale is also necessary to see ourselves in a truly scriptural way. If we are too narrowly focused on our troubles, shortcomings, and lack, we will never be able to tap into the transformative power available to us when we can envision ourselves as the "overwhelming conquerors" that Paul describes us as (Rom. 8:37). It is only by using a much larger scope than we normally would that we can have profound joy even when actively suffering and exhibit overflowing gratitude despite our current lack.

I love looking at familiar Bible stories through this mindset and perspective lens. These stories take on an added significance when we make an effort to relate to their frame of mind even though their circumstances are foreign to us. Another reason to look at these well-known stories is their ability to help us apply their lessons to our own life. Second Timothy 3:16 says, "All Scripture is inspired by God and useful for teaching [and] training in righteousness; so that the man of God may be...equipped for every good work." So, with that in mind, let's look at some biblical examples of people who can exemplify what having a proper scale of perspective looks like.

The Apostle Paul is the classic example of someone who had every conceivable opportunity to adopt a victim narrative. But, because he drew his identity from what he knew about God, has left us some truly amazing insights about how to fight off a negative narrative. This is a guy who was "beaten times without number, often in danger of death. Five times I received...thirty-nine lashes. Three times...beaten with rods, once...stoned, three times...ship-wrecked, a night and a day I have spent in the deep. I have been on frequent journeys, in dangers from rivers, dangers from robbers, dangers from my countrymen, dangers from the Gentiles, dangers in the city, dangers in the wilderness, dangers on the sea, dangers among false brethren; I have been in labor and hardship, through many sleepless nights, in hunger and thirst, often without food, in cold and exposure" (2 Cor. 11:23-27). It doesn't get much more volatile than that! Yet, when he is encouraging the Corinthians he says, "For momentary, light affliction is producing for us an eternal weight of glory far beyond all comparison, while we look not at the things which are seen, but at the things which are not seen; for the things which are seen are temporal, but the things which are not seen are eternal" (2 Cor. 4:17-18).

What did he say? Light affliction? If you don't understand how he can classify what he had been through as "momentary, light affliction," it is because the concept of "comparison" is the only thing makes this kind of mindset change possible. If Paul were to look at that list of suffering only through a "temporal" (earthly, time-bound) lens, he would have plenty of material to write a victim narrative for himself. But, because he has caught a glimpse of the glory waiting for us, he is able to use an eternal perspective that makes his suffering look puny in comparison. This is also why he can honestly say, "More than that, I count all things to be loss in view of the surpassing value of knowing Christ Jesus my Lord, for whom I have suffered the loss of all things, and count them but rubbish so that I may gain Christ, and may be found in Him...in order that I may attain to the resurrection from the dead" (Phi. 3:8-11).

Again, it is comparison that drives Paul to say something so forceful. Suffering the loss of all things is pretty serious, but when Paul uses the words *"in view of,"* he is using the language of changed perspective. Suffering that kind of worldly loss is devastating unless one has a "view of" the value of what is gained eternally. Finally, he just comes right out and says it as plainly as anyone can, "For I consider that the sufferings of this present time are not worthy to be compared with the glory that is to be revealed to us" (Rom. 8:18).

One of the great blessings of being given the kind of perspective that Scripture provides is that we have something to compare with our present circumstances; we have an "in view of" that lets us de-emphasize circumstances that would otherwise be overwhelming. I trust that Paul can speak with authority about suffering, but I also think it's likely that he didn't start his journey with the same mindset about suffering that he ended with. I can imagine the first shipwreck, beating, persecution, etc., being a different experience from the third one(s). As He repeatedly saw the protection and provision of God, he was given the opportunity to recast his narrative as a victor and overcomer rather than a victim of such miserable circumstances. It is out of this body of evidence he is able to make a profound forecast about the future: "indeed, we had the sentence of death within ourselves so that we would not trust in ourselves, but in God who raises the dead; who delivered us from so great a peril of death, and will deliver us, He on whom we have set our hope. And He *will yet deliver us...* (2 Cor. 9:1-2 emphasis mine). At this point, Paul has fully committed to the big picture and is as past-positive as someone can be. He has seen God raise the dead and has "set his hope" on the certainty that God, having a plan and perspective greater than any we could ever grasp, has left no detail to chance. He *will* deliver us!

The story of the healing of the man born blind is another perfect example of the importance of scale as well as how easily we adopt limiting narratives when trying to explain our circumstances. As Jesus and his disciples are walking one day, Jesus "passes by" a blind man who He knew to be born that way. His disciples ask Him about the origin of the man's blindness and immediately assume that it was either because he or his parents had sinned (John 9:2). Notice how quickly they try to establish a narrative that will neatly explain his blindness. They might as well have asked "Teacher, did this man lose his sight because he's a victim of his parent's sin? Or is he a loser who deserves blindness because of his own sin?" Jesus sidesteps their attempt altogether and instead shows them that their scale is much too small to capture the true importance of the situation. He says, "...neither...but it was so that the works of God might be displayed in him" (John 9:3).

Think about it, the man had spent his whole life blind so that he could one day be at exactly the right spot for Jesus to "pass by" and have his life immortalized into the story of God! The more I know about the quality of God's work, the more perfect every aspect of it appears to be. He not only can manipulate physical matter to restore sight, but He also chooses the timing for maximum effect. I have a feeling this man didn't ever once look back and wonder why God made him wait as long as He did before healing him.

With His answer to the disciples, Jesus shatters the small scale, loser/victim/villain narrative that they are locked in and instead places this man squarely in the epic overcomer/hero category. The man born blind goes on to testify in front of the religious leaders about what happened and rebukes them precisely because their narrative about the identity of Jesus is so wrong. While the Pharisees debate about whether Jesus is a sinner or not because He healed on the Sabbath, the man who was healed says plainly, "He is a prophet" (John 9:16-17). The Pharisees were focused on one particular Sabbath, and because of that, they missed the fact that Jesus is one in a long line of prophets charged with reminding people (oftentimes offensively) about the bigger story of God. In fact, Jesus widens the scope of His narrative as much as possible by calling himself the Lord of the Sabbath (Matthew 12:8).

When Jesus healed him, the man born blind had his perspective broadened to see much more than just what his restored eyes could perceive. Before that, how many times do you think he had to hear people explain his blindness as either the result of his sin or the sin of his parents? Before he was healed, his blindness was an ever-present reminder to all who "passed by" of how sin had limited him. After his healing, his changed perspective was a testimony to the redemptive story of God, who "passed by" at the perfect moment to demonstrate just how marvelous His works are.

These stories are excellent reminders of how important it is that we choose the proper scale when looking at our circumstances. But sometimes a different sort of reminder is necessary, and I was recently given the opportunity to learn this lesson again myself as well as how easily I can be shaken out of the right perspective. So bear with me while we revisit the stock market for a few minutes.

It was November of 2015 when I opened the investment account at my bank, deposited the proceeds from the sale of the property, and turned my advisors loose to do what they're good at. They were optimistic that I was getting into the market at a good time and ran all sorts of computations to show me what to expect over time. I told you that I used to truly believe that the market would tank as soon as my money went in, but the first few months were fairly uneventful. I checked in on the account infrequently, as it grew only a small amount over that time.

Then something interesting happened on the Chinese New Year in 2016. It fell on a Monday in early February and was my first experience with volatility in the market, although I didn't realize that at the time. For some strange reason, the holiday caused the stock market to turn sharply downward for the week, and I was shocked to see that I had lost about $30,000 in that short time. So, in just ten weeks in the market I was that much below where I had started back in November – not an encouraging start! At that rate, I could imagine the money being gone in a very short time.

I took some deep breaths and tried to remember what my advisors told me about looking long term and I trusted them to do what was necessary, if anything, with the account. So I called on my flexible mindset to try recast the loss through the lens of gratitude. I reminded myself of this by praying, "Thank you Lord that I can lose that much and still be amply provided for!" As it happened, the market regained that loss pretty quickly, and I was surprised that I was back on the plus side within a few more months.

As it turned out, I just happened to invest in the market at the beginning of a historically low period of volatility. Aside from that initial blip, the market rose slowly, but fairly steadily, between that time and the Presidential election in November 2016. Some of you may know how remarkably the market has performed since that time. The President has made frequent mention of the record gains the stock market has made since he was elected. It seemed as if the normal ups and downs of the market had vanished and we entered a period of sustained stock market growth that broke many previous records. This was my first extended experience of the stock market and I sat back contentedly as my investments grew at a pace that my advisors would wish happened every year. They would look like total geniuses if they could get those kinds of returns consistently.

During this time I was not spending too much time thinking about what was happening in my bank account; I was still basking in gratitude for God setting me free from depression and negativity. And, because I had limited experience in the stock market, I assumed that what was taking place was not too far from typical. But something changed in December of 2017. I took a small amount out of the account to buy my daughter a car and began to notice the rate the account was growing at. Over the next five weeks it ballooned by almost $60,000. Up to that time, with few exceptions, I had not earned much more than that in an entire year! And something interesting happened inside of me too. I started to let myself imagine that, as the account grew at a rate very rarely seen, I was somehow becoming safer. I noticed myself checking in on the money in more frequent intervals and I started to use the "stocks" app on my iPhone to keep track of the particular stocks I owned.

In early January, my advisor's office called to set up our bi-annual review to see if our plans were still on track. The meeting was arranged for Friday, February 2nd in the morning and, as it approached I imagined the kind of celebratory meeting it would be – the past several weeks in the stock market were among the best ever seen. This is a good time to quote Morpheus in *The Matrix* - "God, it seems, is not without a sense of irony." Because, after another record day on Friday, January 26th (when my portfolio gained almost $10,000 in one day), everything started to turn around the following Monday.

The market lost 430 points from its high on that Friday to the morning of the meeting with my advisors the next Friday, which equated to roughly a $12,000 loss in the first four days of the week. I recalled the Chinese New Year setback and summoned up the same sort of gratitude for what I still had left, which was more than plenty. As we met in their office, I calmed myself by saying, "It's alright, it just went from an impossibly good last five weeks to a very good last five weeks." At least one concerned investor called while I was in their office wondering if it was time to sell before the market fell much further. We all laughed about those nervous Nellie's who were on the verge of panic because the market took a little (2%) dip.

Well, that's how I felt in the morning anyway. By the end of the day, the Dow had dropped 665 points further, which translated to another $18,000 loss in just that one day! I was stunned and started to wonder if those people selling knew something that I didn't. It seemed that, after almost two years of hiatus, volatility had suddenly reappeared with a vengeance. Throughout the weekend, I tried to take my mind off of the surprising last week and put it back on the big picture, but I found it very difficult not to think about what was in store for Monday. I kept a close watch on what was happening as the market opened and was progressively battered as the Dow fell lower and lower through the day. It turned out to be the single worst one-day point loss in the history of the stock market, dropping almost 1,600 points at one point before closing 1,175 points down in a single day of trading. Another $33,000 vanished from my account that Monday and I started to share in the panic that was sweeping the market.

My focus was now almost entirely on the short-term fluctuations happening on Wall Street. I started checking obsessively and was scouring the internet for clues about when the hemorrhage would stop. No one could offer any solid answers and, as stock prices tumbled, the safety I had allowed myself to feel as the money grew was under attack from all sides. I just happened to be meeting with my therapist for the last hour the market was open that Thursday, and while we were discussing how troubled I was becoming, we watched the market slide 1,082 points and I said a painful goodbye to another $25,000. All together I had lost close to $90,000 in two weeks, and I was now kicking myself for not being able to see this drop coming. I mean, after my account went up by $60,000 in five weeks, why didn't

I just cash out with that unbelievable amount of profit? I was not happy with the answer – it was greed. And not just for money, but for the safety that it had come to represent. I had allowed money to insinuate itself into playing a God-like caretaking role in just the previous couple of months.

Even after the market bottomed out that day, I still could not help myself from focusing most of my attention on the money that had fled my account so fast. I found myself doing various calculations about the money that was left (which was still plenty) in order to settle myself inside and predict how long it might take to return to where it had been. And the volatility that had shaken the stock market was now active on the inside of me. I had lost a good deal of the peace I had previously, and the truly troubling part is that, if you had asked me before the stocks dropped why I had peace, I would not have said anything about the money in the bank. But here I had lost almost all my contentment because of the volatility in the stock market.

As I hunted for clues about what to expect going forward, I learned that these sorts of drops are not uncommon and happen on average every two years. I also learned that when the market drops by more than 10% it is called a "correction." And, while this drop was not the largest in history by any means, aside from actual crashes it was by far the fastest and most volatile ever. And, as my finances were undergoing this unprecedented turmoil, God took the opportunity to give me a correction of my own. Near the end of the drop, as I was at my most distracted and obsessed, I suddenly remembered the story of King David taking a census of the people of Israel and how he had provoked the anger of God (2 Samuel 24). I hadn't read this, or even thought about it in years, but, at the same time, a question materialized in my head that highlighted the fallacy that I had bought into as I watched the money grow. I heard, "What are you counting on, Pat?" Now, I'm not going to swear that this was the voice of God, but I have a hard time believing I had some obscure story that I hadn't read in years *and* that question both popping into my head at the same time by pure coincidence.

Just like David had provoked God by counting the "fighting men" of Israel, I had gotten His attention by counting the "soldiers" in my bank account. And while it is up for debate about why God was angry with David, I felt certain that we had both made the mistake of thinking that our security lay in something besides God. David had no reason to number his soldiers because God was the only thing that he needed to win any battle he was called on to fight. This is the same God who told Gideon he had "too many men" and whittled his army down to just 300 soldiers (Judges 7), who He then used to defeat an entire Midianite army described as "thick as locusts" (v. 12). The only reason David would have numbered his army was that he lost sight that God alone had gotten him where he was and it would be God alone who kept him there.

In my own way, I had miscalculated just as David had. Despite knowing better, I let something unseat God and convince me that my safety and well-being were assured by how much money I had available to me. I had become Wile E. Coyote, and my plan to catch the roadrunner of security had just blown up in my face! This is doubly ironic because, until my late 40's, I had very little, if any, extra money in the bank and had never been seriously tempted to equate money with security. I had neither! But, because I lost focus on God and let money take on power it does not rightfully possess, I found myself in a very unpleasant story. Instead of gratitude about the abundant provision God has supplied me during this season, I was angry at myself and had difficulty sleeping through the night. I had literally started "counting on" something besides God and, as a result, my perspective got smaller and smaller over a remarkably short period of time. I paid the inescapable price that comes with a perspective that focuses on the short-term and pushes God to the background – I lost touch with His closeness and love that I felt just a few days earlier. And no amount of money was worth that!

It has only been a few weeks since this happened and I wish I could say I was paying attention to the same smaller degree I was before Christmas, but this volatility still has much more of my attention than I would like. After a pretty quick (partial) rebound after the correction, the Dow has dropped 1,200 points in the past four days and taken back almost $30,000. It's Friday and I'm happy that I can spend at least the next two days free of the temptation to check on the stock market.

There is a name for believing that our well-being relies on something other than God – it is called idolatry. And the really insidious part is that even things that are good can become idols. The health and well-being of our marriages, kids, careers, or bank accounts can slip in front of God and become idols without us even realizing it until they are shaken in some way. It is difficult to keep all these things in the proper perspective and the temptation to put faith in something that is not God is second nature for us. So, everybody fill in the blank with your own name and say this with me, "What are you counting on, _____?"

Another hard lesson learned the hard way for me. A faulty perspective will always end up counting on something that is faulty. And the sharp ups and downs of life (volatility) will tempt us to divert our eyes from the true source of calm in the storm. Peter was able to walk on a raging sea as long as he was looking at Jesus, but as soon as he "saw the wind" (Matt. 14:30), he fell into the ups and downs of the waves around him. And, I'm hoping I never have to answer the question Jesus asked Peter after rescuing him - "Why did you doubt?" (v.31). Because there is no good reason in the world!

ARTISTRY

For we are God's handiwork, created in Christ Jesus to do good works, which God prepared in advance for us to do.(Ephesians 2:10)

Again he said, "What shall we say the kingdom of God is like, or what parable shall we use to describe it? (Mark 4:30)

"I've changed my mind!" is usually not a phrase we associate with personal growth or breakthrough. But transformation and breakthrough cannot be had without a change of mind, usually a profound change of mind. When the Apostle Paul wrote, "Be transformed by the renewing of your mind...," he was identifying the single most important element of change, the changing of what we think. How many people would like to "change their mind" about whether they would stay angry about some grudge they are holding? Or about the role alcohol, food, or drugs play in their lives? Imagine how many people would like to change their minds in a way that would rule out the need for the profound sadness or anxiety they experience in life.

In Revelation 4:1, John writes "And the voice I had first heard speaking to me...said, "Come up here, and I will show you what must take place after this." It's as if John will not be able to comprehend what Jesus wants to reveal to him without a *change in perspective*. In the book of Isaiah, God says, "My thoughts [are higher] than your thoughts" (Isaiah 55:9) and John's revelation has much to do with being lifted to that higher place where his vision can be greatly expanded. God wants to show him the future, and he must get a different view of events for it to make sense.

When we talk about changing our mind, it is not the previously known facts that are different. It is our perspective of those facts that changes. Even if we change our mind because some new fact comes to light, it is only because that new fact provides a different viewpoint to look at the situation. How many times were you certain that someone was dead wrong about something until one new little piece of information comes to light and totally vindicated the person you were judging? I'm ashamed to admit how many red lights I've sat at waiting to make a right turn, and the person in front of me won't just turn even though they're signaling. I quickly conclude they are of inferior intellect until the pedestrian they were waiting to pass in front of them becomes visible to me. Then I have to repent for cursing someone completely without cause.

In that situation, my assessment reversed because my changed viewpoint allowed me to see the situation more fully. And here's something true of everyone – we don't see most situations fully. We are usually missing the most important viewpoint of all (God's) and are desperately in need of a "come up here" encounter. It is hard to overstate the impact that a changed perspective can make. In fact, the whole redemptive history of Israel owes its existence to the unusual perspective change of one man.

Joseph was sold to the Egyptians by his brothers when he was a young man because they were jealous of his relationship with their father (Gen. 37:4). Joseph was favored by his father Jacob above all his siblings and, to make matters worse, he had told his brothers of several dreams that seemed to indicate that they would one day be his servants. Not long afterward, while he and his brothers are out tending their family's livestock, his brothers consider killing him, but decide instead to sell him to a passing caravan of traders. After this, he winds up working in the house of an Egyptian official named Potiphar and thriving because "the Lord was with him and...gave him success in everything that he did... (Gen. 39:3)." When Joseph was imprisoned after being falsely accused of rape by Potiphar's wife, he naturally assumes a leadership position there and prospers for the same reason (Gen. 39:23).

Through a series of seeming coincidences, Joseph's gift of interpreting dreams becomes known to Pharaoh, and, after impressing Pharaoh by interpreting his troubling dreams, Joseph finds himself in a position of authority second only to Pharaoh himself. He is given a wife who ends up bearing him two sons, and the names Joseph chooses for his children symbolizes his change in perspective. The first he calls Manasseh, which means "God has made me forget." Joseph chooses this name because God has caused him to forget "all my trouble and all my father's household" (Gen. 41:51). And the other son he names Ephraim (which means "fruitful") because he says, "God has made me fruitful in the land of my suffering" (Gen. 41:52).

Now, it's clear that Joseph does not mean that he has literally forgotten his troubles or family. What he means is that God has changed his mind about what kind of story he will tell about his life's history. The facts about being betrayed by his jealous brothers, separated from his loved ones, falsely accused by Potiphar's wife, imprisoned for years without cause, and having to start from scratch in a foreign country could easily have caused Joseph to cast himself as the victim in his story. Instead, God causes him to "forget" those facts and see the injustices done to him in a different light.

As a result of de-emphasizing the wrongs he suffered, Joseph creates a different narrative as overcomer of what others inflicted on him, victor because of his triumph over resentment and bitterness, and hero who prevails against the odds by keeping his faith intact. If one desired to create a story of barrenness and desolation, Joseph's life could provide enough material to support it. But Joseph, with God's help, chooses to "forget" (change the importance of) that body of evidence and to focus on the elements of his life that support a "fruitful" interpretation. There is not much mentioned in the story about Joseph's internal struggle with bitterness, resentment, or sadness, but anyone who can put themselves in his place can imagine how much forgetting God helped him to do.

One of the more astonishing events in the Bible occurs when Joseph's "forgotten" brothers reappear in Egypt as a result of famine. They come seeking to buy grain and don't recognize that they are addressing the brother they betrayed and sold into slavery many years earlier. Joseph tests them and takes his time revealing himself to them so he can see what kind of people they have become in the interim. When his brothers finally find out that they are dealing with the one person on earth who has all the power, as well as the motive, to justifiably have them killed, they are understandably terrified. Even before they know it's Joseph, they interpret the difficulty he is giving them as divine retribution for their sin involving their brother all those years ago.

Then comes the time for the clash of perspectives! When Joseph tells his brothers who he is, they are convinced that he is going to destroy them; their perspective is focused only on their own limited and self-serving story and leaves God out of the picture entirely. But, because Joseph has allowed God to adjust his narrative about the previous circumstances of his life, he can clearly see the larger story – God's redemptive plan for the nation of Israel and beyond. Because Joseph has already had a "come up here" experience that changed him from victim to overcomer, he says to his brothers, "...do not be distressed and do not be angry with yourselves for selling me here, because it was to save lives that God sent me ahead of you... it was not you who sent me here, but God" (Gen. 45:5, 8). The "forgetting" God has worked in Joseph allows him to set aside the natural desire for retribution which, in turn, brings the wisdom and provision of God fully into view. The main difference between Joseph and his brothers is the scale they are looking at events with. Joseph is using a wide lens that allows him to see the long-term plan of God and be gracious to his forgotten family, while his brothers are limited to a petty scale that ends up being self-serving, doubtful, and manipulative.

Ironically, when their father Jacob dies, Joseph's brothers begin to question that Joseph could really be as forgiving as he seems and again start to fear for their lives. They appear to contrive a scheme to assure that Joseph's anger will not rekindle against them. Because they don't believe Joseph's explanation that their betrayal was part of the plan of God, they doubt the sincerity of his forgiveness. So they send a message to Joseph that their father's dying wish was that Joseph "forgive the transgression of your brothers...for they did you wrong." They continue to try to manipulate Joseph by going on to remind him that they are servants of the same God as Joseph's father (Gen. 50:17). When Joseph hears this, he weeps because he sees through their attempt to guilt him into forgiving them, something he had already done before he ever knew he would see them again. Because Joseph's brothers lack the proper perspective, they are limited to feeling fear, mistrust, and anxiety, but Joseph's perspective allows him to access all of the emotions that make this story possible: gratitude, forgiveness, and hope.

Remember, one of the things Joseph had to do was make peace with forgetting his family of origin; Joseph did the suffering, grieving, and "letting go" necessary to make this reunion something other than a bloodbath. It's obvious he senses their fear because he reaffirms his conviction that God has orchestrated the entire event in the service of His greater purpose. Joseph reassures his brothers by saying, "Do not be afraid, for am I in God's place? As for you, you meant evil against me, but God meant it for good in order to bring about this present result, to preserve many people alive" (Gen. 50:20).

And it should be mentioned that the salvation Joseph is preserving here is not just his own family and their descendants (who become the nation of Israel), but he is safeguarding the lineage of Jesus and, by extension, the entire eventual population of the eternal kingdom of God. Talk about a bigger story than just some kid being sold to a random caravan in the middle of a remote desert! The hard to fathom truth about the life of Joseph is that God was "with him" and "causing him to prosper" while he was being betrayed by his brothers, tossed into a pit, sold into slavery, and falsely imprisoned just as much as when Joseph is second in charge of all Egypt. The calendar just needed to flip a few pages forward for it to become evident. In fact, it is impossible to separate the first season of injustice and deprivation from the second one of incredible blessing and personal transformation; they were both orchestrated by God for the greatest good possible.

Well, these are great stories, but how do they apply to the kind of change we are trying to make? We looked at the story of the man born blind in the previous chapter. When Jesus declared that he was born that way to demonstrate the works of God, He was exercising something called the *artist's prerogative*. The idea is that the meaning and message of any particular artwork is solely at the discretion of the artist who created it. The artist alone gets the privilege of deciding which words describe the intent of his creation. He can splash paint on the wall and declare it to be a representation of man's inhumanity to man, or anything else he wishes – it is his right as the artist. This is why it is so important that God has said we are His "handiwork, created to do good works" (Eph. 2:10). It means that He alone can choose the words to apply to what he has created. God makes this clear when he says through Isaiah, "Shall the potter be considered as equal with the clay? That what is made would say to its maker, "He did not make me"; or what is formed say to him who formed it, "He has no understanding"? (Isaiah 29:18). And yet that is what we (the clay) frequently say about the potter (God).

One of the more marvelous privileges that God allows us is the ability to collaborate with Him about what our lives will look like. We are encouraged to "work out [our] salvation with fear and trembling; for it is God who is at work in [us]..." (Phil. 2:12-13) We are, to a degree, acting as "artists" who are, line by line, constructing a story with our actions as well as our interactions with others. God delegates to us a certain authority to determine the nature of the story we are telling about our lives and, more importantly, the degree of collaboration taking place between God and us in the writing of the story. We are free to declare, "He has no understanding!" and live according to that statement.

The Greek word *poiema* is translated "handiwork" in the Ephesians passage heading this chapter and has connotations of a fabric or tapestry produced by a weaver. This is an apt analogy about what the kingdom of God look like. Just as a weaver intricately intertwines threads of different color, texture, and length to create his artwork, God weaves together the lives of everyone ever born to express His virtuosity in creation. And the tapestry He creates is not limited by time in any way. The lives of people who lived hundreds, or even thousands, of years ago are still able to influence the tapestry today. Because God is not affected by the complexity of how all these lives interact with each other, the size of the "tapestry" quickly becomes so immense that we cannot see all of it at one time. We have to walk around it trying to observe its nuances and beauty, but, because our scope is limited, it is difficult to assess the overall quality of what He is producing.

And our temptation is to focus more intently on just the few threads that we can see intersecting our own. We are intimately acquainted with the section of carpet that we inhabit, and we are

248

constantly trying to reconcile what looks like some ragged ends present in our lives with what we have been told is the impeccable wisdom and care of God. If we are honest, when we look closely at our lives, there appear to be some areas that are irreconcilable with what we have been told about God. Many of us have experienced things that we have difficulty believing a loving God would ever allow to exist in His "handiwork."

This is why the idea of scale is so important for us to grasp. Because, when the tapestry is examined up close, and we focus on the losses and suffering we have undergone, it is easier to conclude that we are forgotten losers, persecuted victims, or entitled to vindicate ourselves with villainous behavior. The section of rug you are looking at might be quite dark, plain, or rough when seen in isolation. But, if you can give yourself permission to consider another, higher perspective, you can set the stage to have your own "come up here" insight. When we are finally able to consider the tapestry from that higher perspective, only then can we see the true magnificence of God. This is the One who invented the concept of beauty itself as well as the eye that can observe it - how could what He makes be anything less than breathtaking in its grandeur?

It's important to remember that God is not just producing an artwork in each of us individually. He is also producing an artwork of us corporately. God was "with Joseph" as he grew into his position, but the purpose was so that "many lives could be saved." If God was to grant us an audience to explain why our section of the tapestry looks a bit undone from up close, He could easily explain that, because of the connections with other "threads" that we are both aware and unaware of, our life must necessarily contain the circumstances that it does. But, if we're honest, our curiosity would not be satisfied there. He would have expanded our scope just a short distance beyond what we currently see, and we would naturally want to know why those farther circumstances had to occur as they did as well. We would want what

Job wanted – either to have the painful events of our lives justified by God or to justify ourselves and prove God to be an unfit potter. The truth is that, because of the inter-connectedness and complexity of the human experience, it would take literal lifetimes for Him to fully explain the reasons why your history unfolded as it has.

That is why He calls for faith. Not because He enjoys keeping us in the dark or withholding important information from us, but because, without faith, we cannot be free to enjoy life as the gift it was meant to be. We will constantly be demanding satisfaction to our curiosity and usually disappointed with partial answers. Because the truth is that knowing *why* something painful occurred, or lingers, cannot heal our pain. Knowing why you have a toothache doesn't help at all with the discomfort caused by it. Remember that Romans 8:28 says He causes "all things to work together for good to those who love God [and are] called according to His purpose," and, because we have serious limitations when trying to get a glimpse of "all things," it is next to impossible to see how anything good can come out of our most painful experiences. It is also important that this passage does not say that He will turn something evil into something good. It says that God, in His incredible ability to manage even the most trivial circumstances of our lives, will cause the result of the "working together" of "all things" to be good.

Joseph doesn't say that his brother's evil was actually good, he uses his own artists' privilege when he says that the meaning of it cannot be discerned by looking at it as an isolated incident; considering the over-arching intention of God is the only thing that reveals just how glorious the plan was all along. When their evil is looked at in the context of God's larger scale, the meaning and motives of their betrayal are subsumed into something good. For the ones who have been "called according to His purpose," there is not one moment of our lives that will be left out of that transformation. Good will gravitate all meaning and purpose toward it until, one day, evil is totally drained of the power to harm us ever again. Just like He did for Joseph, He will ensure that the final story that is told about the painful events of your life will cause those who hear it to rejoice and praise God. And He will do the work necessary for you to joyously say, "He has caused me to forget all my troubles!"

For us to experience the kind of peace that He knows we need to live as His children, He simply says, "Trust Me!" in response to many of the questions that seem so important to us. Because we would lose so much precious time in the pursuit of answers, He offers the assurance of His incredible goodness in place of answers that will not lessen our pain in the least. Faith, in this context, is the relaxed assurance that the events of our lives are in no way random. Instead, everything that has happened, and will ever happen, is designed to enhance the unfolding beauty of His handiwork in us. Trusting God in this way also keeps us in contact with the reality that the few, seemingly inconsequential, threads that comprise our lives are absolutely indispensable for the larger story of God to be expressed.

Without faith, we will be tempted to conclude that whatever story our lives are telling is, to some degree, divorced from the one God is telling. I imagine Joseph felt that way sitting in prison for years wondering what he'd done to get so far from the plan of God. I've heard a lot of people affirm that "everything happens for a reason," but not many say that it's for a *good* reason! Joseph couldn't see that the evil his brothers had done was redemptive in the eyes of God because he had not been given the privilege of seeing the whole story yet. And there is another marvelous aspect to the artwork that God is creating; it's the truth that, if we were able to see the entirety of His handiwork, no portion of it would strike us as less stunning as any other. The final product will be equally glorious throughout no matter if it is a central, well-worn portion (like the story of Joseph) or some peripheral, less-used part of the carpet.

Try to imagine how Joseph would have felt if he had known the future God had planned for him while he was tossed into that pit or sitting in prison; I'm pretty sure he would have found something to celebrate while he waited for the inevitable deliverance to happen. How would you feel about your life if you were convinced your story was intertwined to that degree with the story of God? Would you continue to ascribe to a negative narrative about yourself or others? What would your artistic privilege cause you to say about yourself and the circumstances of your life? If you knew that He was planning a future that was no less glorious than the one He arranged for Joseph, would you be able to "consider it all joy" as you go through your current difficult circumstances?

Because the truth is that you are free to disagree with God about what He is making and whether it was necessary to make it through the means He has chosen. And, if there is one thing I can assure you of it is this - that when you are finally able to see what He is doing from a high enough perspective, there will be only one response: gratitude. You will be so overwhelmed with the wisdom and kindness of His work that you will forget to complain, question, or doubt anymore. You will thank Him with every cell in your body for every moment of His involvement in crafting the story of your life and the pain, even though it might be intense, will become a "light affliction." The eventual, unavoidable, emotional state of every believer is one of inexpressible gratitude. There is really only one question worth asking – "Why not start thanking Him now?"

I could be ashamed to say that, for most of my life, I would have answered that question by saying, "Because of blah, blah, blah!" When I consider how stubbornly I held on to my malnourished view of God and what He was willing to do on my behalf it makes me cringe. The outside of my life doesn't look too different from what it used to before my latest transformation. I worked in settings where I could assist others to make their own difficult changes and I still do. I have the same basic self-care routines. But, what goes on inside my head is what is so different. I have an entirely different language now to employ in the pursuit of change. And I describe what the transformation I've been through feels like in this way.

Imagine you were treading water in the deepest part of the ocean and someone suddenly hung a hundred lbs. of lead around your neck. You thrash around wildly for a few seconds but, after you tire, you find yourself sinking quickly below the surface. As you sink, you feel the pressure begin to build in your ears, and your lungs start to burn as oxygen deprivation sets in. Eventually, you pass through enough water that no more light can reach you, and you wonder just how deep you can sink. And imagine that, even though your lungs were screaming for air, and the pressure beyond what a human could stand, you were unable to die. Picture yourself sinking so far down that there was no way to distinguish anymore which way you were going.

Over the next decade or two, you feel something periodically tugging at the weights around you, and you notice, at some point, that you are floating in a near weightless state, but still without any sense of whether you are facing toward the light or away from it. But by now, you are so deep underwater that you are certain there is not enough time left in your life to get back to the surface under your own power. Keep in mind that you are still acutely feeling the lack of air and crushing pressure and wishing that they alone had the power to snuff out your life.

Now imagine that, after having given up all hope that anything could find you or that you could find your own way back up, you began to sense that you were somehow approaching the surface again. And, as you gain momentum upward, the burning in your lungs creates an urgency to get to the surface at all costs – nothing else matters! Suddenly, you burst through and, after what seems like a true eternity underwater, finally are able to suck in the fullest and sweetest breath of air that you have ever known. Life has just flooded your body so gloriously that you feel you had never known what a breath felt like until now.

And imagine if you could stay in the excitement of that first breath for the rest of your life! That every moment after you surfaced felt as sweet as that one. That is the best way I can describe what He did for me at that roulette table four years ago. I have no way of knowing whether everyone else feels as excited about what He is doing as I do, or if it is because I spent so many years near death that just being normal feels like heaven. All I can say is, as a result of the "working together" of "all things," He has made the past four years so sweet that it would be worth ten times the anguish of the first 48. If it were necessary to go through what I did in order to get where I am now, I would gladly do it again.

I can now testify in agreement to what Jesus said about Himself in Luke 4:18. He quotes Isaiah 61 and tells those present what His mission is. He mentions only part of it to those present, but I can say with certainty that the rest applies as well. "He has sent me to bind up the brokenhearted, to proclaim freedom for the captives and release from darkness for the prisoners...to comfort all who mourn, and provide for those who grieve...a crown of beauty instead of ashes, the oil of joy instead of mourning, and a garment of praise instead of a spirit of despair" (Isaiah 61:1-3). He was not exaggerating!

The Shawshank Redemption is my favorite movie. And not just mine; it's consistently ranked as one of the best-loved movies of all time. Morgan Freeman plays Red, who is in Shawshank prison for a murder committed in the course of a robbery and Tim Robbins plays Andy, who is wrongly convicted of double murder entirely because of circumstantial evidence. If someone were to ask me, "What is the movie about?" I could recap the plot by saying, "It's about a banker who is wrongly imprisoned for the murder of his cheating wife and her lover. In prison, he is abused by the guards, raped by other prisoners, and, because of his skill with finances, he's enlisted by the warden to run his scam providing cheap prison labor to local construction projects. When a new inmate provides clues to who really killed Andy's wife, the warden contrives a situation to have him killed to keep the exculpatory evidence from coming to light. Finally, after 19 years, Andy turns the tables on the warden and escape with the warden's stolen money. The end of the movie shows him fixing up an old fishing boat in Mexico."

Whenever I discuss this with other people who have seen the movie, I ask them if those are all true facts about the movie. They agree that I've covered the basic facts. But when I ask people if they would be inclined to see the movie based on my description, they are unimpressed. It sounds like a dozen other ordinary prison movies. I've chosen words that are factual, but they don't capture what makes the movie so admired, and they don't inspire anyone to rush out and see it.

But there is more than one way to answer that question. When I get the opportunity to tell people about Shawshank my eyes light up as I tell them that it's because the theme of the movie is my life's story – the struggle to keep hope alive! Let me explain. About midway through the film, Andy is thrown in solitary confinement for commandeering the prison's P.A. system to play music for the inmates. When he is released after two weeks, his friends are sure he will come out scarred, but he is oddly cheerful instead. When they ask him why, he points to his chest and tells them, "There's something [inside]...they can't touch." Red asks what that is and Andy replies, "Hope!" Red sternly chastises him and says, "Let me tell you something, my friend. Hope is a dangerous thing. Hope can drive a man insane. It's got no use on the inside." Red fully appreciates the torment that hope can be when no action can be taken to improve one's situation. When one is sentenced to life in prison, hope must be jettisoned to get through the tedious and dreary routine that life becomes. Sounds a lot like how a depressed person would cope with things!

After Andy escapes, Red is paroled and attempts to manage life outside of prison for the first time in many years. He actually considers committing a crime that will send him back to Shawshank because he misses the comfort of having someone there to tell him what to do. He's become institutionalized and says he wants to return to prison because it's a "terrible thing to live in fear." Before Andy escaped, he told Red about something he would leave for him under an oak tree in a nearby city, and as Red considers going back to Shawshank, he says that the only thing stopping him is the promise he made to Andy to find what he left there under the tree for him. Red makes the trip and finds a tin buried near the tree that has some cash and a note in it. The note reads in part, "Remember, Red, hope is a good thing - maybe the best of things. And no good thing ever dies. I will be hoping that this letter finds you, and finds you well." The note forces Red to revisit the one thing that has been such a threat to his prisoner mindset – hope. Andy reminds Red that hope is not something that can be killed and encourages him to make the trip to their pre-arranged meeting spot in Mexico.

Red's next line in the movie is one I've had to encourage myself with many times over the years, "Get busy living, or get busy dying." Because the truth is there is no middle ground. We are either doing the things that allow life to flow into and through us, or we are distancing ourselves from life. Before hope came alive in me, I had to make a determined effort to do the things of life that I was being coached to do. And, even though I didn't believe that those actions would ever pay off for a loser like me, I was so sick of doing the things of death (which had no chance to succeed), that I did the things of life even though I thought they could only succeed in theory. Get busy living means to do the things that hope requires of us. The little actions that declare our conviction that, despite its difficulties, life is worth living and that there is a heroic narrative motivating us. To get busy dying means the opposite, to shrink back, remain paralyzed, and mark time with no hope that our actions add up to anything worth fighting for. Red decides that taking the risk to meet his friend in Mexico is his only real choice if he is to find a life worth living. Returning to Shawshank and its institutional "care" is tantamount to death, maybe worse.

In the final scenes of the movie, we see Red buying a bus ticket that will take him to the Texas border with Mexico. As Red rides toward Mexico, he speaks the last few lines of the movie and gives us a glimpse into his new mindset. Looking out the window of the bus he says, "I find I'm so excited I can barely sit still or hold a thought in my head. I think it's the excitement only a free man can feel. A free man at the start of a long journey whose conclusion is uncertain...I hope I can make it across the border...I hope to see my friend and shake his hand...I hope the Pacific is as blue as it has been in my dreams...I hope."

Now, when I take the time to describe the movie this way, as an epic battle that is near universal in its application, people have a very different response. Those who haven't seen the movie express interest and, many times, those who already love the movie say, "I hadn't noticed that! I'm going to have to watch it again." The theme that is most inspiring to me is Red's journey from someone who has ruled out the existence of hope to someone who relishes finding it alive inside of him again. He undergoes a transformation from a futureless loser imprisoned for life to someone embracing the risk necessary to create a different story. Even when I was such a committed pessimist, Red's willingness to risk letting hope back into his life spoke to me in profound ways. I couldn't watch the last scene without crying. I still can't.

So why does this matter? Why spend the time talking about a movie? I like to tell people about Shawshank because we all are living our own personal Shawshank Redemption. We all find ourselves limited, or even imprisoned, by sin. We all want to transform into something different. We all need our thinking renewed. And we all get the privilege, the *blessed* privilege, to choose the words that accurately describe the story we are in. We can choose to focus on the dreariest and most tragic events of the "plot" to try to prepare for setbacks we are certain lie in the future - I did for many years. If we do choose those words, that narrative, let's be clear about what we are choosing. We become negative about the past, subtly train ourselves to attend mainly to the facts in the present that confirm a negative bias, forecast a general continuity of a negative story in an attempt to reduce anxiety, and get "sick comfort" out of living without the demands that hope places on us. We become institutionalized prisoners in the confines of our own mindset and, like Red, rebuke anyone who tries to advocate for the necessity and beauty of hope.

How different the outcome of doing something as innocuous as using a different set of words to describe the same life. Instead of a movie no one wants to see (including myself), the heroic narrative provides abundant motivation to continue the fight. It's no accident that Red says he can't sit still or keep a thought in his head. He says it's the "excitement only a free man can feel." When we give ourselves permission to change the story, we become free in a way that inspires others to pursue their own Shawshank Redemption! In a blink, just by using our artist's privilege to change the story that explains our life, we move from powerless prisoners on a miserable death march into heroes with everything to live for. Life transforms from a relentless burden into a magnificent gift!

When someone does this and decides that it will be the heroic aspects of their past that will define them rather than the abuses, losses, or shortcomings, they have *reinvented* themselves. Reinvention is nothing more than changing the story we tell about the facts of our past and what they mean about our character and

258

potential; the facts remain the same, it is how we relate to them that changes. And, no matter how devastating the facts of the past, there is always a perspective that allows us to fully transcend the pain and anguish they can represent. We get to employ our own artist's privilege to determine what the past represents, and how we choose to narrate our lives will either keep us locked in bitterness, regret, and blame or free us to live as the heroic overcomers God says we are.

FINALITY

Do not conform to the pattern of this world, but be transformed by the renewing of your mind. Then you will be able to test and approve what God's will is—his good, pleasing and perfect will. (Romans 12:2)

So we are back where we started - change is hard. And I find myself faced with a frustrating irony. Before my own "come up here" experience, if someone had come to me and said, "You know, Pat, you have way much more power to change how you think and feel than you know," I would have said, "You have no idea what I'm up against! This thing comes and grabs me by the throat, carries me off to its lair, and eats me alive." If you had told me I had any choice at all in whether to think positively or negatively, I would have chuckled dismissively. Because, for a long time, I sensed no choice. I was as addicted to negative thinking as I ever was to food, marijuana, or cocaine, maybe more so. And, just like drugs and alcohol rewire the brain in devious ways that condition it to crave destructive things, I had created deep mental "ruts" that kept me thinking in self-destructive ways.

But, I know that there must be choice on our part, otherwise Scripture would not so forcefully encourage us to change how we think. God would not ask us to do something we couldn't. And I would encourage anyone reading this to imagine what would change if the verse above became true for you. Because "renewing your mind" does not mean being refreshed so that you can continue to think the same polluted thoughts as before. It means to change your mind about many of the things you currently act on as if true, even though they are not. So how would you know if your mind was renewed? What kind of thoughts would you have? What kind would not show up again? What would the main characters of your story be?

I sometimes use an analogy of a sculptor working on a block of marble to illustrate the transformation process. When you watch an artist work by hand on a block of stone, he will make many hammer strikes that appear to have very little effect besides a few small chips flying off into the air. It is tempting to think that, at the rate he is working, he will never make any appreciable progress. But, after many blows, there comes one strike that dislodges a large slab of material and dramatically changes the character of the stone. It then becomes clear he was hammering on a fault line in the stone which, due to the cumulative effects of the hammer blows, finally causes a sudden, pronounced change.

I fought against the depression and futile thinking for many years and made only slogging progress. I tried medication, therapy, exercise, prayer, and everything else I could with little effect. And then, the one strike that happened at the roulette table dislodged a huge chunk, enabling me to suspend my previously held biases and quickly change the lifelong narrative I had constructed. I found it suddenly possible to narrate the events of my life with a completely different tenor of voice. Rather than the accusatory, judgmental, and harsh words I spoke over the "film" of my life previously, I had the ability to sincerely choose kind, affirming, and encouraging words to speak about what I was worth.

As I look back at the journey, I can say with certainty that the circumstances I grew up with, coupled with what must have been a genetic predisposition to depressive thinking styles, left me with no choice about what mindset I would use to interpret the world. I was screwed for sure. There is a story about how elephants are trained that may or may not be true. They say that if a young elephant is restrained with a rope that he cannot break, he eventually learns not even to attempt to break the rope even though, as a fully grown adult, he could easily free himself. It may be that mindset is something like that as well. My mindset was so firmly set early in life that I never even questioned its validity until I was 48. I tried to fight off the depression my whole life, but I didn't realize that, because my depression was a main character in the story I was choosing to tell, it was going nowhere until my story changed. As long as I held to the loser narrative, depression and futility were inescapable.

That is possibly the most important thing to consider about the narratives we assign to ourselves – the kind of characters that belong in the story with us. If I choose a loser, victim or villain narrative, I invite all the unsavory types that belong in such stories along for the ride. These stories are fertile ground for depression, anxiety, addiction, anger, and hopelessness. And because they are main characters, they show up in every chapter and color every line of dialog. Peace of mind, contentedness, and gratitude make only cameo appearances.

Conversely, the victor, overcomer, and hero narratives consistently bring characters like joy, excitement, and courage into the story. If addiction or depression find their way into these narratives, it is only to teach or remind the hero of some necessary lesson. These dark characters make an appearance to sharpen the hero's focus and provide the training he needs to tackle even greater challenges in the future. In a positive narrative, even serious setbacks like lasting disability, social injustice, and illness are recast into opportunities for personal, spiritual, and relational growth; these are the circumstances that reveal the hero in us. Without challenge the hero remains unrecognized.

In the end, it was so easy to change my mindset that it is hard to believe it wasn't possible much earlier in life. It pains me to think about how much time I let the tiny little rope of my childhood bind my fully grown mind. I hope that some who read this will find the courage to confront whatever faulty mindset they currently act on as if true. Because this is the truth I've found to be so liberating – it does not matter what has happened to you, it only matters what story you tell about it.

I can imagine someone saying, "That's easy for you to say! You don't know what I went through." It's true, I don't, and I used to say the exact same thing to anyone who suggested I had some choice in the matter of what to think and feel. But this idea of controlling our own narrative is something that has taken center stage in our culture recently. More and more people are becoming aware that there is something very powerful in our choice of words to describe who we are and what we are worth.

I just saw some of Larry Nassar's accusers at his sentencing hearing saying this very thing in many different ways. In case you don't know, Nassar, while working as a doctor at Michigan State University and as the national medical coordinator for the U.S. gymnastics team, molested hundreds of girls under the guise of medical treatment. All the young women tell their stories in powerful and heartbreaking ways, but the testimony given by Gwen Anderson illustrates perfectly the outcome of choosing the right narrative. She said, in part, "We are going to move forward, we are going to live our best lives, because we are fighters and we are strong. We overcome impossible odds, because that's what we were trained to do, because that's what we know how to do - because we are gymnasts...I seriously struggled with the decision to allow myself to be recorded and shown in public because I was scared that my students would see me at my weakest moment. They would see me as a victim. But I've come to realize that this moment is not my weakest moment, this is my moment of strength. This is my time to close the chapter of being a victim and open my chapter of being a survivor, and that standing here today, facing the man who molested me as a child and share my story, is my time."

The judge, amid controversy, had allowed all of Nasser's victims to tell their stories at the sentencing hearing, whether they were part of the proceeding or not. Several of the women mentioned that the judge had privately encouraged all these women to reject the label of victim and instead to identify themselves as survivors. I am all in favor of that, but I would go a step further. Survival doesn't capture the full picture of what these women have done. Many of them have gone on to win Olympic medals, finish their degrees, or take the risk of starting families of their own. These women are true victors, overcomers, and heroes! Listening to their stories, it is clear that it will take considerable effort for them to do the "forgetting" that will allow them to find a fruitful narrative again. But, with God in the picture, and plenty of sources of grace and truth, it is only a matter of time for that to take place. That's how powerful controlling the narrative is.

And I'm not talking about some "law of attraction" kind of power to control reality with your choice of words or purity of your thoughts. That's nonsense! The power I'm talking about is far greater. It is the power to choose whatever perspective is beneficial when you look at what has happened in your life. The past will always remain unchanged - the facts are the facts. But your orientation to them is entirely in your discretion. And how you orient to them will dictate what kind of thoughts and feelings are available to you going forward. When painful memories revisit and bring along accusatory thoughts like "You'll never fit in!" or "No one will want you because of what happened to you!" the artist's privilege allows us to erase those messages and assign whatever meaning we choose to be reminded of instead. Anxiety can remind you that something unpleasant might be about to happen outside of your control or it can remind you to thank God that He has promised that everything He allows to touch you is only for your ultimate good. You get to decide which one it will be!

My hope for those women abused by Nassar is that when those memories revisit them, and attempt to remind them of how vulnerable, unsafe, or damaged they are, they will instead be able to "thank" those same memories for reminding them of how powerful and pure they are to have survived and still be able to laugh at anything. That may sound trivializing of their pain, but my own experience has taught me that there is no amount of suffering and anguish that cannot be transformed into "light affliction" by choosing the perspective that God makes available to each one of us. God does not shrug and sheepishly apologize for giving us circumstances that He cannot work for our ultimate good!

When I was in the loser narrative, I had a whole set of facts to support that story that I could recount to a listener at a moment's notice. I had learned to convey the tragic episodes of my past in a humorous way, and I kept those memories so accessible I was essentially rehearsing the trauma, loss, and futility I had experienced to that point. After God stepped in and allowed me to change my narrative, it didn't take long until I found myself surprised at how far those memories had receded from my awareness. The facts that I thought were so defining and foundational were suddenly of far less value in telling the story of my life to others (and myself). Joseph's ability to reorient to the facts of his history allowed him to transcend the evil that his brothers had done to him – the meaning of it changed. And, because he did the work necessary to find a "fruitful" narrative, his brothers could have done very much more evil to him and the outcome would have been the same. The "forgetting" Joseph did would have covered that too.

I recently had one of the more fruitful experiences of my life and it would never have happened without the kind of perspective change we've been talking about. I met Lisa on her fifth visit to treatment. She was a beautiful woman in her mid-twenties who dazzled me with her ability to think deeply about the important things in life. At our first meeting, over the course of an hour or two, she recounted just some of the horrific abuse that had been done to her by her father and other trusted adults. There was every sort of dysfunction possible in her family, and she had moved out at an early age, gotten addicted to heroin, and had several near-death experiences due to overdose. After she had spent the first hour telling me about her awful history, I asked her to fill in the blank, "Because of my past, I am _____." She filled it in with "damaged goods" and began to cry as she told me that she couldn't believe that anyone would find her a worthwhile person even to know, much less love.

Over the course of 3-4 months, I watched her live out that identity in various ways. She started a romantic relationship with a peer in treatment who really just wanted someone to keep him company while he got high. Despite knowing he "fit the pattern" of the kind of bad relationships she had been in previously, she couldn't bring herself to resist his advances and, before long, found herself heartbroken again while he left treatment to relapse and sent her text messages offering her drugs if she would join him.

She gravitated to friends in treatment who would take advantage of her generosity and poor boundaries. She found herself in high-risk situations because these "friends" would get into trouble and need her to bail them out. And, because of her low self-esteem, she felt powerless to say no to protect herself from their irresponsibility. On more than one occasion, she tried to arrange to relapse, but had been thwarted by strange circumstances. As she gained ground against her primary addiction to heroin, her immaturity tried to express itself with a previous eating disorder and codependent attachments to her housemates.

All during this time, we talked about her narrative and the power it had to influence her choices and decisions. She recognized that she had been choosing the company of the kind of people that belong in a "damaged goods" story, and responding to others as if she was more

266

damaged than everyone else. She purposely left herself undefended against malicious people and re-experienced the same things that had damaged her in the first place. As she got more sober time, she began to grieve at how much the lies that were embedded in that story had cost her. And she began to see that believing them was optional. She continued to attend support group meetings, got a sponsor, worked the 12-steps, and slowly but surely, she was able to get the "new past" we touched on in an earlier chapter.

After several more months in the treatment center's structure, she was delighted to tell me that she had met a young man who was different from the others. This one actually valued her and, to her surprise, she believed him when he said kind things about her worth! She had decided to return to school to pursue her long-neglected dream of being an artist and was thrilled to tell me she could hold on to hope for the first time in many years. It had taken over a year of sustained effort, but she had made a significant dent in her "damaged goods" narrative. We laughed as we talked about her graduating to just being "goods" now. And I rejoiced with her about finding someone who treated her according to her new identity. She ended up moving to the Midwest with him, and our farewell was very bittersweet.

Not long ago I got a text from her saying that she was writing a paper for a class at school about "the person who has had the greatest influence on your self-concept," and that she had decided to write it about me! She told me that I had been the "driving force" behind her sobriety and that I had "saved her life." When I heard this, I couldn't help but shake my head in wonder! What an awesome God who can take someone whose self-concept was as tortured as mine and use them to play a positive role for someone like Lisa. And none of that would have taken place unless He had set me free to "forget all my troubles" and put me in the very place where I could find a "fruitful" outcome to my story. Hearing her say that to me was something that, just a few years earlier, would have been completely beyond my ability to "ask or even imagine."

I can't fully convey how gratifying it was to watch someone else's identity change as a direct result of the intervention God had done on me. The only difference was the time scale involved. What He had done for me in a few minutes, He did for Lisa over the course of a year. And she was getting it 20 years sooner than I had! I smile when I think of how many people she will impact as she takes what she has learned and passes it on to others.

When my story was disconnected from His, when I thought that there was no overlap between His victory and mine while I was still alive, I was telling the drabbest version of my Shawshank Redemption story – (say this in a robotic monotone) "Jesus was God in the flesh who died for my sins so I can go to heaven and be released from the misery of this world." I spent many years echoing the words of Job, "Will You never turn Your gaze away from me, nor let me alone until I swallow my spittle?" (Job 7:19). That's what I thought about the involvement of God in my life. I remember thinking, "If this is what Your love feels like, please hate me for a while!"

Now that my eyes have been opened to the kind of story that God is writing, and the high honor granted to us because of our place in it, every bit of the pain, dismay, and anguish seems utterly glorious and I am unable to thank Him enough for making me the object of His handiwork. And the part that boggles me more all the time is that He allows us the privilege of choosing something as important as the "words of our testimony." We can choose to look with a small scale at the abuse, mistreatment, tragedy, or misfortune that has befallen us and reap frustration, resentment, and blame while demanding answers that ultimately cannot heal our pain. Or we can consciously exercise faith and choose a larger scope that allows the "forgetting" of our troubles and lets our pain finally recede into the past where it belongs.

I've attempted throughout this book to put the spotlight on some of the particular ways that transformation can occur as a result of "renewing our minds." The kinds of thoughts that we allow to set up residence in our minds have downstream consequences that can mean the difference between looking at life as a tedious routine or a spectacular adventure. They can be the difference between accepting the challenges of life with gusto or retreating into a cell of despair and closing the door behind us while we pretend it is locked. They can be the difference between believing what God says about our incredible worth and potential or living on a treadmill of performance trying to earn the approval of others so we can feel we belong.

The solutions we've discussed revolve around doing our part of the "renewing our mind" process. This first means we become aware of our faulty narratives and ways that our thinking conflicts with what God says about us. This is not always as easy as it sounds; these stories can feel deeply true even though they are highly distorted. Adopting new positive behaviors allows us to look back on a new past that will support a hopeful forecast going forward. Finding supportive structures that can provide grace and truth over time is paramount in the pursuit of self-control and spiritual growth. Consciously reprioritizing will help us find gratitude in a consistent way. And learning to use the science behind habit formation is helpful to establish a practice that makes healthy habits routine; craving doesn't just have to work against you.

I hope you heard me emphasize the need for other people in the change process. Without close and meaningful relationships you will thwart many of the ways God means to heal you. You will only be able to "let go" and grieve fully if you are part of a community that you can draw comfort from in your dark times. And meditating on the numerous Scriptures that teach us what things to focus our attention on and what things to avoid prepares us for our own "come up here" experience where He can enlarge our perspective and give us a glimpse of the future. The rest is in His discretion. There is no way to force His hand to change you, even if you've done everything listed above and more. The best piece of advice I can give you is never to quit and to encourage yourself with every means available until you have your own momentous encounter with Him. This Scripture is as true as every other – "Let us not become weary in doing good, for at the proper time we will reap a harvest if we do not give up" (Galatians 6:9).

And, whatever way you find your thoughts working against you right now, I will stake my life that God will eventually do "exceedingly, abundantly beyond" what you think possible in your wildest imaginations. It may take, as in my case, 48 years of hacking through some very thick and demoralizing mental jungles, but, I can assure you that if He makes you wait that long, the relief He brings will be sweet enough that you will not second-guess His timing.

We are meant to greet each day like children racing downstairs on Christmas morning, certain that there are all sorts of gifts awaiting us! As adults, we know that not everything that we "open" daily will be pleasant; there are all sorts of ways that bad news can present itself to us. But, when our mindset is flexible, and we have the right scale of perspective, we can rejoice greatly knowing that every gift waiting for us is meant only to bring us greater maturity and to allow the hero in us to express itself to the fullest extent possible. If that is true, absolutely true, why should we allow ingratitude, anxiety, or anger to limit our happiness for even a fraction of a minute?

Above all, renewing our minds is not about how to think better when things are going our way. It is about how to think when we are directly opposed by circumstances in life. It also requires doing one of the scariest things a human can do – leaving behind one's current identity and adopting an entirely different one. This new identity accepts without question what Scripture says about our worth and importance to Him. Best of all, it comes with an expansion of our faith that rests on complete reliance that what is currently beyond our imagination is exactly what God has in mind for us sooner or later.

Ultimately, God will make it possible for us to find the same perspective that Joseph was finally able to grasp – "What [seemed] meant for evil, God meant for good..." The story does not end until every one of us gets to say that. And there is not one of us that will be excluded from that triumph. The day will arrive for each of us when we will "come up here" and see everything differently. The things that now seem impossible to reconcile with what we know about Him will suddenly make such perfect sense we will wonder how we couldn't see it all along. At its simple core, renewing our minds means we echo those words of Joseph with glee long before the outcome is seen - we say them by faith from the start.

36851925R00171

Made in the USA
San Bernardino, CA
24 May 2019